Grandparenting a Child with Special Needs

CHARLOTTE E. THOMPSON M.D.

Jessica Kingsley Publishers
London and Philadelphia

First published in 2009
by Jessica Kingsley Publishers
116 Pentonville Road
London N1 9JB, UK
and
400 Market Street, Suite 400
Philadelphia, PA 19106, USA

www.jkp.com

Library of Congress Cataloging in Publication Data
Thompson, Charlotte E.
  Grandparenting a child with special needs / Charlotte E. Thompson.
    p. cm.
  Includes bibliographical references.
  ISBN 978-1-84310-906-8 (pb : alk. paper) 1. Grandparents of children with disabilities--United States. 2. Grandparenting--United States. 3. Grandparent and child--United States. 4. Children with disabilities--Care--United States. I. Title.
  HQ759.9.T56 2009
  649'.1510973--dc22

                              2008042685

British Library Cataloguing in Publication Data
A CIP catalogue record for this book is available from the British Library

ISBN 978 1 84310 906 8

Printed and bound in Great Britain by
Athenaeum Press, Gateshead, Tyne and Wear

**To
all the grandparents
who care for grandchildren with
special needs**

Contents

Section IV You Need Time Too

Section V Help From Others

Appendix

Acknowledgments

I owe a great debt of thanks to several outstanding physicians. When I was an intern at Children's Hospital in San Francisco, the year before the Salk polio vaccine was introduced, Dr. Edward Shaw, an extraordinary physician and teacher, gave me my first real introduction to the problems of individuals with disabilities. Dr. Shaw's compassion and knowledge were the foundation on which I based my care of children with special needs. In later years, Lord (Dr.) Walton, Professor Victor Dubowitz, Professor Caroline Sewry, and Dr. Roger Terry taught me much about muscle diseases and muscle pathology. Dr. Paul Vignos and Dr. James Drennan shared their wisdom about the orthopedic and rehab care of patients with disabilities, Dr. Linda Gorin was my teacher about rheumatoid diseases and Dr. Margaret Thompson increased my knowledge about genetics, as did Dr. Milan Blaskovics about metabolic diseases. To all I owe my deepest gratitude.

I would also like to express my deep appreciation to Juno Duenes and Elaine Butler at the Support for Families of Children with Disabilities in San Francisco for sending out my questionnaire about caring for a child with special needs. Ana Volpi also has my sincere thanks for sending the questionnaire to two parent groups of children with neuromuscular diseases. My great thanks to all the parents and grandparents who took time from their busy days to answer the questions. Their task is a difficult one, which they do with great love, skill, and determination.

Those who graciously took time to answer the questionnaires were: Colleen Kerr, Laura and Marianne Plosser, Deanna Dicke, Shane Numberg, Sally Spencer, Ilene Candreva, Christina Conn, Anne Sullivan, Gay Grossman, Virginia Rutherford, Martha Gay Stewart, Diane Neuman, Kay Welsch, Amanda Quayle, Susan Fahning, and Sandy Brown. Marilyn Maidens offered wise advice about several grandparenting problems.

Dr. George Kaplan, pediatric urologist, kindly reviewed and made additions to the section on urological problems and CPA Mark Lindsay added his wisdom to the section on the tax benefits for grandparents. To both, I want to express my appreciation for giving of their time and expertise.

I would also like to say great thanks to my grandson, Alexander Thompson, for his wonderful computer skills and for not being too dismayed at his grandmother's lack of technical ability! My daughter, Jennifer Thompson, has helped in countless ways with suggestions, wisdom, and knowledge from her previous experience with the agency she founded to find jobs for teens with disabilities. My son, Dr. Geoffrey Thompson, was always available to solve computer or other problems and read over parts of the manuscript. His help was invaluable. Kimberly Walter also offered advice and assistance for which I am very grateful, and Barbara Hinton helped in numerous ways. A very special thank-you goes to Moreen Fielden, a wonderful teacher, headmistress, parent, grandparent, and special family friend who kindly reviewed the entire manuscript.

And last, but certainly not least, my deep appreciation to Lily Morgan at Jessica Kingsley Publishers in London for her patience and kindness in overseeing the entire manuscript and to Helen Jackson, Claire Cooper and Paula Peebles for their help in so many ways. My great thanks to all who helped make this book a possibility.

Introduction

Grandparents awaiting the birth of a grandchild usually don't care if it is a boy or girl as long as the baby is healthy. If a child is born with a birth defect or disability, some grandparents are like the Rock of Gibraltar, while others distance themselves or even refuse to acknowledge the new baby.

As grandparents we are important to our grandchildren and they are important to us. We can cause great pain to a grandchild with special challenges and his or her parents if we don't offer and provide our unconditional love and support. It is always a challenge to be a grandparent, as I have learned, but as long as we can develop the wisdom to know when to help and when our help will cause problems, we can love and enjoy our grandchildren no matter what the challenges. Communication with kids can be difficult if we don't understand the stresses of today's world for kids. Life has changed greatly since we raised our children and to be the best grandparents possible, we must stay abreast of what is happening in our grandchildren's world, as well as the world in general.

I hope that the information in this book will make grandparenting a child with special needs much easier. As a practicing pediatrician for fifty years with the last thirty years spent caring for children with disabilities, I have learned how much parents need all the help and support they can get. It can be a long, lonely journey caring for kids with special needs, particularly if there is no support or the parent is single. As the mother of two children, a grandmother and step-grandmother, I have learned a great deal about the practical aspects of caring for children. The parents and grandparents who kindly answered my questionnaire also provided some helpful information.

Every child, with or without a disability, is a special, unique human being. By looking for and helping foster this sense of uniqueness, parents, grandparents and grandchildren will reap endless rewards.

Section I

SUPPORT FOR THE WHOLE FAMILY

Chapter One

Coping with the Diagnosis

As a grandparent waiting for the call or news that a new grandchild has arrived, you are excited, but also fearful. There is always the worry that the new grandchild will have a problem or even not survive. What a great relief it is to receive a call that everything is fine, but if the caller says there is a problem, your heart jumps up into your throat. Immediately, you want to rush to be with the parents. If this is not possible your anxiety level can go over the top and you will find yourself on a roller coaster of emotions. This can be devastating and not helpful to the parents or you.

There are ways to get life back in balance again and I hope that my experience helping countless parents and grandparents through the ordeal of a painful diagnosis can allow you to cope more successfully.

The very first step after you have been told about your new grandchild is to take a deep breath and remember that some wonderful new medicines and ways of treating disabilities and problems have been found. When I was a medical student, leukemia in children was fatal. Now with early diagnosis and treatment, most of the children live full and happy lives. Diabetes, too, was fatal until a medical student working in his professor's lab discovered insulin.

If you are a computer person, you will most likely want to look for as much information as you can find about the particular disorder. The Internet can be helpful, but remember there is a great deal of medical misinformation on the Internet. Talking with doctor friends and agencies specializing in the particular disorder or problem may be more helpful. Once you have a better understanding of the condition, you will know how to offer the best support to the parents.

If a baby has to be in the intensive care nursery for a long period and you can relieve the parents from time to time, that will make a great difference. If you are nearby, providing meals and doing errands will lighten the parents' load or you could ask what other help is needed. If there are other children at home, you could offer to take care of the siblings for a few days. The brothers and sisters will most likely be frightened by the way their parents are reacting and unable to understand what is happening.

As you offer support to the parents and siblings, remember that you need to do your own grieving. Unless you allow yourself to grieve, the numbness and pain you surely are feeling could erupt as medical symptoms later on. By recognizing the different stages of grieving that Dr. Elisabeth Kübler-Ross[1] outlined many years ago, you can handle the feelings as they arise and not be surprised or have some unforeseen consequences.

THE STAGES OF GRIEVING

Shock, numbness, denial, bargaining, rejection, hysteria, anger, and guilt are all normal reactions, but the most immediate ones are shock and numbness. Both of these reactions are nature's way of allowing us to regroup after a heart wrenching occurrence in order to develop some coping mechanisms.

Grandparents who have had to deal with many problems in their lives often have excellent coping skills, while grandparents who have been sheltered and protected from life's tragedies may crumple and expect others to care for them. I've seen the grandparents of children born with minor disabilities fall apart, while other grandparents on being told of a major problem or disease are able to think of the parents and child and not themselves.

If you are a strong grandparent who has weathered many storms you must still allow yourself to grieve. The best way to do this is to take a few minutes several times a day to feel the grief and cry or just allow the pain to surface. Many people handle grief and pain by becoming extremely active. An accident may result or you may harm yourself in other ways as developing increased blood pressure or other medical problems.

You need time to take in what has happened and if this is your first, long-awaited grandchild, the pain and grief may be so overwhelming that it is almost incapacitating. You feel as though you want to hide and pretend the tragedy has never occurred. You may also feel as though you want to cry and cry, but the tears just won't come.

Some parents and grandparents remain stuck in a deep, black hole with their pain and grief and never pull themselves out. They go on with their daily tasks and routine, but hurt so much that they slowly distance themselves from their child or grandchild and no longer find much joy in living. Talking to a partner, a close friend, or a counselor can help bring the grief, pain, and rejection to the surface and allow you to move on with your life.

One mother of a child with a progressive disorder told me that you never accept a terrible diagnosis, but you just have to adjust to the reality of it. She did and her son in his brief sixteen years brought her much happiness. Your grandchild may also bring you unexpected happiness and joy. Often families find that learning how to handle their grief and pain results in increased closeness and better communication.

Anger, too, can cause medical problems if it is not expressed and older grandparents or those with medical problems must learn to express their anger to keep from getting into trouble. Exercise can be helpful, as can talking to other grandparents who have had similar problems to handle. Writing in a journal is therapeutic for some people and others find that poetry, handwork, or art work make a great difference. By allowing yourself to really feel the pain and anger and talk about it, you will be surprised how many other grandparents have had to deal with the problems of a grandchild with special needs. Twelve percent of children are born each year with some type of disability and 150,000 babies are born with birth defects yearly, according to the March of Dimes.[2]

Rejection of a grandchild with a disability or special problem can hurt you, the parents, and the child. Every child is a special wonderful human being. If you can see the baby or child and not the disability you will be offering the child and the parents a great gift.

HANDLING A DIAGNOSIS LATER IN CHILDHOOD

If a grandchild has seemed perfectly fine at birth or in the first few years and then has a tragic accident or the diagnosis of a progressive or incurable disease, grandparents need to allow themselves to grieve so they can offer support to the parents and other children. Some grandparents refuse to accept a less than "perfect" grandchild and either will reject the diagnosis or the child. Some insist that the parents go from doctor to doctor or medical center to medical center to try and find a different diagnosis. *One mother told me that her "wealthy mother-in-law tried to make a crooked stick straight and caused major problems."* How sad for the parents, the child, and the grandmother.

Another mother told me that one of the grandmothers refused to see her grandson in a wheelchair. The boy always had to be seated in a regular chair or at the dinner table before his grandmother arrived. I can't imagine doing that to a child or his parents.

As grandparents we are extremely important to our grandchildren and their parents. We can make the decision to find ways to handle our grief so we can offer help and support to our grandchild and the parents or we can cause great stress and unhappiness. The decision is ours.

Chapter Two

Providing Help and Support to Parents

One of the hardest things about having a grandchild with special needs is knowing when to help, when to say something, and when to keep quiet. Some grandparents hover so much that they become a nuisance. How do you know how much help and support to offer? If you live close by, the right answer is critical. If you make a nuisance of yourself, there could be lasting repercussions.

A grandmother, who was retired, but had been an outstanding nurse, found it extremely difficult not to hover when a new grandchild was having heart surgery and then had complications. She told me "Talk about feeling frustrated and helpless. After years of being trained to help and then not being allowed to, makes it hard to cope. Yes, the parents should be in charge, but the waiting is hard to endure. I have been knitting aimlessly and bicycling."

If the parents are not functioning well after receiving a devastating diagnosis and want assistance, grandparents can step in and offer help with meals, child-care, running errands, researching medical information or spelling a parent who is staying by a hospital or intensive care bedside. It is hoped that the parents will be able to say if they want help. If things are falling apart in the house, offering to pay for someone to come in and clean or provide child-care can be life-saving. It may be easier for parents to have paid help rather than having a grandparent nearby. Grieving is very personal and many parents are not willing to let grandparents see how much they are hurting or not coping well.

If there are other children in the family, a grandparent or grandparents can help greatly by taking the siblings out for a meal or a fun few hours. Siblings often are forgotten when parents receive an unexpected diagnosis. Their lives and needs are just as important as the child with special needs and they will suffer greatly if the parents focus all their attention on the child with a problem.

OTHER WAYS TO HELP

One grandmother made an important contribution by researching family medical history for several generations. The child's diagnosis had been unclear until the grandmother found both pictures and histories of several family members with a similar problem. Once the doctors had this information they were able to sort through possible diagnoses and come up with the answer.

A grandfather accompanied his daughter and grandchild when the child had an appointment with me. By explaining the problem he had with an anesthetic after a long surgery, the diagnosis of a muscle disease was much more likely. (A potentially fatal condition called Malignant Hyperthermia is associated with several of the muscle disorders.) *This also provided information about precautions the parents should take if this child or their other children had surgery.*

Another grandmother made the probable diagnosis of diabetes in her five-year-old grandson when the child's doctor had missed it. He did not check for diabetes by doing a yearly urinalysis, despite a strong family history of the disease. The grandmother became suspicious when she noticed that the floor was sticky around the toilet bowl whenever her grandson visited! She thought that sugar in the urine probably made the floor sticky and insisted the boy be tested for diabetes. She was right and what a smart grandmother!

Often telephone calls can become a major nuisance if friends and neighbors call after hearing the devastating news. A grandparent can be very helpful in returning phone calls if the parents ask them to do so. Buying them an answer machine can also be a life-saver, because there will be many times when the parents just are not up to answering calls from worried family, friends, or neighbors.

Providing transportation for siblings to and from school, activities, or doctor and dentist appointments can be very helpful. It also gives grandparents an opportunity to talk to the brothers or sisters and listen to their concerns or worries. Kids pick up on tension in the home and always know if something is going on. It is important they are told whatever information they can handle depending on their age. That way they won't fear they did something to cause the problem.

HANDLING PARENTS' REJECTION OR ABUSE

Some parents simply refuse to accept the diagnosis of a problem in one of their children and walk away. Sometimes this is the mother and sometimes the father. In one study of babies born with spina bifida, eighty-five percent of the fathers left the home.[3]

I had one patient with cerebral palsy whose mother had deserted the family when she was small. The father was an excellent, caring parent, but unfortunately he was sent to prison because of some financial difficulties. The child with cerebral palsy was left in the care of her older brother and it was an extremely difficult time for both of them. The mother was not heard from again. I wish there had been grandparents to help. They could have made such a difference.

There are situations where a parent feels guilty because the gene that caused a particular disability was present on the parent's side of the family or the parent was a carrier of the gene. I have heard parents argue vehemently about who was responsible for a child's disability and sometimes the argument was held in front of their child. A problem like this often ends in separation or divorce and loving grandparents could make a great difference to a child who feels he or she is responsible for the parents' break-up.

The majority of the parents of the special needs children I have cared for have been single parents. Many were amazing in both their ability to cope and the dedication they showed their children. Unfortunately, many of the children had grandparents who did not stay in touch which made it very lonely for the special needs child and single parent. What a difference grandparents could have made if they had been able to take over some of the day-to-day tasks and responsibilities and offer emotional support.

One single mother had left the East coast and come to California because her parents would not accept her pregnancy. When the baby was born with a serious congenital deformity, the mother became very depressed. I tried to find some counseling for her as I feared for both the mother's and baby's lives. The infant had no future because at a few months of age he was found dead in bed. I've always wondered if the mother didn't take things into her own hands.

Tragically, many children with disabilities are abused, physically, emotionally, or sexually. The abuser can be a parent, a step-parent, a sibling, teacher, or teacher's aide. The abuse can be in the form of bullying, hitting, beating, or neglect. Some children are not given adequate food or fluids and others are left alone for long periods to cope as best they can. Abused children are more easily preyed upon because they may lack the ability to get away or not understand what is happening. Statistically, children with special problems or disabilities are abused more than children who can run away or fight back.[4]

Unfortunately, even when abuse is reported to child protection agencies, the social workers are so overloaded that little monitoring is done and deaths have resulted. In the U.S., we frequently see tragic newspaper accounts of children who were found dead from abuse even though they were known to child protection agencies. They were either forgotten or deleted from the list of those to be monitored.

If you notice changes in a grandchild's behavior and have concerns that some type of abuse is occurring, please take action now. A call to a child abuse agency can be made from a public phone and your name need not be given. There are also Internet resources and other places that can offer advice and support. One in the United States is www.childwelfare.gov and another is the National Child Abuse Hotline at: 1-800-4-A-Child. In the U.K., the Foundation of Survivors lists multiple agencies and resources for protection against abuse for kids with special needs. The Web site is www. freewebs/jameyphillips/usauksupportresources.htm.

Some signs that abuse may have occurred are:

- bruises that can not be explained by a fall

- burns

- fractures

- cuts

- bloody spots on underwear

- a change in behavior as crying jags, or increasing withdrawal from others

- a change in habits

- a sudden fear of men

- extra clothing to hide signs of violence

- a new fear of parents or adults in general

- unwillingness to be touched

- secretiveness

- an increased desire to bathe

- wearing extra clothes to bed.

If you speak up and get a child help and protection, you could save that child's life.

There are times, however, when abuse is suspected and instead there is an undiagnosed genetic problem. I have had experience with two families where the parents were accused of abusing a baby because of bone fractures and criminal charges were made. I was able to show that both children had osteogenesis imperfecta or "brittle bone" disease. In this disorder, even a small movement can cause a break or fracture. There are varying degrees of involvement, so a diagnosis may not be made right at birth.

HANDLING PARENTS' DENIAL

If the parents are in denial about a child's problem and you suspect there is something wrong, what can you do? If there is good communication and the parents will listen: I would plan your strategy and perhaps after a good dinner when the parents are relaxed, I would talk about your concerns and suggest an appropriate medical or other professional visit. This suggestion should only be given when the parents are not pushed for time.

Two grandparents, both child development experts, soon realized that one of their grandchildren had a special problem. However, both parents were in denial and refused to seek medical advice. When the child started kindergarten, her excellent teacher insisted that testing be done. This showed the child did have the problem the grandparents feared and the little girl was put in a special class. The grandparents were willing to pay for some additional after-school help, but once again the parents refused. The grandparents decided they could do no more and suffered every time they visited the family.

I think one of the hardest things about being a grandparent is that you have limited say and limited control unless you have full-time care. Many times you have to bite your tongue and say nothing. If there is a question of a possible physical harm to a grandchild, I'm sure you would speak up and hope you will be heard. Establishing a good relationship with both parents is very important and sometimes takes a lot of work. Most parents want the best for their children, but may be too busy or overburdened with other problems. They may also feel you are interfering and trying to exert control over their lives.

DISTANT GRANDPARENTING

If you don't live close by the family, you can still offer support. This could be providing financial help, researching family histories, medical professionals and facilities or other tasks the parents ask of you. Knowing when to call is important so as not to overburden the parents. Cards and notes can offer support or if you have no financial worries, you could arrange for some meals to be delivered or pay for a cleaning service. Both would most likely be appreciated. Thinking about what you would need and like to have done in a similar situation should give you ideas about how you can provide the best assistance and support.

Chapter Three

Helping Siblings Cope

When a child has special needs, it takes a great amount of energy to keep up with all the various appointments, school meetings, and activities. Even when there are two parents to manage everything, time spent with any brothers or sisters can be extremely limited.

It is very difficult to be the sibling of a child with special needs and, as a brother or sister, you can feel ignored and unloved. Grandparents can help greatly by stepping in and driving siblings to school, activities, appointments and friends or just spending time with brothers and sisters talking, listening, and having fun.

If a brother or sister has always been the center of the parent's universe until a new baby arrived, it can be doubly hard to take a back seat. It can help greatly if small, special gifts from the new baby can be delivered to the sibling at home. A grandparent could help make this possible, because often when an infant is hospitalized for a long time, many mothers almost live in the hospital. This is not healthy for them and not healthy for any other children. Grandparents can also help by taking the parent's place at the bedside for a while, so he or she can get some rest and, it is hoped, spend time with the other kids and their mate.

Often the siblings of a special needs child will start acting out, develop stomach aches or other medical problems, in order to get attention. If this occurs, some time spent with a grandparent can be life-saving. A grandparent, who is retired, can be a great gift to a lonely, lost child. Finding a common interest is important. Working on a hobby together, visiting a favorite park or recreation area can be fun and take the child's mind off the troubles at home. Going to the library or a bookstore and then sitting down to read a book together can be great fun for little children. Cooking and baking together will be long remembered. Planting flowers and working in the garden will help grandchildren develop a love for nature and this can be therapeutic for everyone. Woodworking is also fun and creative.

Most kids like to play games and having a special shelf for games in your home is a good idea. Kids love to have their grandparents play games with them and even if you don't enjoy playing games, it will pay off royally. Television is often used as a baby-sitter by busy parents and anything you as a grandparent can do to get your grandchildren away from TV is important. The same is true for Game Boys, computers, and Nintendo.

Most kids these days get bored with the many toys they are given and don't know how to entertain themselves. If you need some ideas about how to get your grandchildren away from the TV and other electronic things, an excellent book is *Unplugged Play* by Bobbi Conner (2007).[5] The book is filled with great ideas for games and having fun using simple, everyday things.

Many parents are both working one or two jobs to make ends meet, so meals are usually fast-foods, often eaten in front of the television. Sometimes each person watches TV in his or her own room while eating, I am told. Family meals are important in order to discuss the day's activities, successes, worries and to keep everyone communicating. If this doesn't happen, kids can get into all kinds of trouble because they think no one cares what they are doing.

Grandparents can make a great contribution by teaching siblings how to set a table nicely and by helping them practice their table manners. *One grandmother says her small grandson takes great pride in helping to set the table and even draws and colors pretty placemats for the table. He knows that when he comes to grandmother's house he is expected to sit at the table during mealtime, practice good manners, and both listen and talk to the others who are there. What a lucky little boy!*

ONE-TO-ONE TIME

If you have one or more grandchildren, in addition to the special needs grandchild, taking one child at a time to visit a park, go on a merry-go-round, or to buy an ice cream cone will give you a chance to find out if the child has worries or concerns. It is important to listen carefully and also watch the child's body language.

Often siblings overhear conversations that they don't understand about their brother or sister and need explanations. Also, they may feel guilty because they are healthy and their sibling is not. Then, too, kids often feel they somehow caused the illness or disability. These concerns can have a lasting impact if they are not brought out into the open and put to rest. A grandparent who has time to listen may be exactly what a child needs to get rid of any fears or anxieties.

TEACHING THE STEPS OF INDEPENDENCE

Siblings often don't learn how to do everyday tasks because their parents get so wrapped up in the needs of the child with a disability or illness. Grandparents, who have the time and patience, can play an important part by teaching their grandchildren how to do basic chores. This way they can start to learn the steps of independence. Most children with disabilities can also do some chores if the chores are adapted to their level of ability. Kids with learning disabilities or those who have trouble focusing should have their chores broken down into manageable parts. Some may need a chart to show what they have completed and what still needs to be done. A box of stars that you can buy at a stationery store would help. Each time a chore is completed, a star could be put next to that task. This takes a lot of patience and a lot of attention on a grandparent's part, but is a way of ensuring that a child learns about responsibility and the importance of completing what he or she has started. The following is a list of chores by age that kids can do if there are no disabilities.

Chores for Children

Ages 3–5 years	*Ages 5–7 years*
Dust	Make beds
Set table	Sweep steps and floor
Empty wastebaskets	Fold clothes
Put away toys	Sort clothes
Sweep	Water plants
	Care for pets

Ages 7–10 years	*Ages 10+ years*
Clean bed and bathrooms	Load dishwasher
Help make lunches	Change beds
Empty dishwasher	Wash windows
Make dessert, salad	Iron simple things
Wash windows	Help fix dinner
Load washing machine	Mop floors
Vacuum	Yard work
	Clean bathroom
	Empty garbage

A fun way to get kids to do chores is to give them a ticket for each chore completed. When a certain number of tickets are earned, a special treat can be in store such as a trip to get an ice cream cone. Another good idea is to have a chore chart for each grandchild. You can list the chores for each day and then put a check on the chart when a chore is completed. A certain number of checks would equal a special treat.

Money management is important for all kids to learn, particularly in these days of many things to buy, multiple enticing TV ads, and the bad economy. Rather than just giving your grandchildren money, it is important they do some chores to earn the money. This way they learn you are not a cash machine and that money doesn't "grow on trees."

Some people think kids should just be given an allowance because they are part of a family. I disagree, because I think children need to know how hard it is to earn money. If they start learning this at a young age, it will be easier for them to become financially independent when they are older. Children who are given too much at an early age often think they are entitled to everything they want as they grow up. Earning their own money gives kids a feeling of competence and importance. If you just give them money, they will never know the joy of earning their own money.

❀

One grandfather gave each older grandchild a small amount of money and said he would match whatever money he or she could earn from interest on savings account or stocks and bonds. Then he spent some time teaching the children about money management. It was a fun time for the grandfather and the kids. The grandfather had a hard time relating to children in other ways, but found this to be a way he and his grandchildren could have a common interest.

SIBLING GROUP MEETINGS

I've held group meetings for siblings of special needs kids and found these to be very eye-opening experiences. Many of the kids felt as though they weren't important to their parents and many were angry they had to do chores when the sibling with a disability did not. We lanced a lot of anger in those groups and I was glad that the kids were able to share their feelings with me and each other.

There is an organization in Seattle, Washington, that puts out a newsletter for the siblings of kids with special needs. It can be accessed at: www.seattlechildrens.org/sibsupp/resourcespage.htm. Their newsletter would be helpful for grandparents in the U.K., as well as the U.S. It is hoped, too, other special organizations and agencies pay special attention to siblings. If not, this could be something you as grandparents could investigate or even instigate. Many siblings carry a life-long burden when they have a sibling with special needs. A large percentage of kids who have siblings with disabilities go into the healthcare professions.

One doctor, who sought counseling, told me that her psychiatrist said, "You have been carrying your disabled brother on your back all these years. No wonder you feel used and angry. You've always had to be the strong one and your sibling got to do anything he wanted and seems to have been the one running your family."

ESTABLISHING A LONG DISTANCE CONNECTION

If you live at some distance from your grandchildren and they can come for a visit, this can offer a wonderful opportunity to spend some one-to-one time with a grandchild. Another way to spend time with a sibling of a special needs child is to plan a trip. This not only gives the grandchild some extra attention, but for a time he or she can forget about the problems at home. It is fun to plan a trip with a grandchild and he or she will feel proud to be involved as much as possible in the planning. This should include a budget. Kids don't need to go to fancy hotels or expensive tourist attractions. If they can spend some time with their grandparents and learn about other people and cultures, that will long be remembered. *My children were introduced to Indian dances and customs by their Arizona grandparents and have special memories of these occasions.*

If it is not possible to have grandchildren either visit you or for you to go on a trip together, there are other ways that you can keep a special connection. *One grandmother has a set time each Sunday when she talks with her grandchild. Another grandfather discovered there is a video set-up where he can have a camera at his grandchild's house and another at his house and they can talk with each other. This is done at a regular time once a week and has made a great difference in the child's life. The two have established an enduring bond.*

In this day of amazing technology there should never be an excuse of not keeping in touch with grandchildren. Older grandchildren can send e-mails, as can grandparents. Postcards, snapshots, small, unusual gifts, videos, recorded messages sent on a tape, fun cards, and letters are inexpensive and important. Those of us who have never known our grandparents missed a great deal. *I saw my only living grandparent just once when I was about four and have only a faint picture of her in my mind. However, I do have a postcard that she wrote me and several pieces of her furniture and some dishes. These are special to me and to my children.* Getting to know grandparents and other relatives gives children a sense of their history and a feeling of having roots which we all need in today's topsy-turvy world.

FINDING HELP FOR A TROUBLED SIBLING

There may come a time when you sense that a sibling of your special needs grandchild needs professional help. This can be a very delicate subject to bring up with the child's parents. They may be denying the problem or be so busy and preoccupied with the needs of their jobs or other children that they don't realize or don't want to see that there is a problem. A special problem can occur if one twin dies and the other twin is left without his or her best friend. In this case, some very special attention and/or counseling may be needed.

Some children are so sensitive that they develop true emotional or psychiatric problems when they live with a special needs child. They may feel left out and not important or feel that they did something to cause the problem. If this is the case, some counseling is definitely needed.

One teenager was left at home to baby-sit his six-year-old brother. He let the child go swimming in the family pool, but for a few minutes kept his eyes off the child. It just took those few minutes for the little boy to probably hit his head and end up in the bottom of the pool. The brother quickly pulled the child out, but not before considerable brain damage took place. The family never recovered; the parents were later divorced and a few years later the sibling committed suicide.

If you sense there is a critical problem with one of the brothers or sisters, you could ask the parents to join you for coffee, lunch, or dinner and delicately talk about your concerns. If the parents are resistant, they might give you permission to discuss your concerns with the child's pediatrician or teacher. Permission may not be granted and it is possible that you cannot do anything about your concerns. If you have full-time care and legal custody, then you can consult the child's doctor and teacher and then see to it that counseling is received. If your grandchild is greatly troubled and does not receive counseling, he or she could pay a high price.

Two siblings of special needs children come to mind when I think about any who developed serious emotional and psychiatric problems. Both had a sibling with a severe disability. The one boy had three brothers, all in wheelchairs. I finally had to have him hospitalized in a psychiatric unit where he received extensive therapy.

The other sibling got into all kinds of trouble and finally as a teenager had a serious car accident from which he never recovered. He also was involved with drugs.

There was only so much that I could do to help both of these boys, but if they had had loving, involved grandparents, it could have made a great difference. Both mothers were divorced and doing the best job of parenting that they could while working full time.

If there is not extra money for counseling or good insurance, then a community mental health clinic could be consulted. Often a social worker connected with a special needs organization, agency, or hospital can offer help or at least suggest other places where counseling is available. In the U.K., help can be found at www.sane.org.uk or www.mentalhealthcare. org.uk.

Many U.S. sites now have HELP or 211 lines where you can call and inquire about available resources. If a sibling develops serious emotional or psychiatric problems and doesn't receive help, the consequences can be serious. By recognizing the problem and seeing that counseling is received, you could save that grandchild's life.

You could also save the life or mental health of your grandchild with special needs if a sibling teases, torments, or physically injures a child who is unable to fight back. If a child is deaf, can't verbalize, or is blind, siblings may find sneaky ways to make the brother or sister suffer. Often a sibling does something wrong, but makes it appear as though the child with special challenges has committed the offense or the destructive act. Some kids know how to put on a smiley, ingratiating face, when they actually are being underhanded and destructive.

A parent or parents may be too stressed or busy to recognize what is going on, but if you, as a grandparent, sense that there are problems between siblings, it would be most important to speak up. You may not be able to ensure that something is done to change the situation, but you could try to teach the grandchild who is being attacked some basic rules of self-defense. It could help greatly to enroll your grandchild in a martial arts class that is specifically designed for kids with disabilities.

One child with a disability, who was also small and thin, became angry about even little things. His grandparents suspected he was being picked on by his older brother and paid for him to be enrolled in a judo class for kids with special needs. He began to look forward to the classes and developed a good relationship with his teacher. As the boy gained confidence in his ability to defend himself, his older brother stopped picking on him and the boy became a much happier, less angry child.

The grandchild who is doing the abusing could feel that he or she is not getting enough attention or could have some mental health difficulties. Both of these problems could be helped by grandparents who keep their eyes and ears open and try to see that some changes are made or medical care is received.

Chapter Four

Multiple Birth Grandchildren

It is not unusual these days to see several sets of twins and even triplets in small and large communities. In the United Kingdom, there are ten thousand multiple births a year. In the U.S., the National Center for Health Statistics states that twin births have increased seventy-four percent between 1980 and 2000 and five times as many triplets and other multiple births now occur as compared with past years.

A family in our small town had one child, then triplet girls, and finally a set of twins. The grandmother moved in and became a permanent resident for several years. How lucky the parents were to have another full-time pair of hands with five children under age three all in diapers! Fortunately, all the children were healthy.

When there are multiple births, the possibility of one of them having a disability is higher than the average. This is particularly true if the babies are low birth weight or born prematurely. Twenty-five percent of premature babies may have some type of problem. This may be cerebral palsy, blindness, learning disability, or a congenital abnormality. Cerebral palsy occurs in twenty-five percent of infants born with a birth weight of less than one kilogram or 2.2 pounds and is eight times higher with twin births and forty-seven times higher with triplet births.[6] A grandparent who lives nearby could be a life-saver if he or she is willing to help out.

If there are financial problems in handling multiple birth babies, there may be some help in the U.K. from the health benefits agency and tax department. Resources and support are also available from the TAMBA special needs group at www.tamba.org.uk or at 0800 138 0509. The Web site www.newlifecharity.co.uk offers advice about infants born with birth defects. Other helpful Web sites for babies born with birth defects in the U.S., Australia and Canada are given in the Appendix.

Feeding–Because twins or multiple birth babies can be smaller than a single baby or may be premature, feeding may be a little more difficult. If the baby is bottle-fed, you want to be sure that the size of the nipple hole and the nipple itself works well for that particular baby. A rocking chair is comfortable to sit in to feed an infant. The room should be quiet without loud music or a blaring television.

No infant likes to be rushed to finish eating and most need at least twenty to thirty minutes to take a bottle. An infant should never be propped to take a bottle because babies like to be held to feel secure. Also, a bottle should never be left in a bed or crib for a baby to suck on, which I'm sure grandparents remember from having their own babies.

If there are problems with spitting, it helps to keep an infant upright for about twenty minutes after a bottle is taken. The baby can be put in an infant seat to stay upright after a feeding. If there is a lot of spitting or regurgitation, the formula may be wrong or if it is breast milk, the baby's mother may have eaten something that disagrees with the infant. Some drugs get into breast milk and some foods that a mother has eaten can give an infant an upset stomach. If there is a lot of spitting up, this is something to discuss with the parents or the baby's doctor. Medication for GERD or regurgitation seems to be prescribed quite freely these days, which is of concern. In my experience, when the right eating techniques are used and the formula is appropriate, medication should not be needed or needed infrequently.

One grandmother helped out frequently with her daughter's twins and loved caring for them. She told me that she would take the two babies and sit in the middle of a sofa with a baby on either side to feed them. She burped them individually and always had the phone close by in case there was an emergency or she needed help. The parents both worked and were very grateful for the grandmother's help.

Burping can be a problem with some babies. One mother of twins found that using Mylicon drops was the only way she could get one of her twins to burp. Your baby's doctor might have another suggestion. It is important that the nipple hole be just the right size for each baby, so milk doesn't come out too slowly or too fast. At least now, parents and grandparents don't have to make formulas from scratch, as many did in the past. Powdered formulas are convenient to use for traveling because they can just be added to water and take little space.

Bathing can be a real problem if you have more than one baby to bathe. It is always important to remember to check the water temperature. This is particularly true if a baby has spina bifida or a loss of sensation in the legs. If either the telephone or doorbell ring when you are bathing a baby, it should just go on ringing. An answering machine and a sign on the front door would both be helpful.

If you have someone to help, a good system is for one person to bathe a baby, while the other one dries and dresses the infant. This way, you can get the babies bathed in record time and keep them safe and warm. Having some music playing while you bathe a child can make the time more pleasant. Most babies love a bath, but if there are sensory problems, it can make your job a great deal harder and take more time and patience. You will need to be sure you are relaxed and not in a hurry. A towel or small mat in the bottom of the sink or tub will help keep a baby from slipping.

Dressing—Parents who have identical twins or multiple births have to decide early on whether to dress the children identically or to give them different outfits or at least different colored outfits. *One older identical twin told me "My sister and I were always dressed alike except for half a dozen times in high school. I regret that to this day."*

I'm sure it is hard to establish a separate identity if you are an identical twin, so parents and grandparents need to make a conscious decision about how to handle this question. As grandparents, we can create real problems if we don't respect the parents' and older twins' choices.

Crying—Most grandparents handle a baby's crying better than new parents because they have already had experience with crying babies. Your old parenting sense will probably kick in as you handle a new, crying baby. The most important thing is to not become anxious and knowing that crying is part of what a little baby does. Remember that there are different kinds of cries: the hungry cry, the angry cry, the miserable wet or dirty cry, the tired cry, and the hurting cry. If you are caring for a new grandchild, it won't take long, I'm sure, for you to begin to identify which cry is which. No infant needs to be picked up the instant he or she starts to cry.

If a baby has been fed, changed, burped and it is time for a nap or bed-time, then it is wise to wait for a few minutes to see if the infant will settle down. Babies born into families with lots of children don't get as much attention as a first child, so they usually learn to quiet themselves since they don't get picked up right away.

Sleeping—This is easier with multiple birth babies when they are little and each just needs a snug bassinet. As they get older and need bigger beds, extra room will have to be found. Babies should not sleep in the same bed and never, ever sleep in the parents' or grandparents' beds. Babies have suffocated this way. It is best for them to be in a room of their own and not in the parents' or grandparents' room. A monitor can be purchased, so any distress sounds can be heard. If a baby has apneic spells, a good monitor would be important to have so you can be aware of any breathing problems.

Remember that babies now should sleep on their backs, which is different from what we were told when our babies were small. This position has been shown to reduce the incidence of SIDS or Sudden Infant Death Syndrome. (Smoking also increases the risk of SIDS.)

IMPORTANT MEDICAL TIPS FOR BABIES WITH AND WITHOUT SPECIAL NEEDS

If the baby has an **obstructed tear duct**, try massage and warm compresses *before* allowing the duct to be surgically opened. Gentle massage at the inner corner of the eye will often open an obstructed tear duct. This can be a problem in any baby.

Boy babies can develop a large collection of a cheesy substance called **smega under the foreskin of the penis**. By gently pulling back or retracting the foreskin, if this is possible, the smega can be removed. Baby girls also may have a cheesy material between the folds of the labia. Sometimes, too, in the early days they can have a little vaginal discharge and even a little vaginal bleeding.

New babies may have a **milky discharge from the nipples**. The breasts can also be enlarged or engorged in both boy and girl babies. This usually lasts just a short while.

An infant or child with a **high, unexplained fever** should always have a **urine specimen checked**. This is particularly true for babies with spina bifida and those with congenital urinary abnormalities. (Special infant and small child urine collection bags are available.) Meningitis can occur in babies and little children and if there is any suspicion of this, a spinal tap should be done. This is not a difficult procedure in an infant or child. A child with a shunt or hydrocephalus is particularly at risk for meningitis.

Q-Tips should never be used in a baby or child's ear. They can cause damage and push wax down into the canal. The external ear can be gently cleaned with a wash cloth. A physician can clean an ear canal under direct vision by looking through an otoscope and using an instrument called an ear curette.

Bowing of the legs is normal in babies and little children, but the legs should begin to straighten out once a child starts walking. A difference in leg lengths is important to notice in babies, particularly in girls, because this could be due to a **congenital dislocation of the hip**. If this is identified early, the hip can be treated and corrected.

Babies and little children may **develop flatness of the head** because of sleeping on their back. Once they start moving around and turning over, this should disappear. Special molding helmets for normal flatness appear to be overused these days. There are some congenital abnormalities of the head that need treatment. For these, there are special helmets and once in a while surgery will be needed, but this is rare.

Most **hemangiomas,** which are red and raised small, soft collections of blood vessels, get smaller or will disappear as a child grows older. A pediatric dermatologist always needs to be consulted before a physician does anything to one of these. Otherwise severe scarring may result.

Any baby who is **not making sounds by three months of age** should have a hearing exam in a pediatric hearing center. Older children with frequent ear infections and delayed speech should also have their hearing checked in a pediatric hearing center. In the U.K., the NHS Newborn Hearing Screening Programme offers hearing testing soon after birth and over 1600 babies are screened daily. In the U.S., thirty-eight states now mandate that the newborn's hearing must be checked before they leave the hospital. There can always be an error in the testing, so if a baby is not making sounds by three months, a repeat testing should be done in a pediatric hearing center, not a doctor's office.

Babies who are **teething** usually don't have elevated temperatures. They can be fussy and miserable, but should always be checked for an ear infection or other cause. Cold teething rings, rubbing the gums with a clean finger, and teething biscuits all help.

An infant or child can have an **ear infection without having an elevated temperature**. The child may just be a little fussy or an older child may pull at the ear. If a baby or child has a cough or cold, be sure a doctor checks the ears. Ear infections are often associated with a respiratory infection.

If a **baby boy does not have a good urinary stream** or the opening at the tip of the penis seems to be off-center, the doctor needs to be alerted. This could indicate a congenital abnormality of the urinary system. Baby boys may have their scrotums filled with fluid. This is called a **hydrocele** and is quite common at birth. The fluid usually absorbs by six months. If it persists into later years, surgery may be necessary or it could indicate other urinary abnormalities.

Diaper rash can usually be cleared by keeping the diaper area as clean as possible and using zinc oxide ointment or Eucerin's Aquaphor. If a baby has spina bifida or a skin disorder, it is even more important to keep the diaper area clean and dry.

Milia is the term for **tiny white spots** that occur around the nose in newborns. The spots should disappear in a few days or weeks and need no treatment.

Thrush is a fungus infection in the mouth caused by monilia. It can be treated with special medicine that your doctor prescribes. When an infant is on antibiotics, the risk of monilia is increased.

Some **diaper rashes** are also caused by monilia and have a different appearance from the usual diaper rash. The monilia rash is usually red and raised and needs anti-fungal cream for treatment.

EQUIPMENT

Equipment can become very expensive if everything new is purchased for multiple birth babies. Fortunately, there are twin clubs where used equipment can be borrowed, rented, or purchased inexpensively. Most of the multiple birth clubs have newsletters that may have ads for used equipment. The Internet is also a good place to look for beds, strollers, and other needed baby equipment. You want to be careful that any used equipment has not been painted with lead-based paint that the babies might chew on as they get older.

SUPPORT GROUPS

Support groups are very important for parents and grandparents of multiple birth babies. In the U.S., the Triplet Connection offers help and resources at: www.tripletconnection.org. Their telephone number is (209) 474-0885. Twin Services has suggestions and help at www.twinservices.org. Their telephone number is (435) 851-1105. In the U.K., help can be found at www.twinsuk.co.uk.

Online chat rooms are a good way to share information and keep parents and grandparents from feeling so isolated and depressed about the constant needs of multiple birth babies. These can be helpful for grandparents both in the U.S. and the U.K.

As the children get older, it is important that each child receive the same attention. A child with special problems often monopolizes a parent's time, so if a grandparent can help out with the other children or with the special needs child, then it is hoped each child will get some good one-to-one time.

Chapter Five

Parents' Separation and Remarriage

If your grandchild is in a family where a divorce has occurred or is occurring, your role as a grandparent can be greatly changed or be threatened. A new partner or spouse may resent your presence or be suspicious of you as the parent of a previous partner. This could put your relationship with a grandchild in serious jeopardy.

In the U.S., divorce occurs in fifty percent of marriages, whereas in England the rate is considerably lower, twelve to twenty-six percent, and appears to have gone down in the last year or so. In Ireland, it has increased a little.

By keeping the lines of communication open and being as pleasant as possible, it is hoped that you will be able to have an on-going relationship with your grandchild. A card or even a small wedding gift could help close any rift. Also, an offer to baby-sit or provide transportation for your grandchild's various appointments or school functions could help keep your relationship intact.

If you are financially able, offering to pay for some special tutoring, if it is needed, art lessons or sports activities could help maintain your place in the family structure. A family membership to a museum, or swimming program might also keep your foot in the door. If a step-grandchild has a special problem and you have expertise in that area, your assistance could be invaluable.

One grandmother was a specialist in the needs of children with special problems. A grandchild was having trouble focusing and was becoming a behavior problem at home and at school, so the parents asked the grandmother if she could arrange for some testing to see what could be done.

The grandmother knew the staff in the learning disabilities center at a big University Medical Center and made arrangements for the grandchild to have some psychoeducational testing. The tests showed a marked learning problem, as well as an attention deficit disorder. Medication was prescribed and the boy was helped immensely. The youth started focusing better in school and his grades improved. The parents were delighted and told the grandmother that their family life had become pleasant and manageable.

Before long, however, an extremely large bill arrived from the University Medical Center. The parents asked the grandmother to review the bill and she saw that the charges were excessive. The woman called the doctor in charge of the testing program and he referred her to the CEO of the hospital. The grandmother finally reached the man, after several attempts, and her conversation with him resulted in a new bill on which the charges were greatly reduced. The parents couldn't have been more grateful. The grandmother's ability to see her grandchild was ensured and she continued to have good relationships with her daughter and the new husband.

If a couple have separated or divorced, it is extremely important to keep negative thoughts to yourself about the parent who is not your son or daughter. It is particularly wise to never make a derogatory comment about the other parent to your grandchildren. Kids caught between two separating or divorcing parents suffer greatly if the parents use them as battling rams or each parent tries to outdo the other with gifts for the children, expensive treats, or vacations.

A grandparent always should try to stay as neutral as possible and use a mate, friends, or a counselor to express feelings of unhappiness or anger at the situation. Parents have many unforeseen problems going through a separation or divorce and your role should be to help as much as you can, stay in the background, and bite your tongue about saying anything negative. If you live at a distance, you will get much less fall-out from a separation or divorce, unless you cause problems with frequent intrusive phone calls or send letters containing inflammatory remarks.

As a grandparent of a child with special needs, it is particularly important that you try to be as pleasant as possible to the other parent and his or her family members. If you can be the peacemaker, that will accomplish a great deal. In time, it is hoped, much of the pain and anger will dissipate and the needs of the children will be made of prime importance.

CHILD CUSTODY

If your grandchild's parents have never married and then split apart, serious custody issues can arise. Sometimes one parent will take a child and quickly disappear to another state or even out of the country. If there has not been a marriage and then a legal divorce, this can create a difficult problem. In one-third of child custody battles in the United States, a registered marriage has not taken place. A good family attorney with experience in child custody issues should be able to help. Sometimes the only way a missing parent and child can be traced is if a cell phone, bank card, or credit cards are used.

In the U.S., if a parent resides with a child in another state for six months or more, this becomes their home state and legal proceedings have to be carried out by an attorney in that state. A family attorney in your area or town can work with the out-of-state attorney, but this can become very expensive. Immediately, a warrant for the missing parent and child should be posted with the court and an experienced family attorney should then follow through on legal proceedings to have the child brought back to the previous place of residence.

In the U.K., the National Association for Child Support at www.nacsa. org.uk offers advice and resources about child custody issues.

KIDNAPPING

In ten percent of cases in the U.S. when a child is taken from the home, it is by a stranger. If this occurs the local police and FBI can be involved. The National Center for Missing and Exploited Children Web site is at: www.missingkids.com and their number is: 1-800-843-5678. There is also an American Association of Lost Children at 1-800-I AM-LOST and American Children Held Hostage at 516-232-6240.

In the U.K., if a child is taken by a parent or someone else, help can be found by calling the NPIA Missing Persons Bureau at 0808 100 8777. Their Web site is http://uk.missingkids.com. If they can not be reached, the local police should be notified.

Several years ago there was a tragic newspaper account of a little child who was playing in his grandmother's fenced front yard. The grandmother was in the house and when she checked on the child, he was gone. The child was never found. So as grandparents we have to be constantly vigilant. Most people think of kidnapping as something that occurs to someone else. It can happen in a department store, as happened to a friend, a mall, or anywhere. So if a grandchild is in your care, you have to have eyes in the front and back of your head and be aware of what is happening all around you.

I was walking with my granddaughter, Heather, one day and she was not in the best of moods. She had wanted to stay longer at her friend's house, even though we had agreed on a specific time for me to pick her up. The child was trailing behind me, so I kept turning around to be sure she was still close. Heather didn't understand why I needed to do this, but when I explained I was responsible for her safety and that if anything happened to her, I would be devastated, she came up beside me and peace was restored.

Men's bathrooms can be scary places to let a little boy go into alone and I've sometimes asked a pleasant man or guard to check on my grandson when he was small, but old enough to go into the men's bathroom by himself. I would wait outside the door, look at my watch, and if I started to get uncomfortable about the amount of time Alexander was in the bathroom, I took action. It is far better to be safe than sorry.

It is understandable that grandparents would want to just enjoy fun times with their grandchildren without any of the pain or heartaches, but in today's world that is becoming more and more difficult. If we can just stay on our toes and enjoy and treasure the fun times we have with our grandchildren, then it is hoped that the difficult times will pass more quickly. We have much to offer our grandkids and their parents, but only if we take care of ourselves, keep up to date on what is going on around us, do our best to stay in the background, and not interfere unless an emergency occurs or if we are in charge of grandchildren either part-time or full-time.

GRANDPARENTS TAKE OVER

Chapter Six

Grandparents in Charge

If you have part-time or full-time care of a special needs grandchild, you must find ways to take good care of yourself while caring for your grandchild. It has been reported that caretaking grandmothers have an increased incidence of heart problems.[7] While it is true that grandmothers get younger and younger these days, many older grandparents and even great-grandparents are caring for grandchildren, part-time or full-time.

I've had fairly elderly grandparents bring severely disabled grandchildren to my office. They have full-time care because the parents are teenagers, divorced, separated, in the military, dead, in jail, convicted of child abuse, jobless, or have drug problems. Most of these grandparents did not have much in the way of financial resources which added greatly to their stress. However, all were loving and doing an excellent job of caring for the special needs grandchild.

One older grandmother worked a night shift, so cared for her disabled grandchild in the daytime, while her husband took over the care of the little girl during the night. The father had died in an accident and the mother was in prison because of drug use. No grandparents could have been more loving despite minimal funds and health problems.

In some ways, it is easier to be a full-time caretaker rather than a part-time one. When you are in charge, your word is the one to which the grandchild must pay attention. Kids are great about manipulating adults and kids with special needs often have developed manipulation to a fine art. It is true that many have to learn how to use manipulation to some extent to get their needs met. However, all kids want boundaries and can get into trouble if they don't have them.

DISCIPLINE

Many grandparents say they just want to love their grandchildren and have fun with them. That is fine if you see your grandchildren just now and then, but if they live with you part-time or full-time, that doesn't work. Kids want an adult in charge and want to know the boundaries. If they do, they feel loved and secure. Some parents and grandparents feel that discipline is punishment and yet loving discipline is what kids need and want. Kids who are spoiled and out of control don't feel loved. Many patients have told me that they wished their parents would give them limits, because then they would know what was expected of them. They would also know that their parents cared enough to make rules or limits and stick to them.

If you are in charge just part-time, the kids at some time will probably say, *"But mother or daddy lets me do so and so."* A good answer to this is, *"That's fine in your house, but in our house these are the rules."* Kids can be very flexible if they know the rules, the rules are fair, and you are consistent about sticking to them. It is very hard on kids if there is not consistency because then they are never sure exactly where they stand.

It is often helpful to sit down with a grandchild or grandchildren and have a family conference. You can have a specific agenda and discuss rules, problems, chores, or perhaps allowances. The conference can be tailored to what a child can understand, but even a four-year-old can feel quite grown up if he or she is included in the conference and knows their opinion will be valued.

Discipline is particularly hard with special needs kids; as for example autistic kids who now and then or even quite frequently have "meltdowns." Parents and grandparents tell me that when a "meltdown" happens, the best thing to do is to have the child go to a special area or room and have the time to try and get in control. Any sharp or potentially dangerous objects should be removed from the child's reach or vicinity. Special toys and books can be in the room and sometimes favorite music will help. A child who is a computer whizz may find that focusing attention on the computer will help get things back in balance.

It will help if you can explain to a grandchild why you have made a specific rule or set certain limits. I think adults talk down to children too much. Kids can be quite adult in understanding things, depending on their age and intellectual ability, if you have established good communication and the children love and trust you. If a child is developmentally delayed, your expression or tone of voice should get the message across that you mean what you say and that you won't put up with a naughty, out-of-control child. Kids should always know you still love them; you just don't like their behavior at that moment.

It is often particularly hard for grandparents to discipline a child with a disability or problem and these kids can grow up spoiled and whiney. Kids with special needs want to be treated just like the other children.

One mother told me the story that one day she spoke angrily to her son, who was in a wheelchair, when he did something he knew was wrong. She started to feel terrible about what she had said when she saw a big smile appear on her son's face. He was delighted to have been treated just as his brother and sister would have been treated. This mother said she learned a big lesson from that experience.

Many parents these days use "time-outs" as a form of discipline. For grandparents, this may be a new concept and one that does not work for you. If a child knows you mean it when you say "No" and you are consistent, your voice should be your best form of discipline. However, if a grandchild has serious emotional or other problems that need more than a firm "No," then you will have to find the form of discipline that works the best for you and your grandchild. Spanking, particularly in anger, can hurt a child badly. By having a child go to a room you have set up, you can get control of your anger. By setting a timer, your grandchild will know he or she is free to leave the room when the bell rings if there have not been any further problems.

If a grandchild has serious behavior problems or does a lot of biting, hitting, kicking, spitting, screaming, has breath holding spells, or temper tantrums, you may need some extra help. Medications can cause increased stimulation and a change in medication or elimination of one or all drugs may be needed. If a child psychiatrist is overseeing your grandchild's care and you are not happy about the doctor's interest or attention, you might want to get a second opinion. It is too easy for a doctor to prescribe medicines without looking for underlying problems. Sometimes a child will have some other problem such as diabetes, hyperthyroidism, anemia, or some other condition that causes irritability and poor behavior. There could also be some interaction between drugs that is causing a bad reaction. Sometimes, too, a child can have two problems, as for example a muscle disease and also a learning disability or attention deficit disorder.

BEHAVIOR PROBLEMS

Behavior problems can be related to a grandchild's principal disability or to something entirely different. The behavior problem may be corrected quite easily or it may take some special laboratory or other tests. Over the years, some of the reasons I have found children to act out, be irritable, yell, be withdrawn, have temper tantrums, hit, and throw things are:

- hunger or poor diet, eating mainly fast-foods
- fatigue
- frustration from an unrecognized problem such as a communication difficulty or decreased hearing
- too high expectations by parents, grandparents, and teachers
- lack of sleep and no regular bedtime
- allergies not recognized or inadequately treated
- overstimulated
- reaction to medicine
- visual problem
- parents' divorce or separation
- lack of consistent discipline
- boredom in a very bright child
- no regular routine
- death of a pet, sibling, or family member
- parental tension and quarrelling
- little time with parents
- unrecognized learning disability
- parental illness
- fear and anxiety
- not enough time to play or quiet time
- emotional problem
- metabolic problem
- diabetes, kidney problems, or anemia
- infection
- severe constipation

- attention deficit hyperactive disorder

- heart problems.

Some children respond very well to play therapy or art therapy. An art therapist could be consulted or a child psychologist who does play therapy. Both of these are fun for kids and the results may be excellent.

SUGGESTIONS ABOUT COPING WITH YOUR GRANDCHILD'S UPS AND DOWNS

When a child has a special problem, he or she can be greatly hurt by an unkind or careless remark. If there is a hearing loss or severe developmental delay, the impact will be different, but an individual's body language can be just as telling if he or she pulls away or acts in an unkind fashion. *One parent told me that "People do a lot of hurting without knowing it and you have to teach your child how to handle the hurt."*

If a grandchild asks about why he can't do or eat what other kids do, it is important to answer the questions as honestly as you can. If the diagnosis is a serious or potentially fatal one, it will be more difficult to think of just the right answer. By being as optimistic as you can and trying to give your grandchild hope that answers will be found for his or her particular disorder, you can save the day. No one knows what the future holds and a new treatment or medicine that could be potentially life-saving could be announced tomorrow.

Many kids with disabilities know they are different and want to hide away in their rooms and spend their days on the computer or playing games. If they are not able to keep up with other kids, hiding may be their way of coping. Thus, it is important to find ways such as swimming, martial arts, art, or other activities in which they can excel. Every child has special qualities and if you can help bring these to light and find something in which a grandchild can excel, you can change the child's life.

If the hiding or retreating becomes increasingly worse, it might be time for some counseling. If you or a counselor can get a grandchild to open up and express feelings, that would be a major step forward. It is important to be realistic about a child's future and not place expectations upon the child that cannot be fulfilled. Every child should be accepted for their strengths and weaknesses, no matter what they are. If you always stress what your grandchild can do and not what can't be done, that will be a major contribution. You will give a grandchild the best quality of life if you expect the family rules to be followed, chores to be done, and each individual to be treated with respect.

ASKING FOR HELP

Having either part-time or full-time care of a grandchild with special needs can be very stressful at times, even though you love being with the child. It is important to anticipate what could be harmful not only to your grandchild, but also yourself. If you get too tired or anxious, this can impact your health, your driving, and even make household accidents occur.

If you are an older grandparent, it is important to know your limits and ask for help if you need it. Sometimes just having a friend or teenager spell you for an hour or so can make a difference. You need to take time for your own on-going activities and having some fun with friends or your mate. Exercise can also help.

Organizations such as Big Brothers and Big Sisters can be a great resource. Their Web site in the U.S. is: www.bbbs.org. In Canada, the Web site of this organization is: www.bigbrothersbigsisters.ca.

This organization screens their applicants and if one individual doesn't work out another one might. These volunteers can be a great help if you need a day off or a few hours to yourself. It is good, too, for kids to develop friendships with other caring adults. Kids with special needs often feel very isolated.

Trading child-care with another parent or grandparent can work out. That way each of you can have some time off. If you are not good to yourself, you won't be able to take care of your grandchild or yourself.

Transporting kids who need special equipment such as wheelchairs, braces, or oxygen tanks can be physically taxing and can raise some safety issues for you and your grandchild if you are not wise and ask for help when needed.

One large teenager with severe cerebral palsy had older grandparents. They both had health problems and just getting her from place to place was a big problem. The grandfather had a friend who was a motorcycle enthusiast and through him the couple developed a relationship with the local Harley-Davidson motorcycle club. The members were great about being on-call to help the grandparents and even made the teenager an honorary member. So reaching out to as many people as you can, if you need help, pays off royally. Trying to do everything yourself may create big problems and you could pay an enormous price by trying to be all things to all people.

TEACHING VALUES

Most grandparents have had their ideas of values and ethics tested at some point, particularly if they have worked outside the home or in large institutions or corporations. *I took a class one evening entitled "Ethics and Morals" which was taught by an executive of a local, major corporation. In the second class, the instructor defined Ethics as "whatever was appropriate at the time." I was extremely bothered by the man's definition and decided to speak up. It was interesting that only two others in the class were bothered by the definition. I dropped out of the class shortly after that and was not surprised to read several years later that the large corporation for which the man worked was in trouble with the government for misusing funds from various contracts they had received.*

I believe, as grandparents, that we can make a real contribution by trying to instill a good sense of values in our grandchildren, particularly if we are in charge. As role models, our grandchildren will note if we are kind to others; keep our anger in check or find acceptable ways to let it out, such as pulling weeds, hitting a golf ball or tennis balls; are responsible; and are involved with our family, friends and community. Even children with limited awareness or developmental delay can be taught acceptable behavior and kindness to others. Our society has become so "Me" oriented that any way we can show our grandchildren a different way of living will be making a real contribution.

SAFETY

Grandparents who have their special needs grandchildren for just a few hours, part-time, or full-time, need to be sure that their houses are safe.

One grandmother had a balcony on her house and left the sliding glass door open just a little. She didn't realize her grandchild could get through the narrow opening and over the child went to the cement below. The grandmother never really recovered from the child's severe head injury.

Children with visual difficulties need ways to know that certain areas are unsafe and specific objects are unsafe. Grandparents can work out a system for a grandchild and the book, *Children with Visual Impairments*, edited by M. Cay Holbrook (2006), gives some good suggestions about how this can be done.[8]

SAFETY CHECK LIST

1. Grandmothers' purses can be a source of danger if they contain medications. So it is always wise to put purses up high when a child is in the house.

2. Kids who are hungry will eat or drink all kinds of things. If caustic or poisonous substances are put in food packages, containers, or unlabeled bottles, a child may think it is something good to eat or drink.

3. Polishes, dishwasher soap, and cleaning compounds should all be up high and not under the sink.

4. Medicines should be in a locked cabinet or in a place where a child can not get into them.

5. Pacifiers can come apart and cause choking and should never be on a string around the neck. This could cause strangulation.

6. Vinyl on cribs and playpen rails can be pulled off, chewed, and choke a child.

7. Old playpens or cribs often contain lead paint and children may chew on the painted areas.

8. Hot water heaters should be turned down below 120 degrees Fahrenheit.

9. A child must never be left in a bathtub and the water should be tested before a child is given a bath. (This is particularly important for spina bifida kids or those with decreased sensation in the legs.)

10. Toys that are hung from the crib on a string have caused strangling, as have window blind cords near a crib that a child can reach.

11. Alcohol and cigarettes should never be left where a child can get into them. Children will ingest both of these and can have some bad results.

12. Wall heaters and floor heaters need to be surrounded by a strong, safe enclosure, so children can't burn themselves.

13. Smoke detectors need to be installed in prominent places and fire extinguishers should be easily accessible.

14. Swimming pools need to be surrounded by a fence or covered. (Be sure a child can't slip under the cover. This has happened.)

15. Fishponds can be dangerous if a little person slips and falls into one and no one is around to rescue the child.

16. Fire resistant clothing is a must, particularly in Halloween costumes.

17. Electrical outlets should be covered. Special covers can be purchased for these.

18. Electric cords need to be checked to be sure they are not frayed.

19. Hot pot handles should be kept turned away from the edge of the stove.

20. A coffee or teapot cord should never be left dangling where a child can grab it.

21. Gates should be installed at the top and bottom of all stairs for small children.

22. Toys need to be checked to ensure no small parts can be pulled off. Small kids will swallow almost anything.

23. Post emergency numbers by the phone. These should be: the grandchild's doctor, the poison center, ambulance, and nearest hospital.

24. CPR (cardiopulmonary resuscitation) is important for all grandparents, baby-sitters, and family members to know. In the U.S., hospitals, the American Red Cross, and some agencies offer CPR courses. Two Web sites that could be helpful are: www.RedCross.org and www.EmergencyUniversity.com/CPR In the U.K., online courses are offered at: www.safekids.co.uk/CPRChildren.html.

25. Garages can be danger traps and access should be denied unless an adult is there to supervise.

26. Old refrigerators should never be left where a child can climb into them.

27. Toy chests with heavy lids can trap a child.

28. Open windows can be tempting if there is no screen or guard.

29. Bedside table drawers containing medicines can be tempting for kids.

30. Peanuts and hard candies are not safe for little kids because they can cause choking.

31. Hot and cold water handles need to be clearly marked.

32. Bathroom rugs should be taped to the floor or be non-skid.

33. A side grab-bar on the tub and a towel or mat in the tub help prevent accidents.

34. Side bars can be placed on toilet seats or you can purchase a raised toilet seat with the side bars already installed.

35. Bath and shower seats can help keep a child firmly in place.

36. Playpens still have an important place in keeping little children safe. (Many parents today think they are too restricting, but it is better to be safe than sorry. Playpens certainly didn't hurt our children!)

37. All kids need to wear helmets when they are on bikes or skateboarding.

38. Kids should be warned to stay away from pool drains. The suction in some pools is so strong that kids have died when they got stuck on a drain or put an arm in one and were not able to pull it out.

39. Button or disk batteries should be put out of a child's reach. They can be ingested or put in the nose and cause serious problems. The batteries come in hearing aids, toys, watches, calculators, running shoes, small electronic devices, and greeting cards. (In the U.S., there is a 24 hour National Button Battery Ingestion Hotline at 202-625-3333. In the U.K., call NHS Direct at 0845 46 47.)

40. Car seats must be appropriate for the age of the child. If there are any transportation requirements, these should be discussed with your grandchild's doctor. In the U.K., the specific requirements can be found at: www.childcareseats.org.uk/law.

41. In the U.S., if an adapted vehicle is needed, a brochure can be obtained by calling 1-888-327-4236. Also, the Association of Driver Rehabilitation Specialists can be contacted at 1-800-290-2344 if there are questions about what can be done to make or be sure a car can safely transport a grandchild. The American Academy of Pediatrics at www.aap.org has a two page list of guidelines about *Transporting Children with Special Needs* and some good advice is offered. The National Highway Traffic Safety Administration at www.nhtsa.gov also has good suggestions about safe car seats.

42. Moving–If a move is necessary and you are caring for a grandchild, this is a time to be particularly aware of safety precautions. Kids can get into amazing things when there isn't the stress of moving, but if boxes are everywhere and movers are coming in and out, this is a time to be particularly on guard. It would be best if you can arrange to have a friend or hire a teenager to watch your grandchild. That way you can check on what the movers are doing to be sure things are handled the way you want.

43. Time of day–Another particularly dangerous time is first thing in the morning when a child may get out of bed before you and you haven't had your morning tea or coffee. Early morning and before dinner are the two times of day that kids get into the most trouble. Before dinner, everyone is usually tired and hungry and these two things make safety precautions and awareness even more important.

I was going down a steep hill in San Francisco early one Saturday morning when a little child darted out in front of my car. Fortunately, I was able to quickly stop, so the child was not hurt, but I had to take a few deep breaths and sit still for a few minutes before I started the car. A grocery store was across the street, so I suspected the child was hungry and looking for something to eat. I wondered if the parents were still in bed and didn't even know the little boy had sneaked out of the house.

TEACHING PERSONAL SAFETY

Many parents and grandparents hover over and protect a child with special needs so much that they are denied the opportunity to learn how to assess and protect themselves from dangerous situations. You don't want a child to be fearful of strangers and the outside world. Instead, you want them to learn how to be observant and aware of potentially harmful individuals and strangers. By teaching children to look and feel confident and watch out for predators or those who might cause them harm, you are giving them a great weapon. An important task of parenting is to teach children to look a stranger in the eye and get away as quickly as possible if their instincts tell them something is not right.

Kids with special needs are particularly vulnerable, because they may have limited ability to move, may have poor awareness of harmful situations or be developmentally delayed and be completely unaware of possible harmful situations or people. In this case, an accompanying aide or neighborhood friend would be an important asset.

If a child is able to enroll in a kids' special needs self-defense class it could be life-saving. However, it would be important to check with other parents or grandparents to be sure the instructor is someone who has had experience teaching kids with disabilities and would be aware and sensitive to any special problems. Karate and other forms of self-defense can help create self-confidence, a good self-image, improve strength, flexibility and also be a good way to make friends.

FEEDING GRANDCHILDREN

Grandmothers, who have planned and cooked countless meals, are usually ready to do less cooking once their children are grown. When grandchildren come to visit or stay, then the whole food question arises again. This can be a particular challenge if your grandchild is on a special or restricted diet. The various, fairly new diets include: gluten-free, ketogenic, low salt, low fat, low calorie, allergy-free, and diabetic. Fortunately, there are many good cookbooks that can help, as well as agencies with caring staff members.

One grandmother sent me a holiday card with the note that she and her husband had moved to a retirement community and her greatest joy was no longer having to cook! She had been an excellent parent and loved to cook when her children were growing up, but finally had decided that she had had enough.

So when grandchildren come to visit or live with you, meals once again become important. Many kids these days are being raised on fast-foods because both parents work outside the home full-time or the parent is single and also works full-time outside the home. Grandparents can make a great difference in a grandchild's nutrition if they try to set an example of good eating and offer a nutritious breakfast with some protein: eggs, sausage, yogurt, beans, or oatmeal and not just cold cereal or a pop tart.

It has been well documented that breakfast is the most important meal of the day. Also, individuals who eat a good breakfast with some protein and not a lot of sugar do better in school and work than people who eat their big meal at the end of the day and little food during the day. Breakfast eaters also find it easier to maintain a healthy weight.

Teens, in general, I have found, are the worst about eating breakfast. If you can sit down and eat breakfast with a teenage grandchild, that can make a difference. Nuts, instant oatmeal, little sausages, bacon, pieces of cheese, or yogurt will provide a quick and easy breakfast. *My children always liked "eggs in a frame." You cut a round hole in the center of a piece of bread, put some butter in a skillet, heat the bread on both sides and then put in the egg to cook. Kids may also be able to make this for themselves as they get older.*

Because breakfast is usually rushed on school days, you can have everything ready the night before and then just quickly heat things or zap them in a microwave if you have one. Beans and cheese or scrambled eggs wrapped in a tortilla can provide breakfast on the run, as can an ice cream cone filled with yogurt and fruit or some granola. Pitta bread can also offer something hot and nutritious if you fill it with scrambled eggs, egg salad, avocado, beans, or tomatoes. You may have to be creative or even a little sneaky to get kids to eat a good breakfast.

Most little kids don't like vegetables, so you may need to mix them with things they like. *One mother told me she put vegetables in a blender and mixed them with different things or put a good spaghetti sauce and cheese over them and served them that way.* For little ones if you mix something they don't like with something they do like, that might work. However most kids don't like mixture, but just like to know exactly what they are eating.

They also want small portions and food that is colorful. A plate filled with all white food or foods of all the same color doesn't make a very appetizing meal. You can make fun salads with half a pear, grated carrot for hair, raisins for eyes, and tomato or melon for a mouth. Half of a potato can be made into a sailing ship with a sail made out of cheese, melon or something else. Cookie cutters can also be used to devise other interesting looking foods. Muffins can have extra bran added if constipation is a problem or you could add dried cranberries, raisins, or other nutritious fillings.

If the children's parents are vegetarians, that can create a problem unless you are also a vegetarian. Dr. Henry Legere (2004, p.116) in *Raising Healthy Eaters* notes that "a child would need to eat anywhere from three to seven times as much non-meat protein foods to get the amount of protein found in a single serving of meat and cheese."[9] This makes giving children enough daily protein a difficult task, but eggs, oatmeal, and beans could help.

Kids prefer raw vegetables, but if there are swallowing difficulties or a child is under age two, you need to be a bit careful about giving them uncooked vegetables. Dipping them in a fat-free salad dressing may make them more inviting, but I would avoid the dips you can buy or make because these have lots of calories. Pretzels, chips, popcorn, nuts, whole peas and beans, pieces of hot dogs, whole grapes, raisins, and carrots may all cause choking if there are swallowing problems.

Healthy snacks could be fruit, yogurt, low-fat crackers, and low-fat cheeses, unless there is a milk allergy or intolerance. Soft drinks, candy, cakes, pies, and cookies could all be given now and then as a special treat.

A multi-vitamin is recommended for all of us these days because we eat so much processed food. Your grandchild's pediatrician could help decide the best one to give.

One of the best ways to get your grandchildren to try some new foods and new ways of eating is to have them help plan, shop, and prepare some meals. Then if you sit down nightly with your grandchildren and have a family dinner, the grandchildren will long remember these special times.

OBESITY AND ASSOCIATED MEDICAL PROBLEMS

With the marked increase in obesity in kids in both the U.K. and the U.S. these days, it is important that kids learn about good nutrition and what foods to eat and not eat. In the U.K., obesity in kids has risen steadily, so now it is estimated that at least one-half million school kids are overweight. Living on snacks, soft drinks, and fast-foods is eventually going to lead to obesity and probably increased blood pressure, and heart disease.

The marked increase in weight is often, too, accompanied by a lack of activity, particularly if your grandchild already has problems with muscle weakness or mobility.

If there is a problem with obesity, keeping a three day record of what your grandchild eats can give you an idea of how many calories are being consumed. Calorie charts are listed in some cookbooks and I've seen little calorie books at grocery store check-out counters. Your grandchild's doctor should be able to give you an idea of how many daily calories would be the best or you could consult a hospital or school dietitian.

Grandparents who take time to plan, shop, and prepare healthy meals will make a difference in their grandchildren's health and longevity. On the other hand, grandparents can become part of the problem. If a grandchild is constantly offered high calorie snacks, big meals, or lots of candy and other treats, a large weight gain may occur.

One grandmother refused to listen to her daughter's plea that she not give the granddaughter so much food when she cared for her after school. Even a telephone conversation from me had no impact. The girl disliked any form of outdoor sports. Instead, she watched many hours of television and her weight gain became excessive. She always had a big meal after school at her grandmother's house and then dinner at home when her parents returned from their jobs. The girl's weight gain became so excessive that she developed something called "sleep apnea." This can be a problem in greatly overweight people. The teenager would periodically stop breathing at night and finally after some special tests had to receive oxygen at night. I'm sure the woman thought she was being a loving grandmother by giving her granddaughter large, tasty meals after school, but instead she helped create a serious problem.

RESPITE CARE

In the U.K, many resources are provided for caretaking and respite. Home Care Officers, who have a wealth of information about resources, are connected with organizations such as the Muscular Dystrophy Association and with special centers and clinics.

Focus on Disability: www.focusondisability.org.uk/children-1.html lists several ways that help is provided. One of the ways is "temporary accommodation," where a child stays with a private family in their home, so the parents or grandparents can have a rest or holiday. The site also states that daycare can be provided for a child who is disabled "in a nursery, with a registered childminder, or for a few hours in a playgroup." They note that the National Health Service "provides a full range of services for disabled children, including therapy, specialized services, specialist aids, and equipment."

There are also organizations in the UK that provide support and services for carers. For example, the Crossroads Caring for Carers at www. crossroads.org.uk and Carers UK at www.carersuk.org.

In the U.S., different organizations provide respite or relief care. They have or can find individuals trained to care for children with special needs. If a registered nurse is necessary, your grandchild's physician can order one. The ARCH National Network offers support groups, legal information, and resources that can be found at www.archrespite.org. Their information can be invaluable.

If you are going to have a respite worker for a few hours or even a few days, it is important that you leave a detailed list of instructions for the worker. The list should include:

- emergency numbers: doctor, ambulance, police, fire department, plumber, and electrician
- your cell-phone or pager number
- U.K. NHS Direct is 0845 46 47
- U.S. Poison Control Hotline is 1-800-222-1222
- neighbors who will be at home or close relatives
- location of fire extinguishers
- location of flashlight
- medications to be taken with the dose and time
- food allergies
- other special instructions as to furnace or air conditioner controls
- instructions about grandchild's special equipment: braces, oxygen tanks, wheelchairs, ventilators, or apnea monitors
- location of first-aid kit which should contain:
  - band-aids of all sizes and shapes
  - a roll of gauze bandage
  - antibiotic ointment
  - ace bandage
  - tweezers for splinters
  - small scissors

- ° cotton balls
- ° Phisohex
- ° surgical tape
- ° Tylenol (paracetamol)
- ° Benadryl
- ° EpiPen for an allergic grandchild
- ° oral thermometer for older children
- ° rectal thermometer for infants and small children.

Another way to get some respite and provide fun and friends for your grandchild would be to locate a good camp for children with special needs. This could be for one day, several days, or a week. There are a wide variety of camps for kids with all kinds of special needs both in the U.K. and in the U.S. For the U.K., the Web site www://fsc.org.uk/programme/list_sn.asp gives a list of special needs camps. Easter Seals (www.easterseals.com) in the United States has special camps as do many other organizations. Some religious groups also have special day or vacation camps that can be fun. It is very important to network with other parents and grandparents to be sure the camps are well-run, clean, have appropriate activities, and enough counselors. The counselors should all have had background checks if they are to be around children. It is also important to find out if a nurse or other medical personnel are on the staff and if a doctor is available when needed.

One of my children went to a week's sleepover camp and came back with a badly infected leg, weight loss, and sleeplessness. I had checked the camp out with other parents, but apparently things had gone downhill since their children had been at that camp. Sometimes no matter how much you investigate things, there can be some unpleasant surprises.

HOUSE MODIFICATIONS

If you have full-time care of your grandchild and a wheelchair is necessary, you may need to make some house modifications. These can be quite expensive or you may be able to find a neighbor or friend who is handy with tools and willing to help. There are also commercial resources for home adaptations and in the U.K. the health service will pay for some home adaptations such as ramps, stair lifts, and easy-access showers. These are paid for by the Disabled Facilities Grant.

A retired carpenter volunteered to build ramps for families who needed them if our Center for Handicapped Children would pay for the materials. Grant funds were used for this purpose and it worked out well for everyone. We also had grand-fathers who built ramps, lowered shelves, and helped with other needed adaptations.

In the U.S., some insurance policies will cover things like wheelchairs, but it is usually a fight to get this kind of help. There is minimal help through the different state organizations for children with disabilities, but it is worthwhile to contact the local office of your state's organization for children with special needs.

The Internet offers information about companies that do house modi-fications. These can be checked out with other families who have had modifications done. The Web site: www.homemods.org gives multiple companies in the U.S. that do house modifications. It is important that a child with special needs have easily accessible places to hang clothes and drawers and shelves where favorite times can be stored. This way a child can be as independent as possible.

CLOTHING MODIFICATIONS

Kids want to look exactly like their peers and not stand out. If you are handy with a needle and thread, you can adapt clothing to fit over back braces, leg braces, and contractures. Sometimes a friend or neighbor will be willing and glad to help. Velcro can be used to replace zippers to make it easier for a grandchild to dress and undress. Fortunately, most kids pre-fer baggy clothes these days which makes it easier to cover all kinds of things.

One family had a kind neighbor who was retired and handy with a needle. She was wonderful about helping the grandmother adapt clothes for her grandchild. The Internet offers many resources for adaptive clothing and there are compa-nies that specialize in clothes for kids with special needs (see Appendix).

HAVING FUN

It is very easy to get caught up in the everyday needs of a grandchild who has a disability or problem and forget to plan time for fun. Even skipping an occasional therapy session, school day, or activity can be important. Kids can begin to feel that life is not worth living if their days are filled with doctor appointments, therapies, or school. It may take some planning and phone calls to organize a fun day or few hours, but it definitely will pay off for you and your grandchild. (Chapter Ten offers suggestions about having some fun times with your grandchild.)

Helping with Dressing and Hygiene

Most little kids love to make mud pies, get dirty, mess with finger paints, play dough or clay. Keeping any child clean can be a problem, but if there are problems with sensitivity to touch, hair washing, bathing, and teeth brushing can become an on-going battle.

If your own children didn't have problems with touch, but your grand-child does, you will have to devise some creative ways to help with bath-ing, dressing, and dental care. Tremendous patience is needed to teach self-help skills to children with motor, sensory, emotional problems, or developmental delay. Occupational therapists (O.T.s) can be of great help in showing you and your grandchild how to do specific tasks. These can include bathing, dressing, and even eating.

Occupational therapists also have many ways to help kids work on fine motor skills and they can determine if specially adapted instruments like a long-handled tooth brush, comb, or shoe horn can make a difference. There are also special tools like button hooks that can be helpful, as can extra large handles on utensils.

Any clothing that you buy should be purchased with the goal in mind of making your grandchild as independent as possible. Being able to dress and undress adds to a child's feeling of confidence and independence. It can also be a great time-saver for you. Buttons and zippers can be replaced by Velcro strips, and Velcro strips can also be sewed on so clothing can open at the sides. Front pant zippers can be replaced by Velcro strips and shoes can be purchased that close with Velcro, rather than shoe laces.

Most kids with disabilities need a specific routine to get up and get dressed. Children, in general, don't do well if they are hurried, so it is important you allow enough time for a grandchild to get ready for pre-school, school, or other activities. It helps if you or your grandchild lay out the next day's clothes the night before. If a grandchild resists teeth brushing or has a fear of water, you can try to make a game out of these. If a child can listen to favorite music on headphones while having his or her teeth brushed that could save the day.

Bathing can be helped by having some fun bath toys or bubble bath. If a child has frequent bladder infections, bubble bath is generally unwise to use. In addition, some bubble baths will cause an allergic reaction in a child with highly sensitive skin.

Skin care can be a problem if a grandchild is a paraplegic or quadriplegic. Daily baths are important for these kids to prevent skin breakdown and body odor. If frequent skin breakdown occurs and the areas become infected, Phisohex can be used for bathing and Neosporin ointment can be applied after a bath to help prevent infections. Phisohex can cause drying of the skin, so it should just be used for a few days at a time. Remember that the temperature of the water should be carefully checked before a grandchild with decreased sensation is put into a bathtub. The water heater temperature should be turned down below 120 degrees Fahrenheit.

Dandruff or seborrhea of the scalp can be an on-going problem for young people who have difficulty washing their hair frequently. There are some good anti-dandruff shampoos that can be purchased over the counter and there are also some that can be prescribed by a physician.

Most little girls love to play beauty parlor, so a shampoo tray like those used in beauty shops can be purchased to help with hair washing. A shower hose in the bathtub could be used for boys or a shower might be the best place to wash the hair, depending on the child. If a child watches another child having their hair washed and it looks like fun, this may help also. *My daughter loved watching herself with a hand mirror as I made bunny ears on top of her head with her wet and soapy hair.* Having a manicure set of their very own can make a difference for little kids who bite their fingernails or resist having their nails trimmed.

If your grandchild has difficulty getting in and out of a bathtub or shower, special bathroom lifts or just a slide board may be helpful. Bath chairs, bath stools and a handheld shower attachment may make a difference. Remember that as kids get older they may be uncomfortable having a grandparent or a parent bathe them. Often a male attendant is needed for a boy or a female attendant or helper for a teenage girl. A rubber bath mat or towel should be placed in the bottom of the tub to prevent slippage and a grab bar on the side of the tub could prevent an injury.

You often have to be creative to accomplish simple tasks and sometimes music will help. Singing or playing a special song as you wash a child's hair, brush their teeth, or cut their fingernails can make the tasks seem like fun and the time go more quickly. Little kids love to do things to music and if you can't sing, there are lots of children's songs available on CDs.

The author Pamela Tanguay, in her book, *Nonverbal Learning Disabilities at Home* (2001), gives some excellent suggestions about teaching self-help skills to kids with tactile sensory problems.[10] However, if you are tired, stressed, or in a hurry, it is better to skip a day's teeth brushing or bathing. A quick sponge bath, if it is really needed, can give you a little more time and could save your energy and patience. We all have our tipping point for fatigue or stress and if we don't pay attention to our own needs, we could say or do things we would greatly regret.

Children with autism and other kids who have difficulties with chewing, swallowing, and smelling different foods can make life very difficult for a caretaker. An occupational therapist or a mother or grandmother who has had experience with these kinds of problems could be a life-saver. Many kids always want the same foods and never, ever want one food to touch another one. It can be hard to find ways to offer a balanced diet if there are food difficulties. A dietitian in a hospital might have some excellent suggestions as can some of the books about feeding children with special problems. A mother or grandmother who has had to solve these problems could be the best one to advise you.

Toileting can be a major problem as kids get older and heavier. There are commodes that can be purchased to be used at the side of a bed or wheelchair. A wheelchair needs to have a detachable arm, so a child can slide over or be transferred onto a commode. Grandparents should be careful that they know how to lift a grandchild and this is something a physical therapist or occupational therapist can teach you. Once you have strained or pulled your back, it can put you out of commission for quite a while and be extremely painful. If you don't take care of yourself, it won't be possible for you to take care of a grandchild.

If a child has a fear of the toilet because of the noise it makes, this may take some extra special patience. Some autistic kids are said to feel as though they are losing part of their insides if they have a bowel movement. A story about a child using the toilet may help or your grandchild could have on headphones playing favorite music. Letting your grandchild pick out a special padded toilet seat could help or one that is in a favorite color.

If brushing teeth creates a problem, I have seen musical toothbrushes. A child could also have on headphones and be listening to a favorite song. Any way you can reduce your stress and your grandchild's will pay off royally. Parents and grandparents of children with special sensitivities may also have some other great ideas. So do lots of networking and research and I'm sure the right answers will be there.

Chapter Eight

Helping Boost Your Grandchild's Self-Esteem

Lack of self-esteem and a feeling of little self-worth are common problems with many kids today as they are inundated with pictures of beautiful models, movie stars, and sports figures who make millions of dollars a year. Many parents and teachers value the kids who are good in athletics or studies far more than they do young people who are honest, kind, sensitive to others, and caring. If young people have poor self-esteem, this can lead to depression, substance abuse, eating disorders, and even suicide.

As grandparents, I believe we can help boost a grandchild's self-esteem in many ways. A grandchild with a physical, emotional, or developmental disability can have a much harder time developing good self-esteem when life is often an on-going challenge with many obstacles to overcome.

Some guidelines to help in boosting self-esteem are:

- **Listen** to everything you say to your grandchild. An offhand, negative remark or statement can have a lasting impact. Most of us remember one or more cutting or early remarks that hurt deeply and became etched in our memory.

- Try always to **look for positive aspects** of your grandchild's behavior and compliment him or her when it is justified. (Compliments must be sincere and not given without cause.) When a grandchild misbehaves, criticize the behavior, but let the child know he or she is still loved and valued.

- Help **set achievable goals**. Mastering these will boost a grandchild's self-confidence and self-esteem.

- **Keep the lines of communication open**. This requires honesty, trust, and that you listen, not just talk. Lots of one-to-one time for talking is needed. Encourage your grandchild to express emotions and opinions.

- **Empower** your grandchild with **decision-making ability** as much as possible. In some cases, this may be extremely difficult.

- Let your grandchild try to **do tasks without your help**. Even small achievements can be important and help boost self-esteem. Each small independent step can lead to the next bigger step.

- Encourage your grandchild to **volunteer** as often as possible in ways **to help** friends and family members. This will build confidence and friendships.

- **Teach mutual respect** and maintain your role as grandparents. You are not just friends.

- **Set limits**. This is crucial. Kids want you to be in control and will become anxious if they have to parent themselves.

- **Discipline in a firm, consistent way**. This is important, though extremely difficult. Kids are experts at knowing which buttons to press and when. Avoid disciplining in anger, as much as possible. Hitting or severely punishing children will create angry, non-communicative young people and can set them on the road to destructive behavior.

- **Build trust** by showing you will always be available to love and help your grandchild.

- **Develop rituals and traditions** that your grandchild can depend on and enjoy. Kids need consistency and as much fun as possible.

- **Teach respect** for others no matter what their religion or race may be.

- **Teach responsibility**. Every child should be responsible for something: pets, chores, homework, or just putting away games, toys, or books.

- Look for and **value your grandchild's uniqueness**. Every child has special qualities which will blossom, if he or she is loved and treasured. If kids are allowed and helped to follow their own path or stars instead of trying to fit into a preconceived mold, much more is likely to be achieved.

- **Respect** a grandchild's **privacy**. We all need time to ourselves. Telephone calls and mail should remain private unless a grandchild has serious emotional or developmental problems.

- Give **regular chores**. This helps develop a sense of responsibility and competence and teaches the steps of independence.

- **Help others** in the community, or at your place of worship. This provides important role modeling for your grandchild. In contrast, prejudice and bigotry leave dark stains on a child's psyche and will make your grandchild poorly equipped to handle life in our multicultural nations.

- **Be flexible**. This is a must for parents and grandparents. The unexpected becomes the norm far too often, so we have to learn to ride the roller coaster of change.

- **Show love** by both words and hugs. This is the key to developing good self-esteem in your grandchild. Children who are raised without limits and expressions of love become rigid adults who are afraid to trust.

- **Celebrate** even the smallest accomplishments. Daily acknowledgment of the struggles a grandchild may be having can make the day go better. A surprise treat, a day off from school or doctors' appointments, or a surprise trip to the zoo or park can make a grandchild smile and know how important he or she is to you.

FEAR AND ANXIETY

Fear and anxiety can cause great shyness and a lack of self-confidence. There can be a fear of one or two things or a fear of the world in general. You may need to talk to a counselor to find the best way to handle your grandchild's fears, but your own good parenting instincts and common sense could be all that is needed. Some general guidelines are:

- Don't make fun of fears, because this will probably make them worse.

- Talk to your grandchild about any special fears. You might say that you were afraid of _____ when you were a child to let the child know that everyone has fears at one time or the other.

- Try to hide your own fears and anxiety. A child wants an adult to be in control and not be afraid.

- If your grandchild is old enough try giving a big piece of paper or a big pad of paper and crayons and ask your grandchild to draw his or her fears. This may be very revealing and can be an easy, fun way to express feelings.

- Bath toys or bubble bath, unless there are skin or urinary problems, can help if there is a fear of taking a bath.

- Visit a firehouse if fire engine noises are scary.

- Leave on a night light or put stars on the ceiling that glow.

- A new, little cuddly pet may help a child.

- Tape a bedtime story with your voice or a parent's voice.

- Show a child how to use a vacuum or other appliances if there is a fear of loud noises.

- Consult a child therapist if your methods are not working.

- Don't allow scary movies, video games, or television.

- Find a child's special interest and help the child to excel in sport, hobby, art, music, or dance. Junior theater is also a wonderful way to make friends and get rid of fears.

If you are concerned that bullying is causing a loss of self-esteem, I would talk with the school principal and teachers. A good Web site that addresses bullying and gives some helpful advice is www.bullying.co.uk.

If you have tried hard to follow these guidelines and feel your grandchild still lacks self-esteem, some counseling or family help may be needed. Some kids have personality or other problems that make even the best parenting or grandparenting unsuccessful. It is much like growing flowers. You use the same seeds, under the same conditions, but are dismayed to find that some seeds produce beautiful flowers, while others produce flowers lacking in color or size.

EVALUATING YOUR GRANDCHILD'S SELF-ESTEEM

1. Is your grandchild extremely shy?

2. Does your grandchild find it difficult to separate from you?

3. Does your grandchild have difficulty handling new situations?

4. Does he or she have trouble sharing with others?

5. Does your grandchild find it difficult to make friends with peers and adults?

6. Does your grandchild have a problem with excess weight?

7. Does he or she constantly worry about gaining weight?

8. Does your grandchild often seem withdrawn, depressed, or moody?

9. Does your grandchild always have to be the center of attention?

10. Does your grandchild bite his or her nails, wet the bed, have headaches, or other nervous symptoms?

If your answer to the majority of these is "Yes," it might be time to think about ways you can help boost your grandchild's self-esteem. Talking to your grandchild's teachers and doctor may give you some ideas about what to do. I hope that some of the guidelines I have outlined will get you off to a good start. Good luck!

Chapter Nine

Handling Social Occasions

No one can live in isolation and have a healthy life. We all need friends, family and times to socialize. Many people, however, as they get older find their world gets smaller and smaller. Medical problems may develop which restrict the ability to drive a car or get around. Relocation and deaths may result in fewer and fewer available friends, so new ways have to be found to get the socialization we all need.

Children with physical, emotional, or developmental disabilities need friends and family, but many have great difficulty socializing. They may be all right with a single individual, but more people can pose a problem. If you, as the grandparents, are the ones in charge, some understanding and sensitivity to your grandchild's limitations in a social situation are important. You may want to invite friends to your house, but are not sure how a grandchild will react.

One Easter Sunday, I asked a good friend about her plans for Easter dinner. She said that she planned to take one daughter and her family to Easter brunch, but couldn't take the other daughter because their son with autism would often act out in social situations or restaurants. I asked if I could spend time with him so the family could all have Easter brunch together. I knew the grandmother had a special room where the boy had his computer and toys and thought I could probably manage the youth. The grandmother replied that she greatly appreciated my offer, but she never knew when the child would have a "meltdown," yell, and thrash around. She said she would have the other family to dinner that night which made a great deal of additional effort for her.

Sometimes the smallest thing can set children off, so you have to be prepared. The Autism Society of America gives some excellent suggestions on their Web site: www.autism-society.org about handling autistic children in social situations. These could also work for kids with many other special problems.

One of the excellent suggestions they give is to take a child for a short walk if he or she gets upset in a social situation. Taking along a favorite stuffed animal or toy is always a good idea. I would add that some role playing and talking about the up-coming event might help, plus looking for places and situations where your grandchild feels comfortable. Then you could gradually try introducing the child to larger social gatherings.

EATING OUT

I think all children need to learn how to act in social situations. Eating out with a child can be a disaster unless you talk about your expectations and what behavior will and will not be accepted. You also need to eat fairly early, so there won't be as many diners, choose a restaurant that is child-friendly and take along some crayons, a small pad of paper or a favorite toy. *My children still remember a Thanksgiving dinner when they were about ten and twelve. We were invited to join a good friend and her two little children to have Thanksgiving dinner at a very nice restaurant. Her parents were the hosts and the dinner was delicious. However, the meal was frequently interrupted by my friend's two little boys, ages three and five, getting down from the table, running around the restaurant, and then climbing back and forth under our table! Neither their mother nor the grandparents said anything to the children and my children were amazed that the two little boys were allowed to get by with this kind of behavior. It made quite an impression on both of them! They knew that I would never have allowed them to act that way. The children and I had many holiday meals in restaurants since I was divorced and working very hard. It was more fun for us to have a celebration out than for the three of us to eat alone at home.*

Some good opportunities for socialization for your grandchild are the Special Olympics, therapeutic horseback riding programs, and special ski schools for kids with challenges. In the U.K., the Special Olympics Web site is www.specialolympicsgb.org. Many agencies also have social functions for their members. Kids often feel better knowing other kids who have their same kind of problems. I have connected patients who have a special disorder with another child having their same condition. Many became pen pals and loved having a friend who could understand what they were feeling.

There are a large number of camps now for kids with disabilities both in the U.K. and the U.S. In the U.K. there is a good list of available camps at the Web site: www.fsc.org.uk/programme/list_sn.asp. In the United States, there is a list of camps for many different needs at the Web site: www.Kidscamps.com. Camps are available for children with many different problems: asthma, diabetes, heart problems, and autism to name a few. If a child can go to a camp with kids who have similar problems, it often makes socialization much easier. Long-term friendships can be established and a camp experience might be something that could be enjoyed year after year.

Before deciding on a camp, it is important to check on the ratio of staff to campers and the experience of the director. I would also want to be sure that someone is responsible for the campers at all times, so a child can't wander off, get hurt or get into mischief. The availability of medical care and emergency services would be another thing to investigate and the location of the nearest hospital that cared for children.

Outdoor events with other families work for some kids: picnics, barbecues, and swimming. All you can do is try different things and be prepared to leave if your grandchild gets upset or out of control.

If you decide that you want to attempt a birthday party for your grandchild, I would limit the party to just a few friends or family members if there is difficulty with socialization. A birthday party in a park where the kids can run and play can be fun. Be sure you have lots of helpers. Teenagers are often a great help at events like this.

A good way to have a holiday party is to have one especially set up for children in your yard or patio, if you have one, and then food and drinks for the adults in the house. Some helpers could supervise the kids in the patio where there could be refreshments, games, art materials, or whatever would be appropriate for the kids' ages.

If there is a particular agency that has been helpful with your grandchild, perhaps you could volunteer to help with a holiday party or organize one if no plans have been made for an event. A group of grandparents could get together and sponsor a fun occasion.

I was active in a grandparents group at my grandchildren's school and offered the use of my house for a grandparents tea to be held on a Sunday afternoon. The school provided the food and I just had to have the house and patio ready for everything to be set up. Grandparents brought their grandchildren and the guests were greeted at the door by my two grandchildren, I had games for the little ones and a table for art work. It was very little work for me and turned out to be a fun occasion for everyone. Similar parties could be held in a condominium club house, a patio, or a park.

A group in San Diego, California, has started The Miracle League of San Diego. They bring kids with disabilities together to play sports and the kids all seem to get along. There are sixty other Miracle Leagues across the United States which have similar programs. Another group in San Diego has started a Surf Day Camp for kids with disabilities. Volunteers help the kids surf and everyone seems to have fun and get along.

An organization in England connects kids and families with other kids and families who have a child with the same disability. It is "Contact a Family." Their Web site is www.cafamily.org and the telephone number is 0808 808 3555.

If it is important for you to be at a social event and your grandchild is invited and wants to go, it would be wise to take along a helper, in case the child needs some time away. If your grandchild knows the rules and what you will and will not accept, this will help. However, when a child is tired or hungry, all the rules often go by the wayside. I would be sure a child has a snack low in sugar before a social gathering. A little protein can go a long way to keeping most children grounded. You might also take along a snack and a favorite book or toy.

Often brothers and sisters are the only playmates a child with special needs will have. This can put a burden on the siblings. Perhaps they want to invite a friend to play, but feel obligated to include their brother or sister. I think this is something that needs to be decided on an individual basis. Many siblings are great about managing the brother or sister with special needs, but at some point it can be unfair to expect them to always have to include a child who may have some difficulties with socialization or mobility problems. *I know of families where another child was conceived with the sole purpose of having a playmate for the child with a disability. The mother of one child told me that she and her husband expected the new child to take over the care of the sibling when they were no longer able to provide care. I tried to tell this mother that I felt she and her husband were putting an unfair burden on the second child, but I'm sure my words had no impact.* I knew their decision would have a life-long impact on the second child.

It is not fair to you as caretaking grandparents to greatly restrict your social occasions because you have a grandchild with special needs. If you can find someone to come into your home and help out with your grandchild while you entertain friends, that could be an answer. You also might be able to trade baby-sitting with another parent or grandparent of a special needs child. This will require some networking and perhaps contacting the staff in the agency that has resources for your grandchild's special disability. Another resource that some of my parents and grandparents have found useful is to hire a college or medical student to help out. If you can find a student with a special interest in kids with special problems or disabilities, this can be a real plus. If you try to eliminate friends and social times with them because of your caretaking role, you could pay a high price. Taking care of yourself is all important, so you can do the best job of caring for your grandchild.

Chapter Ten

Having Fun with a Grandchild

Childhood should be a time to feel safe, loved, and free of pain or anxiety. A grandchild with special needs may miss a great deal in childhood unless you and his or her parents find ways to make the years fun and memorable, despite on-going challenges.

Most kids prefer spending quality time with their parents and grandparents as opposed to going to expensive amusement parks or receiving lots of toys or gifts. If you choose to go to an amusement park, a family pass is usually much less costly.

A child's special memories of his or her growing years will be doing something different or creative with you; learning about the stars, playing games, cooking, or doing arts and crafts projects. Many things can be adapted without a great expenditure of money, though you may need to do a little research and use some creativity. This will be especially true if your grandchild has difficulty focusing, sitting still, or has developmental delay. If a child has muscle weakness or spasticity, there are many ways to make adaptations

One grandchild with cerebral palsy delighted in remembering all of his many family members' birthdays. His grandmother helped him make creative cards to send and this became the child's special thing. The grandmother had to find some special ways for the boy to be able to color and write, but it was a fun project for both of them.

Another grandfather, who was a tailor, taught his grandson to reweave fabrics. The youth was able to do this despite considerable muscle weakness and this skill later became a source of income.

ARTS AND CRAFTS

Most kids, even from an early age, love to use crayons, paints, and color-ful markers. A roll of white shelf paper, still available in most hardware stores, is great for making posters, banners, and pictures. The paper can be taped to a big board or a kitchen wall or spread out on the floor. All art supplies should be non-toxic and water soluble. Large brushes, size ten to sixteen, are easier for little children or older kids to use if they have limited hand mobility. Finger paints are messy, but can help develop good tactile sense and little children love them. You can buy or order special holders for brushes, crayons, and pencils if a child has difficulty holding these. Cottage cheese cartons or disposable plastic containers can be used to hold paint brushes after they are cleaned. Cleaning up and putting the art supplies away should be part of the project. This teaches responsibility and will let your grandchild know the importance of putting things away in the right places after they are used.

If kids draw pictures of their family or themselves, you might be able to get some insight into how they are feeling or how they see themselves or their family. Hanging or even framing a picture or two or having an art exhibit for the family is a way to offer praise and help your grandchild's self-esteem.

Non-toxic modeling clay or play dough is good to help fine-motor coordination and is fun to use. You can also make dough by mixing flour, salt, and water. Potatoes that are cut in half make good stamps if they are pressed onto colored ink pads. Stickers are fun to use for different pictures and cards and collages can be made with all kinds of things: pieces of wood, beans, scraps of paper or pictures from magazines. Scraps of mate-rial can be made into small quilts or doll clothes and many packaged arts and crafts are available for sale. Pipe cleaners can be twisted into different shapes or used as part of other projects.

Puppets can be purchased or made with small paper bags or pieces of material and can be used to put on a fun puppet show. A cardboard box can be turned into a puppet theater, or a grandparent who is good at woodworking could make a real puppet theater. Big cardboard boxes make good playhouses and a good tent or fort can be made by draping a sheet over a card table.

My children and grandchildren had fun making piñatas out of big paper bags and then decorating them. We filled the piñatas with wrapped candy, little toys, and a few coins for special occasions. The Halloween piñata was a particular favorite. (A piñata is part of the Christmas celebra-tion in Mexico and is usually made of papier-mâché. Some piñatas are quite elaborate. They are hung from a tree or rope and then hit with a big stick to see who can be the first to break the bag. Children who use wheelchairs, but have good arm strength, can participate along with the other kids.)

Hobbies of all kinds are a way to learn about the world and even make some friends. Stamp and coin collections are easy to put together. Having an easily accessible place for games and art supplies is a good idea for grandchildren. A deck of cards can fill many hours with fun for some kids. Any way that you can keep a grandchild away from watching television, doing computer games, or playing Nintendo is important.

A dress-up box can be a source of outfits or costumes for fashion shows or plays. Even older kids may enjoy helping put on productions and kids in wheelchairs or with limited motor or intellectual ability can still have fun dressing up and writing or acting out the plays.

I have a big box with old jewelry, hats, bright clothing, nightgowns, and other garments that my children and grandchildren used to give plays or fashion shows when they were small. I also have a shelf with games and toys that is used now by friends and former patients who bring their children to visit. If you don't have old clothes or jewelry, these can usually be found in thrift stores.

HORSEBACK RIDING, SWIMMING, AND SKIING

Horseback riding is both fun and therapeutic. In Denmark, this is routine treatment for kids with Duchenne muscular dystrophy. It is particularly good for stretching tightness or contractures of heel cords (the tendons at the back of the legs). Many therapeutic horseback riding programs are now available in the U.S. and most kids love to be involved with the horses. Volunteers walk alongside a child and the kids are firmly anchored in their saddles. Most of the programs do not charge, but are supported by donations or grants.

Swimming is the best exercise for kids with muscle weakness or spasticity and helps others develop self-confidence and feel better. Some private therapeutic swim programs are available and these are usually directed by a physical or recreational therapist. In the U.S., there are also swimming programs connected with large centers for the disabled such as the Recreation Center for the Handicapped in San Francisco. Some hospitals or Rehab Centers also have therapeutic swimming programs, as do some Easter Seals facilities.

There are some wonderful ski programs for children with disabilities and even blind children are being taught to ski. The kids each hold on to a guide and have a wonderful experience swooping down a snowy hillside.

PETS AND PROBLEMS TO AVOID

Pets can help children learn a sense of responsibility and be a source of great comfort and pleasure. Dogs who are Canine Companions are wonderful friends and helpers for many kids with disabilities. To receive these remarkable dogs, a child and parent or grandparent are required to have a two week training period. There are also other requirements that must be met for a child to qualify for one of these special animals. The dogs are taught to pick up items, help navigate doorways and sidewalks, and accomplish things that a child is unable to do. The U.S. Web site is: www.cci.org and in the U.K., the Web site is: www.canine-companions.co.uk.

No one other than your grandchild should pet or play with the Canine Companion. Friends and strangers often want to do so and you may have to be quite firm in asking that they keep their distance.

The one caution I would have about pets is to be sure they are checked regularly by a veterinarian because a sick animal can spread disease. Roundworms, tapeworms, and hookworms are the most common parasites that pets carry and all of these can infect humans. If a child does not wash his or her hands after handling a pet or often puts things in the mouth, there can be a risk of infection. Also, a grandchild should never kiss a pet around the nose or mouth because of the risk of infection. In addition, cat scratch fever is a real entity and kids can become quite ill if they are badly scratched by a cat. Another precaution if you have cats or dogs and also a sandbox for a grandchild is to keep the sandbox covered when it is not in use. Turtles can be a problem because they can spread Salmonella, which causes diarrhea, and a sick bird can cause pneumonia due to infection with psittacosis.

Easy pets for children are colorful fish. Even one or two fish in a small fishbowl can be fun. A grandchild can have the responsibility of feeding the fish and also help with maintaining the fishbowl or aquarium. It is fun to visit a pet store and see the different animals and varieties of fish.

TREASURE HUNTS

Treasure hunts can be simple or quite elaborate. They are fun to have indoors on a rainy day and just take a little imagination. One thing I have done is cut out pictures from a magazine and glue them on to small index cards. You can have two teams of kids or a grandchild can go on a treasure hunt alone. The treasure hunt begins by giving the first child or team the picture of an object which is in specified rooms or areas. The children go to that object, find another card in or on it and so on until a prize is found under or in the last object. The prizes can be simple or can be more expensive.

COOKING AND BAKING

So many families live on fast-foods these days that kids rarely get a chance to cook or bake. Even little children love to make cookies or cupcakes. These can be iced and decorated with some of the readily available colored sprinkles or other decorations. Mixes or ready-to-cut cookie dough are available and easy to use.

My children and grandchildren all loved making a Crazy Cake and I've given the recipe to many friends for their children and grandchildren. My daughter tells me she still makes the cake once in a while when it is cold or raining. The recipe is:

Crazy Cake

1½ cup flour	6 tbl. cooking oil
1 cup sugar	1 tbl. vinegar
3 tbl. cocoa	1 tsp. vanilla
½ tsp. salt	1 cup cold water
1 tsp. baking soda	

Put the dry ingredients into a flour sifter and sift right into an ungreased eight inch square cake pan. Make three holes in the dry mixture and pour cooking oil into one, vinegar into the second, and vanilla into the third. Then pour cold water over all and stir with a fork until the mixture is evenly blended. Bake 35 to 40 minutes in a 350 degree Fahrenheit oven. Invert to cool on a cooling rack and then remove from the pan or ice the cake right in the pan.

Most kids these days have never made fudge or had a taffy pull. These old-fashioned treats will long be remembered and are not that difficult to make. You can use pre-packaged fudge mix, but making it from scratch is not that hard. This would be a fun thing to do on a cold or rainy day.

All kids, even those with mental or physical challenges, should be able to fix a sandwich or simple meal as they get older. This is an important step in growing up and becoming as independent as possible. Boys need to learn some basic cooking skills as well as girls. Grandparents with the time and patience to help a grandchild with cooking can make a great contribution.

Learning to make foods of different nationalities can be fun and will give a child from another country or culture a sense of their roots. It can also teach kids about other people and other cultures.

GARDENING

Children love to plant a vegetable garden and watch as the plants grow. If you don't have a place for a garden, you could use a window box or a container in a sunny spot near a window or in a patio. Certain plants will attract different birds or butterflies and a hummingbird feeder will provide much enjoyment for a grandchild. Watching these amazing little birds come for their dinners will be fun for both grandparents and grandchildren.

Pulling carrots from the dirt from seeds you have planted can be very satisfying. If you love gardening, this joy can be passed on to a grandchild or grandchildren. Watching bulbs start pushing out of the soil in winter and then seeing the flowers blossom can also be special. Bulbs can be planted in a container and kept inside if it is cold and snowy outside.

BOOKS

I have always been the "book grandmother" and have not purchased toys for my grandchildren. Most kids these days receive far too many flimsy toys as gifts. If you give books instead of toys, a child can be started on a lifetime of reading. Even kids with limited abilities can enjoy some of the wonderful pop-up and colorful children's books that are available today in stores or libraries. Every child should have a library card and learn what a wonderful resource a library can be.

If a child has difficulty reading, it is important to discover this as early as possible. It could be that glasses are needed or some testing is indicated to pick up a reading problem. It might also be that a child's brain is just not mature enough to decode the words. Albert Einstein was said to have had difficulty reading and didn't learn until he was seven. Girls usually learn to read before boys, but pushing any kid to read when they are not ready can cause anxiety and stress. Every child has his or her own timetable for growing up and a good educational psychologist should be able to determine if there is a problem or if a child just needs more time to mature.

GAMES

Old fashioned games as Monopoly, chess, checkers, and card games are still fun for kids. You may not like to play games, as I don't, but playing a few games with a grandchild can be fun for both of you. Games do teach sportsmanship and are an inexpensive way for a child to have fun. Puzzles are enjoyable for some kids and are available in different sizes and complexity. Wood puzzles which you can either buy or have made by someone handy with a jigsaw cutter are great for most little kids.

Games with music and old-fashioned games as *London Bridge is Falling Down*, *Ring-a-Round-the Rosie*, musical chairs, and hide and seek can all be adapted for kids with disabilities. Playing post office is fun for little kids, as is banking, having a grocery store, or playing hospital and being a doctor or nurse. A play doctor's kit, mask, and gown can often help take away fears of doctors and hospitals.

If you and a grandchild have a long wait in a doctor's office, clinic, or hospital waiting room, there are some good games to remember or have written down in a notebook that you carry with you. These are:

- **I Spy**—You or your grandchild pick out an object in the room and the other person has to guess what it is. You can set up boundaries in which the object has to be found.

- **List making**—You can list family members or the days of the week or months, but leave one out. Then your grandchild has to figure out what is missing.

- **Tic-Tac-Toe**—If you always carry a small notebook and pen, this old-fashioned game can wile away many minutes.

- **Describing a person**—You can give a description of someone you are thinking about and see if your grandchild can guess who it is.

If you run out of ideas or ways to help a grandchild have fun, there are many books available these days in the library or stores with ideas for activities. It does take a little time and energy to work out the details of some of the projects, but the rewards for your grandchild will be great and you should derive great satisfaction in knowing your grandchild is being creative, having fun, and not turning into a "couch potato."

TOYS

Most little children love having a cuddly, stuffed animal and blocks are always a hit, unless a child has difficulty handling them. The light-weight cardboard blocks are my favorite. They can be used to build forts, walls, and many other structures.

There are companies both in the U.S. and the U.K. that specialize in toys for kids with disabilities. The National Lekotek Center's Web site: www.lekotek.org gives the ten things to think about if you are buying a toy for a grandchild with special needs. Some of the suggestions are:

1. Does the toy have multi-sensory appeal?

2. What is the method of activation?

3. Where will the toy be used?

4. Is it a popular toy?

5. Is it adaptable for a child?

6. Does it allow for creativity?

7. Is it safe and durable?

These and their other points are worth taking into consideration when buying any toy.

Many toys are made of plastic and poorly constructed, so you want to look carefully at any toy you buy. You will also want to check that there are no small detachable pieces which could be swallowed by a little child. Little kids will put almost anything in their mouths. With the recent concern about toys imported from other countries, it is wise to check with consumer Web sites to be sure a toy has not been recalled. In the European Union, toy safety standards are under negotiation and it is hoped they will be enacted in the near future. The U.S. Consumer Product Safety Commission can be found at www.cpsc.gov and a law has now been passed in the U.S. to ensure that all toys meet certain standards. In the U.K, toys are regulated under the Toy (Safety) Regulation Act. This is part of the 1987 Consumer Protection law.

No child needs lots of toys and it is better for kids to be creative in their playtime rather than being given many expensive toys that may not last very long. If a child is given too many toys on birthdays or holidays, some of these can be put away and brought out one at a time on a rainy day or when a child is ill or just having a bad day. A card table draped with a sheet can make a good fort or house and cardboard boxes, cardboard tubes, pots and pans, and small kitchen utensils can all be a source of fun.

TIME CAPSULES

Grandchildren and grandparents might enjoy putting together a time capsule. This could be put in a special place and opened in ten or twenty years. The capsule could contain newspaper headlines of significance, a grandchild's drawing, poem, or story, some snapshots, and mementoes of significance to both the grandparents and grandchildren. It might become a fun family tradition.

SCRAPBOOKS

It is fun to put together a scrapbook for each grandchild and your grandchildren can help. The scrapbooks could contain photographs, school newsletters, award certificates, and other things of importance. My grandchildren love to look at their scrapbooks from time to time. I think this gives them a feeling of importance and of knowing how special they are to me.

FAMILY TREES

An extensive family tree can be fun to put together with a grandchild and may be something that will always be treasured. We all need a sense of our roots and kids love finding out about famous people in their family tree and even rogues! Some historical research could be done by older kids or those who are experts on the computer. If you have old pictures, these could be added to the family tree. You can buy blank family tree charts all ready for you to fill in names and other information. It could be even more fun if you and your grandchild or grandchildren devised your own family tree.

FAMILY TRADITIONS

Every family needs some traditions that can be passed down from generation to generation. If your grandchild has been in a fragmented or dysfunctional family, establishing some traditions is even more important. Some traditions are based on religious customs, while others are related to holidays, birthdays, or other celebrations.

My children helped their grandfather make a wonderful, large birthday board with many holes for candles around the edges. The children signed the back of the board and their grandfather etched the signatures to make them permanent. The large board is special to see when the brightly colored candles are lighted and a delicious cake sits proudly in the middle of the board. I use the birthday board for every birthday dinner and I am sure it will be passed on down the generations.

Your family most likely has had some special traditions and if not perhaps you can think of some that can be used each year and then passed on to the next generation. We all need a feeling of permanence and a child who has many obstacles to overcome needs them even more. Even having a special holiday meal or foods that a child can count on will bring happiness and a sense of order.

HUMOR

Bobbi Conner, in her book *The Parent's Journal Guide to Raising Great Kids* (1997, pp.233-235), talks about how important humor is in parenting children.[11] She says each day we should find "activities that are fun and playful" and to try and "look for humor in the ordinary and even mundane activities." Some days this can be extremely difficult, but kids often say funny things even when they are going through painful or stressful times. Keeping a journal and recording some of the funny or even wise sayings can help the days go more quickly, particularly if they are filled with unpleasant or stressful events. It is also fun to have a child speak or sing a song into a tape recorder. When the child hears his or her voice as you play back the tape, you will probably get some squeals of delight.

ENTERTAINING LITTLE ONES

If you are caring for an infant or toddler, some different entertainment ideas will be needed. Simple toys work the best for little ones, even though many ads want you to believe that even a small child must have the latest toy or gadget. Most babies love to listen to music from a music box or mobile and squeaky toys are fun, as are rattles. Cradle gyms that a baby can play with in a playpen or crib can be very entertaining.

If you want to keep a baby's attention while riding with one in the back seat of the car, having a few finger plays at your fingertips can help the time pass pleasantly. These work well at other times, too, if a little one is fussy. Perhaps you remember *"Itsy-Bitsy Spider"* or similar finger plays from when your children were small. When my grandchildren were small, I found a good book to give me some new ones. It is *The Eentsy, Weentsy Spider: Fingerplays and Action Rhymes* by Joanna Cole and Stephanie Calmenson.[12] It could be ordered through a bookstore or purchased online from Amazon or a used books store, such as www.abebooks.com.

If you want to spend a little money, toy or baby stores have a wealth of things you can buy. One that has worked well for a friend's grandchildren is an activity gym. The gym can go on a rug or you can spread out a mat beneath it. A little one can lie on the floor under the activity gym and play with the various rings and gadgets. Busy boxes are fairly inexpensive and fun, also.

Most toddlers like pull toys, stacking toys, wood puzzles with just a few pieces, stuffed animals, and pots and pans. It works well to have a corner or drawer in the kitchen that contains small, safe kitchen items and some little toys. Little children love to imitate adults, so a small broom, dustpan, or other household items will be a hit with both boys and girls. Expensive toys will often get broken and quickly discarded, so I would suggest sticking with the tried and true items that we used with our children, particularly since there have been so many recent problems with some of the toys imported from overseas. You can always check the consumer safety Web site to see if there has been a recall of a particular toy. It is better to be safe than sorry.

There are beautiful books for small children, but I would be sure they are made of cloth or hard cardboard. It is never too early to develop a love of books. Most children love being read to, but remember that a child may want to hear the same book over and over again! The most important thing is to have some fun and spend quality time with your grandchildren. Your love and one-to-one attention are far more important than the latest in toys or gadgets.

Chapter Eleven

Traveling with a Grandchild

Traveling with grandchildren can be a special, wonderful experience or it can be a disaster without careful advance planning and preparation. If a child has special needs, then even more careful planning is necessary. Fortunately, there are many people and Web sites who can provide much information. Most individuals are extremely helpful, particularly if you explain your grandchild's special needs and how important the trip is to him or her.

Taking one grandchild at a time is advisable. Kids, with and without disabilities, need a grandparent's undivided attention. If an accident or injury happens because a grandparent becomes too tired or distracted, the emotional pain and guilt would be overwhelming.

When kids are old enough to choose a place to visit or some special trip they want to take, their involvement makes it more fun for both the child and grandparents. *One grandmother outlines a budget for each trip she takes with a grandchild.* This way, the child learns about money management and how to make the allotted amount of money last the longest. Many family oriented places are quite expensive, so it is important to check out the entrance and other fees, as part of the advance planning. If a child can look things up on the Internet, a large amount of information is available about fees, wheelchair accessibility, and other important facts. In the U.S., tourist bureaus are found in most large cities and they will gladly mail information if use of the Internet is not possible. Toll-free 800 numbers can be found for these by calling information. Many recreation areas are now wheelchair accessible and have good brochures or provide information on the Internet. These recreation areas can offer special outdoor experiences for a grandchild.

For the U.K., considerable information about travel is available through the different agencies and the Internet offers a wealth of help. Two particular

Web sites to check are: www.wheelchair-travel.co.uk and www.access-travel.co.uk.

TRAVELING BY CAR

If you decide to take even a short trip by car, it is best to plan frequent stops. Most kids, as you will remember, get restless in a car when they can't move around very much. Sometimes there will be a small park where a child can get out of the car and move around a little. If not, there are lots of ways to keep kids entertained.

There are a host of games you can buy for traveling or you can make up your own. Finding out-of-state license plates when you are traveling by car or looking for the different letters of the alphabet have worked well for many children and grandchildren. *Another life-saver a parent taught me was to put together a sack containing several gaily wrapped, small packages. A child gets to open one package every hour. I did this for my grandchildren when they had a long trip and they couldn't have been more delighted. I chose inexpensive items, such as little pads of paper, crayons, magnetic games, and similar things that helped make their long car trip go more quickly.*

AIRPLANE TRAVEL

Air travel is not easy these days with all the security requirements and the large number of people traveling. By calling ahead to find out about the newest restrictions and specific requirements, the trip should go smoothly. Most airlines will allow you to board ahead of the other passengers so you can get your grandchild settled in a seat without having to stand in a long line. Remember that you can't take liquids, anything sharp, or gels or lotions over three ounces.

It is very important that you discuss any medicine needed for the trip with your grandchild's parents and the child's primary physician. Otherwise, the trip can be a nightmare. *My daughter and I were on our way to London when we heard loud screaming soon after the flight started. A large ten-year-old was brought to the front of the airplane kicking and screaming. We found out from one of the attendants that the child was autistic and was terrified of being in a confined space. I offered my help, but the flight attendants said they could handle the boy. The mother was distraught as were all the passengers. The flight attendants tried to restrain the boy which just made him kick and scream that much louder. If a physician had been contacted prior to the flight and a possible problem anticipated, medication could have been prescribed, so the child and all the passengers could have had an easier flight. The boy didn't stop kicking, flailing around, or screaming the entire flight and we all let out a sigh of relief when the plane landed and an ambulance brought medical personnel.*

One word of caution about using medication on a trip is that any new medicine should always be tried for a few days before a trip is made to be sure there are no adverse effects. Some individuals react badly to medicines and if a new drug is given for the first time on an airplane, train, bus, or in the car, there can be a bad reaction. I answered a call on an airline one time for just such a problem.

If a child has a cold or an ear infection, there could be a problem in taking off and landing because of a painful ear. If a decongestant has worked in the past, it would be wise to use it before take-off if your grandchild's doctor agrees. Every infant and child should be swallowing on take-off and landing in order to prevent pain in the ear or an air otitis. A baby can be sucking on a pacifier and a child can be swallowing some water or juice.

If you are traveling with an infant or small child, it would be wise to check about the requirements for infant or child seats for that particular airline. Some airlines require them for certain ages and others do not.

Most airlines require an identification card for kids. These can often be obtained at some children's schools, non-government agencies, in the U.S. at the Department of Motor Vehicles (DMV), passport offices, or police departments. If a special case can be purchased for the card, the grandchild can proudly carry this.

Wheelchairs, walkers, oxygen, and Canine Companions can all be brought on board an airplane if special advance arrangements are made. If your grandchild has a Canine Companion, no one but your grandchild should touch the animal. You may have to speak quite forcibly if a passenger or one of the airplane personnel tries to pet the dog.

Because most airlines don't serve meals these days except in Business or First Class, be sure to take along snacks, sandwiches, fruit, or other tasty treats. I would avoid peanuts, hard candies, carrot sticks, or anything that can lodge in a child's throat. *A two-year-old got a peanut stuck in her throat on one airplane trip I took and once again I had to go to work. Fortunately, all went well, but I always advise parents and grandparents not to give little ones anything hard that can become lodged in their throat.*

ADDITIONAL RESOURCES

In the U.S., The Society for Accessible Travel and Hospitality has information the staff will send you. Their telephone number is 212-447-SATH and the Web site is: www.sath.org. Mobility International also has good information about international travel. Their number is 541-343-1284 and the Web site is: www.miusa.org. In addition, there is a travel information service at Moss Rehabilitation Hospital. They will send information about accessible hotels and transportation for individuals with special needs. Their number is 215-456-9900 and the Web site is: www.mossresourcenet.org.

WHAT TO PACK

I keep a list in my suitcase of things I need to take on a trip. If you are taking a grandchild on a trip, I would suggest two separate lists.

Remember to take:

- parents' letter stating you are authorized to see that a child has medical care if needed

- medications and prescriptions for the medicines in case they are lost or spilled

- passports if you are going out of the country

- thermometer

- eye glasses and prescriptions for them

- contact lenses

- hearing aids

- first-aid kit and band-aids

- inhalers if needed

- oxygen and any necessary tubes or attachments

- wheelchair cushions or any detachable parts

- walkers if needed

- braces (AFOs or KAFOs)

- antibiotic ointment for scratches

- sunscreen

- Wash'n Dris or Handi Wipes

- washcloths (many places do not provide these)

- Ace bandage

- small flashlight

- a deck of cards

- travel games

- paper tablets

- crayons or pencils

- extra batteries for CD players or other equipment

- snacks

- plenty of extra clothing for your grandchild

- books and magazines

- hats for cold or hot weather

- jackets or warm coats as needed (airplanes are often quite cold)

- age-appropriate pain relievers

- insect repellent–depending on your destination

- infant needs: wipes, baby food, diapers, formula

- tweezers, small scissors

- small packets of Kleenex

- a cell phone

- contact information for doctors, dentists or other specialists.

ADVANCE RESERVATIONS

Some tourist attractions require advance reservations. In the U.S., this is especially true in Washington D.C. during school spring vacations and summer-time. *My grandson wanted to see The Mint on our trip to Washington D.C. and I didn't realize I should have written ahead to our state senators or representatives for tickets. Fortunately, a nice man in the line in front of us had two extra tickets, so Alexander was not disappointed.*

Some very busy tourist attractions have family passes that can be purchased or they have special discount rates. Researching these can save considerable money. Spending large amounts of money is not necessary when taking kids on trips. One-day excursions to places of historical interest, museums, parks, the zoo, aquariums, libraries, or a fun restaurant can be memorable. Short train trips can also be a treat. The most important thing is to have fun and spend one-to-one time with your grandchild.

Chapter Twelve

Special Education

A good education can make the difference in your grandchild's self-esteem, life-long happiness, and earning ability as an adult. Because the United States has such a large budget deficit, money for schools seems to be less and less available. A recent study showed that the average reading ability of students who graduate from high schools in the United States is at the eighth grade level and in many cities, there is a fifty percent drop-out rate in high schools.[13] These are heart-breaking statistics. Across the U.S., the drop-out rate is thirty percent.

If you look at programs for kids with special needs, they are often the first to suffer funding cuts. So, if you are the grandparent or grandparents in charge of assuring that your grandchild has the best possible education, you have a real challenge ahead. If you can afford the services of a special education attorney or find an agency that provides this kind of legal help, you are very fortunate. A special education attorney can fight for the best possible education. Sometimes, they can even force the school district to provide a special or private school if a good education cannot be received in the public school.

In the United States today, mainstreaming or putting a child into the regular class is often thought to be the best answer. There are both advantages and disadvantages to this. In some school districts, mainstreaming is a way to save money so special education teachers don't have to be paid. The ideal schooling for a grandchild with special needs is to have some small, very specialized classes and then some fun classes with the other kids. This way they can make friends and still receive the best possible education.

Some parents are insistent that their kids, even those with major disabilities, be enrolled in a regular classroom. This can lead to physical abuse by a teacher or aide or even another student. In addition, tragic deaths have occurred when physical restraints have been used to extreme.[14] A teacher may become overwhelmed if a child with special problems becomes aggressive or even violent. *In one situation, with which I am familiar, a very large boy with developmental delay would pick up a chair and throw it at another child or use it as a battering ram. The teacher and aide were trying to manage almost thirty little kids and couldn't keep their eyes constantly on the boy. Fortunately, our Center's special education attorney was able to have the boy transferred to a small special class where he could be carefully monitored.*

Abuse by teachers or other children may be a particular problem if a grandchild is not able to communicate what is happening. Then each parent and grandparent has to decide whether a small class with only a few other kids is best or a large class where the possibility exists that a teacher may become overwhelmed trying to both teach and keep order.

If parents are insistent that a child be in a regular class, the student can be pulled for some sessions with special education teachers or resource specialists. Some one-to-one tutoring can make all the difference in a child's ability to understand a subject. If a speech therapist or other professional is needed, time with these consultants can be worked in along with regular education classes.

EDUCATION IN THE PRE-SCHOOL YEARS

If you have the care of your grandchild in the first few years of life, it will be special to watch the changes as he or she grows and develops. To help your grandchild have the best chance in life, some special help may be needed depending on the particular diagnosis. If there are sensory problems, speech problems, motor or developmental delay, many services are available.

To find the special services available in your area, I would first call the special education office of your local school district. Easter Seals, too, in the U.S. offers some early infant programs, so calling their local program would be a good idea. Physical and occupational therapists will make home visits and work with small children if your grandchild's special need comes under a program's umbrella of services. There should be no charge for these visits.

In the U.K., I would talk with your doctor or Family Care Nurse to find out what services are available. An agency that offers resources for your grandchild's particular need should also be able to help.

Pre-school nursery schools can offer a chance for you to catch a breath, do errands, or rest. Any pre-school program should be carefully researched. You want to be sure that the teachers have good credentials and their backgrounds carefully checked. Little children should not have more than a few hours of day away from home except in special circumstances. In addition, there should be a teacher for every few children.

Other important questions to ask are how long the pre-school has been in existence, is it accredited, what is the policy about sick children, is medical care available if there is an accident, a seizure (convulsion), or other medical emergency, and how close is the nearest hospital that cares for children?

Some pre-schools are no more than baby-sitting services. I have visited some where the rooms were not clean, there were few fun toys, and the children and teachers looked miserable. So, it will take some networking, some visits to pre-schools, and considerable time to choose exactly the best program for your grandchild. After enrolling a child in a pre-school, it is a good idea to drop in now and then to be sure your grandchild is having fun and getting help with any special needs.

In some states, such as California, children with special needs are eligible for special education help if their diagnosis fits within a particular list of conditions. If it does then the school district must do an assessment, but this cannot be done without the legal guardian's consent. There are a specified number of days when an assessment must be done after it is requested. Then there is an additional time limit for when an IEP (Individualized Education Program) must be developed based on the assessments. Services should then be provided either in small groups or individually.

Some small children are not ready for a pre-school experience and if you, as the grandparent, are the legal guardian, your instinct about this is very important to trust. Parents or grandparents, who have the full-time care of a child, are the true experts with that child and professionals who spend only a short time with a child may know their own area of expertise very well, but they can never know a child as well as you or the child's parents.

The conditions that qualify children, ages three to five, for special education in California and some other states are: Autism, Deaf-Blindness, Deafness, Established medical disability, Hearing impairment, Mental Retardation (Developmental Delay), Multiple disabilities, Orthopedic impairment, Serious emotional impairment, Specific Learning Disability, Speech or language impairment, Traumatic brain injury, Visual impairment, and Other health impairment.

SCHOOL–AGES FIVE AND OLDER

When a child with special needs is ready to start kindergarten, a decision must be made about whether he or she should go into a regular class or into a special education class. To make this decision, some special testing may be necessary. The testing would determine if there are any emotional, learning, auditory processing, or fine-motor problems.

By law in the United States, the school district is required to do the testing. There may be some excellent professionals in school districts who can do the testing, but often they have a long waiting list or are pushed for time. If it is at all possible to have the testing done by an outside qualified professional the results may be more accurate.

Some schools do not want to admit testing results done by outside professionals, but they must do so. Also, your consultants are allowed to attend the IEP or Individualized Education Program. It is probably wise to establish a good relationship with the school of your choice and then before the IEP let them know that your consultants and maybe even an advocate will be attending with you.

The psychological tests do not include an IQ or Stanford-Binet test, but what is needed is termed a "psychological or psychometric profile." This will show if there is any learning disability, auditory processing problem, or other difficulties that will need special help. It takes a well-trained educational psychologist to choose the tests needed to identify particular problems. Also, testing must be done in a child's language, so the results are accurate.

I had a school principal tell me that one of the children in his school did not qualify for special education based on the testing the school psychologist had done. Fortunately, the parents were able to afford outside testing which very clearly showed the boy did qualify for special help and a special class. It made the difference in his life.

Testing should be done on a day when your grandchild is not unusually tired and at the time of day that is best for him or her. If your grandchild doesn't feel well or is coming down with a respiratory infection, the testing should be cancelled until a later date.

Before the IEP, you are allowed to review the records the school has about your grandchild. By law a child with special needs in the United States is to be placed in the "least restrictive environment and receive a free and appropriate education."

THE INDIVIDUALIZED EDUCATION PROGRAM

Each state in the U.S. has different requirements about how soon an IEP must be scheduled after the necessary testing is done. The date must be convenient for you or the parents and you are allowed to have a friend or advocate accompany you. If you plan to record the proceedings, you should notify the principal at least twenty-four hours ahead of time. This probably will not be a popular thing to do, but it is your legal right.

Prior to the date of the IEP meeting, it is wise to make a list of your questions and goals for your grandchild. It is a good idea, also, to have some familiarity with the special education laws. You don't have to be an expert on the laws, but the more you know about them, the better prepared you will be to fight for the best possible education for your grandchild.

I would plan to dress in a professional or conservative manner, so you are taken seriously. On the day of the meeting, be prepared to speak up if you are not happy about the conduct of the meeting or the information presented by the different consultants or teachers. If you do not understand some of the terms the different consultants use, ask them to explain what they mean. If you are timid about stating your thoughts or asking questions, the consequences could result in an inadequate program for your grandchild.

WHO SHOULD ATTEND

The school personnel required to be present are the professionals who did testing, as a speech therapist, psychologist, OT, or PT. Also a special education teacher or the teacher your grandchild will have must attend and someone from the school, as the principal or his or her representative. It may be someone from the school district who is knowledgeable about resources for your grandchild.

Under new IDEA regulations, a professional who would ordinarily be required to attend the IEP can be excused if the parents (grandparents) and school authorities agree. A written excuse must be received from the parent or grandparents. Also, now the IEP meeting can be held with conference calls or video conferencing.

WHAT TAKES PLACE AT AN IEP MEETING

The test results should be presented by the different consultants and any outside testing that you have had done must be admitted for review. This should not be a problem, but I have attended IEP meetings where there was some unpleasantness about this.

All the services that your grandchild is to have must be included in the IEP. The document should clearly state how often the services are to be given and how much time is to be allotted for each session. Unfortunately, even though this is clearly stated, the school districts may later say they didn't have adequate personnel to give the services. By law, they are then required to pay for the services outside the school. You may have to be a bit assertive to see this happen. Once the services are started, you should check frequently to see that your grandchild is receiving all the services designated in the IEP.

If accommodations are needed for the various standardized tests that are now being required in the United States, these accommodations should be written into the IEP. If a child is blind, a test can be read to him or her and extra time can be allowed if it is needed.

An IEP should also list any other services a child will need such as: counseling, recreation, speech and language, Braille services, or routine help such as changing of diapers, toileting, suctioning, or help with catheterization. If computers are needed, then a request for an assistive technology consultant must be written into the IEP. Lucky kids will have computers at home, but children in U.S. special education classes can have computers in school if this is written into the IEP. If a child is non-verbal, it is too late to have computer use not started until ages ten or fifteen years. A computer should be available as soon as a child understands how to use a computer and can manage to use one.

If you want OT or PT to be included, check ahead of time with your state program for kids with special needs to see if they will provide these services. In California, CCS or California Children's Services is required to provide OT and PT if they receive a prescription from a physician. However, often they are short of therapists or they may decide that there is no improvement and so discontinue the services. These can sometimes be continued if your grandchild's physician will write a letter saying they are necessary for educational reasons. This may be to help fine-motor coordination, balance, eye-hand coordination, etc.

It is possible to request adaptive physical education (PE) if it is needed and there are individuals with special training who can provide this. However, the adaptive PE must be written into the IEP and the number of days per week and the length of each session should be included. There are many sports activities that can be modified even for kids with muscle weakness, spasticity, or visual impairments.

If you are not happy with the results of the IEP meeting and feel some services were overlooked, you can refuse to sign the IEP document. You can also sign it, but write a comment next to something that is not as you believe it should be stated. Also, you can take the document home and review it, so that you are comfortable signing it. If you want changes made in the document, they can be made if the school authorities agree. This can be done without a new meeting if everyone agrees. The school may refuse to make the necessary changes or have a new meeting. If this happens, there are specific steps you will have to follow. This is time consuming and may require a legal hearing. Mediation may be required prior to a legal hearing. If you do decide to go this route, you most likely will need a legal advocate or someone very familiar with the rules and regulations. But remember "the squeaky wheel does get the grease" and a child's education is too important to be intimidated by a school system or their personnel.

Once school starts, you should receive regular progress reports and if you see that your grandchild is not receiving the special services that are needed, you can request a new IEP at any time. The request should be in writing to the head of the school district's special education division. It is important to keep a copy and then follow-up with a visit or phone call.

A new IEP should be scheduled every twelve months. The goals from the previous IEP should be reviewed to see if they were met the previous year. If you move your grandchild to another school district, the old IEP should remain in place until new assessments are done and a new IEP scheduled.

RECORD KEEPING

If you are the legal or physical guardian, it is important to keep the school records together in a file in the best order you can. A loose-leaf binder works well for this and in it you can have sections for the school records, outside medical or consultants' records, and anything else that will help your grandchild get the best possible education.

I would also suggest keeping a telephone record of any conversations you have with school personnel. It is often hard to remember what each individual says, but if you have the date, the time, and the person's name, as well as what was discussed, this can be very helpful. I know this sounds like a full-time job and it can be, but I have seen amazing outcomes for kids with special needs when parents and grandparents make their wishes known and keep on top of a child's school progress. Also, the parents and grandparents who have time to volunteer at the school and those who visit the classes regularly will find that their kids fare even better. You might want to check on where your grandchild is seated in the various classes. Some kids want to sit in the back of the room so they won't be called on. If there is a problem with vision or hearing this can create a problem and all the teachers need to be aware of any problems with hearing or eyesight.

IMPORTANT ABBREVIATIONS YOU MAY ENCOUNTER

IEP: Individualized Education Program.

FAPE: Free and Appropriate Public Education.

IDEA: Individuals with Disabilities Education Act.

LRE: Least Restrictive Environment.

IEE: Independent Education Evaluation.

CMH: Community Mental Health.

DIS: Designated Instruction Services.

OCR: Office of Civil Rights (Federal).

DOE: Department of Education (Federal).

SED: Seriously Emotionally Disturbed.

LD: Learning Disabled.

OHI: Other Health Impaired.

OI: Orthopedically Impaired.

OH: Orthopedically Handicapped.

SDC: Special Day Class.

RSP: Resource Specialist Program.

HOMEWORK

Homework can become a major problem if a child doesn't like school, has learning disabilities, difficulty sitting still, or focusing. There are many ways a child with special needs can be helped. A small tape recorder can record assignments, lessons, or special information from the teacher. On-going communication with your grandchild's aide, if there is one, will help, as will sitting down each day and spending time going over what needs to be done. Some schools have "Homework Hotlines" that can be called if there are homework problems. Calculators can be used if special accommodations are made and there are electronic spelling dictionaries and also automatic note takers.

Special tutoring is available online and privately. Companies such as Tutor.com have their programs now in many U.S. public libraries and the program is also available at home with the use of a credit card.

Restricting TV or computer use to one or two hours as long as it is not connected with school work is important. Many kids would play computer or Nintendo games for hours on end unless strict guidelines are established. It is hard to make the rules stick, but you and your grandchild will be saved many battles if the guidelines are established and maintained right from the very beginning.

Chapter Thirteen

Helping a Teen Transition to Adulthood

It is hard enough these days to be a teenager or the parents or grandparents of one without the added problems of a disability or special challenge. When a teen, who has already had many obstacles to overcome, is expected to make the transition to adulthood, the barriers may seem overwhelming. Teens with good self-esteem, who have learned the steps of independence, usually fare quite well. Those with a poor self-image will need extra help and support and grandparents can play an important role for these teens by offering unconditional love and helping in any way they can.

Sometimes parents put such high expectations on kids that life feels like a burden. Kids, too, often put high expectations on themselves, usually to please their parents. It can be a frightening experience to go to college or get out into the real world if they have been sheltered or coddled.

Some parents have great difficulty in "letting go" of their kids, constantly hovering over them and not allowing the kids to make their own independent choices. This is particularly hard if the teenager has a progressive disease or is severely limited either mentally or physically. Grandparents can provide a listening ear and endorse whatever choices their grandchildren make, unless the choices are dangerous ones. Having a neutral sounding board can help teenage grandchildren make the best choices.

If a teen is developmentally delayed, parents and grandparents will need to take a much more active role in the choices they make because it may be difficult for them to evaluate a situation or individuals and be aware of possible danger or problems. It is hoped that some basic social and community skills have been taught, so the teen can communicate with others, make purchases, and safely use community transportation.

If a teen is intellectually able to make choices, he or she may learn more by a few failures than repeated successes. Learning what risks can be taken to yield good results and about good and bad choices will help develop mature judgment.

Once a teen leaves school, the obstacles may seem so overwhelming that depression begins to take its toll. If this is happening to a grandchild and you are close at hand or in charge, then some counseling and perhaps medication may be appropriate. It is very important that a good diagnostic work-up, including a complete physical examination, blood work and urinalysis, is done before any medication is started.

Now that clerks and nurses in America are making most of the decisions about what patient care is allowed in insurance companies and HMOs, many psychiatrists are permitted to see patients for only one or two visits. Unfortunately, some psychiatrists are prescribing powerful anti-depressants without first doing a good work-up or trying some therapy.

Some anti-depressants are currently not recommended for children and teenagers. No parent or grandparent should allow one of these drugs to be prescribed until a complete work-up has been done unless they have complete confidence in the physician and the medication has been thoroughly discussed. Serious effects are caused by some of the anti-depressants and teen suicides have occurred when an adequate work-up and prior counseling have not taken place.

It is important to know the cardinal signs of depression since more and more teenagers these days are having problems with this. The signs of depression to watch for are:

- loss of interest in life

- sleep disturbance

- feeling guilty or negative

- loss of energy

- a decrease in the ability to love family members

- a decrease in appetite

- a loss of interest in appearance

- a feeling of being lost in a deep, black place

- feeling isolated and that no one cares.

I had a patient in his early twenties for whom I strongly recommended psychiatric help because I had fears about his future. Jim, as I will call him, was quite depressed, had considerable muscle weakness, and felt disconnected from his parents and life. He desperately wanted to date and do the things his peers were doing, but could not find a way to accomplish this. His parents were both busy working and saw no reason for Jim to have counseling, despite my urgent pleas. They paid a high price for their decision, because Jim eventually found a way to end his life.

The National Alliance on Mental Illness provides a great amount of support, for parents, grandparents, and young people. They have organizations all over the United States and their Web site at: www.nami.org gives advice on how to find the best professional help, as well as much other useful information. They can be reached at 1-800-950-6264 and if you have a question about a grandchild's emotional state, I'm sure they will be of help.

One medical problem when a teen transitions into adulthood is not only finding other doctors to care for them, but also having the teen's previous doctors educate the new doctors about specific medical or other problems. I find that few doctors in the United States now take the time to pick up the phone and discuss a patient with another doctor.

If the doctors see each other regularly in the hospital or in their office buildings, there can be a good exchange of information. However, sometimes, a patient's privacy is not respected and conversations are held in places that others can overhear. Privacy is all important to a teen, as to any of us, and parents and grandparents need to be sure that a teen's previous doctors have communicated either by sending reports, calling, or e-mailing a new doctor or doctors while respecting a teen's privacy. This all takes time and family members may have to check and re-check that there has been communication between the new and old doctors, as well as other professionals that will be needed.

INTERNET SAVVY AND PRECAUTIONS

Even little kids are using computers these days and for some children with special needs a computer is a life-saver. Many kids with autism and learning disabilities are amazingly proficient on a computer.

For those of us who are not computer whizzes and yet need to know what our grandchildren are doing, here are some tips. Probably the most important tip would be that it would be best for a computer to be located in the family room or a common room where you could easily walk by and see what is going on. If a young person is chatting with someone on the Internet and doesn't want a parent or grandparent to see what is being said, various codes have been devised. The code "POS" stands for "Parent over the Shoulder." It could be "GPOS" for "Grandparent over the Shoulder." This could be because a young person is discussing something inappropriate or something personal. Other codes are bf for boyfriend, brb for be right back, y for why. There is a good Web site that gives other abbreviations. It is: www.safesurfingkids.com/chat_room_internet_acronyms.htm.

Blogs are very popular these days with many teens. The word "Blog" comes from the two words, Web and log. These started in 1997 and initially were written by just a few people. Now they are very popular and are a way for people to express themselves. If a grandchild is spending an extraordinary amount of time writing on a computer, becomes secretive or has a change in behavior, these could be danger signals. Limiting the amount of time that can be spent on a computer, unless it is for homework, would be wise. If a grandchild relies on a computer to stay busy, rather than interacting with other kids, that could lead to trouble.

Remember, though, that kids today are very smart and if you limit computer time at your house, are you sure the computer isn't being used at a friend's house? Keeping in touch with the friend's parents or grandparents is the best way to know what is going on with your grandchild.

Parents and grandparents always need to be aware of any Internet "pals" with whom their children and grandchildren are communicating. Teens with special needs are often lonely and may use the Internet as a way to make and have friends. Unfortunately, one or more of the friends could be a sexual predator. Some on-going discussion of the potential risks of making friends online is important.

Some good rules are: a young person should never give their name, address, or post a photo. Any personal information, such as birthday, e-mail address, social security number, or phone number should also not be revealed. If kids give their IM (instant messaging) password to anyone, it could be passed on or around to others and used in a malicious way. Bullying on cyberspace does occur and tragedies have resulted.

Keeping an online diary is not wise, because the information could be used by others in a destructive way. In addition, anything that is written online should be carefully reviewed to be sure it is the same as would be said to someone in person.

In this day of dating sites, MySpace, instant messaging, and other electronic means of communication, it is hard to keep track of what kids are doing. There are many tragic accounts of those who have started communicating online with a sexual predator, met them, been kidnapped, raped, and murdered. Many of these predators act as teenage kids in order to trap their victims.

You can protect your grandchild to some extent by using different blocking agents. Unfortunately, smart kids often find a way around these or use a friend's computer. Pornographic sites seem to multiply daily, according to the experts. Cyberstalking is also becoming a problem. Having a grandchild's picture and personal information on MySpace is just what a predator needs if he is intent on doing harm.

If your grandchild is receiving sexually suggestive messages online, these should be printed out and reported to your Internet provider. If you prefer to assume that nothing like this could happen to your grandchild, you could have a painful and tragic awakening. As grandparents, we have to be constantly on our toes if we are entrusted with the care of a grandchild. Awareness of what grandchildren are doing daily on the Internet is extremely important for both parents and grandparents.

Some good Web filters and Spam blockers are: Net Nanny, Cyber Patrol, and Child Safe. Some useful Web sites are: www.nationalalertregistry.com, www.SafeTeens.com, and www.WebWiseKids.org. It is a very different world from when we, as grandparents, were growing up, so on-going communication and awareness of what grandchildren are doing online is a must.

DATING, DRIVING, AND DRESSING

Dating, driving, and dressing are the three important Ds of adolescence. **Dating** can be a great problem for teens with special needs if they have been isolated and not developed good social skills. Everything possible should be done to help a teen learn how to relate to others and feel comfortable with his or her body. Clubs, summer camps, religious groups, and the Special Olympics offer good opportunities to make friends and develop skills that are needed to interact with others. Peer groups and finding ways to help others can also make a tremendous difference. Finding a common interest as a hobby or interesting project can help.

Discussion of sexuality or sex education is important for all kids, but must be handled with great tact and understanding if the teen has spina bifida, cerebral palsy, is paraplegic, or has some other central nervous system dysfunction. Sex education programs are given by disability counselors in some medical schools and agencies. If you can find one in your area, this could be extremely important for your teenage grandchild.

No one can live without some touching and warmth. If a teen has a poor self-image and feels isolated, the lack of normal relations between sexes can be devastating. It is particularly hard for those in wheelchairs to feel like "whole individuals" unless they have had strong, loving parenting and grandparenting.

One of my teenage patients refused to get on the school bus that was for the kids with developmental delay. Her bus, that was for kids with physical disabilities, had broken down. She told me that she would have been ostracized and ridiculed by the other kids and they would have thought she was "retarded." Unfortunately, there is prejudice against some groups of disabled kids, even among kids who themselves have a disability. This teenager sadly didn't have parents she could talk to about the problem. How much easier her life could have been if she at least had had grandparents who would listen and help her work through her feelings.

Another patient, a teenager, who used crutches and had no feeling or strength in his legs, told me that girls thought he was "funny in the head" because his "legs didn't work." He longed desperately for a relationship with a young woman, but turned to drugs when his despair became overwhelming. I tried very hard to get counseling for him, but there was little money and he didn't follow through on the appointments I was able to set up for him. His single parent mother had washed her hands of him when drugs took over his life and these ultimately killed him.

Driving is an important goal for most teens. The day they get their first driving license is a cause for great celebration for teens, though not always for the parents and grandparents! The U.S. Department of Rehabilitation will sometimes help with the purchase of a car or van if the vehicle is to be used for work. However, this will take many phone calls, much paperwork and patience. Grandparents can be a big help by offering to make some phone calls, do any of the necessary leg work and offering support. However, it is better if grandparents can stay in the background and let the teen do as much of the investigating and paperwork as possible.

There are used vans for sale that have been adapted for individuals with special needs. In the U.S., a monthly newsletter is put out by the *Disabled Dealer* that lists these vans for sale. Their Web site is www.disableddealer.com. In the U.K., I would check the Web site www.mobilitydisabled.co.uk. Another Web site that might be useful is www.disabledinfo.co.uk. Often vans that have been adapted for individuals with disabilities can be found for sale in the want ads of a local newspaper.

There are many sources for driver's education for those with disabilities and information about these can generally be found on the Internet or in the Yellow Pages. However, careful research should be done before using one of these groups. Some are connected with colleges or rehab programs and are usually excellent resources, but you will want to be sure any driver's education program is accredited and has a good reputation. I would ask a lot of questions and do some networking with other grandparents or parents of kids with disabilities to get their thoughts and opinions about the various programs.

Dressing or appearance is all important to most teens. Every effort should be made to get a teen interested in good grooming and looking presentable. Grooming, daily baths, and showers are particularly important if there is a problem with fecal, urinary, or menstrual odors.

In these days of skimpy clothes, many choices, media and peer pressure to consume, it can be hard for teens with special problems to find appropriate and affordable attire. Clothing can be adapted to handle bowel, bladder, and menstrual problems and every effort should be made to allow girls to be able to dress like other teens. Velcro fasteners can replace buttons and zippers and be very helpful with decreased or limited hand function. Some of the specialized clothing companies listed in the Appendix may have just the right outfits.

Tattoos and body piercing are fashionable now among some teenage groups. In one study, thirty-six percent of young adults were found to have tattoos and thirty-two percent had one or more piercings other than in ear lobes.[15] Both of these can be dangerous, particularly if a grandchild is on steroids (cortisone) or has difficulty handling infections. This study stated that thirteen percent of those who had a tattoo and twenty-three percent of those with a body piercing developed a medical problem. These can be allergic reactions, infections, or even hepatitis resulting from these procedures.

If you are in charge and your grandchild wants to be trendy and have a body piercing or a tattoo, you will have to decide whether to say "No, absolutely not!" or to talk it over and then make your decision.

I had one patient, Debbie, who was being treated with fairly high doses of steroids (cortisone) for dermatomyositis. At one office visit, she said as she entered my examining room, "You are going to be mad at me, Dr. Thompson." When I asked, "Why?" she stuck out her tongue and I saw a small, silver ball in the middle. I did not get upset with Debbie, but told her my concern was for a medical reason. I explained that it was dangerous for her to have had her tongue pierced because of the high dose of steroids she was taking to treat her dermatomyositis and she was putting herself at risk for having an extremely serious infection. Then I added, "If you want me to continue treating you, the ball comes out now and stays out."

Debbie immediately took the silver ball out and I don't think it ever went back in. As her muscle strength returned and her dermatomyositis gradually came under control, I was slowly able to reduce the steroid dosage. Debbie knew I cared about her and we remained good friends, so she listened to what I said and never argued. I think she wanted to have an excuse to get rid of the troublesome silver ball that her boyfriend had convinced her to have put in her tongue.

BECOMING INDEPENDENT

Once a teen has finished high school, the choice has to be made whether or not to go on to college, a trade school, or perhaps a specialized program, such as an art school. Some teens will need a sheltered workshop or will only be able to do jobs such as bagging groceries or other simple tasks. Every job, no matter how easy, will give a teenager a sense of pride and be a source of some income. All kids should be encouraged to get out into the workforce or go on to college after high school graduation if they are mentally and physically able to do so.

In the United States under the IDEIA law, a high school must begin to make plans for transition when a teenager reaches age fourteen. This is called an Individual Transition Plan. Then by the time a student reaches sixteen, definite transition goals and any needed transition services must be written into the student's IEP. The plan must include strategies about how each of the goals can be met. This is called a Student Exit Summary or Summary of Performance. Career, job, and college counseling should be part of this plan and arrangements made for job training or some type of employment if college or further schooling is not desired or a possibility. If residential care will be needed, plans must be made for this.

There are specific requirements for the Transition Planning session. The teenager should be included if he or she wants to attend. There can be more than one Transition Planning meeting during the year, but these should be requested in writing. You are allowed to invite one or more individuals from various community organizations or agencies who could be helpful in working out a Transition Plan. A counselor from the Vocational Rehabilitation office can be asked to attend an IEP meeting in your grandchild's last year of high school to help make plans about job training or special programs in colleges or other facilities. Plans can also be outlined for any transportation your grandchild will need.

Tests are required for admission to most colleges these days. If a grandchild has had special accommodations to take tests in high school, these can be in place for the admission tests if arrangements are made ahead of time. Your grandchild's high school counselor should be able to tell you and your grandchild where to write and what to request if accommodations are needed. These could include:

1. Extra time to take a test.

2. Oral test with the use of an audio cassette.

3. The use of a computer if writing is a major problem.

4. Enlarged answer sheets if there are visual problems.

5. Extra time between tests if this is needed.

Many colleges and universities have programs for students with special needs which may include transportation, aides, and job training. These should be explored and grandparents can play an important role in doing some of the research. Many phone calls will probably be needed, but the rewards can be great for the teen. Once again, a teen needs to do as much of the investigating as possible with support and advice from parents and grandparents.

If accommodations are needed for a student to do well in college, arrangements should be made for these before the teen starts classes. It may be that your grandchild will be uncomfortable about letting anyone know about his or her particular disability. This is understandable, but if there is no disclosure of a specific problem or problems then tests, times of classes, seating in the classroom, plus the use of computers, calculators, electronic spellers, and other things may not be allowed.

I had a teenage patient with a marked loss of hearing in one ear caused by a genetic abnormality. He did not want classmates or teachers to know about his problem and was also quite shy. Because of this, he always chose a seat in the back of the classroom and thus had a hard time hearing the teacher or classmates. Finally, when his mother talked to me about his grades, I asked where he sat in the classroom. The youth finally agreed to let the school personnel know about his disability and from then on he had a seat near the front of the room and his grades improved.

As grandparents, we can make suggestions, but ultimately the choice of what to disclose is up to your grandchild. It would be sad for a teen to do poorly in college just because of embarrassment about letting the teachers and administrators know of a special need. Sometimes talking with your grandchild about the problem or having a counselor do so could be helpful.

Financial aid is available from different sources depending on income, disability, and other special factors. In the U.S., for students with dyslexia, a Web site at: www.dyslexia.com/scholarships.htm is useful. For other scholarships, you or your grandchild might want to look at: www.finaid.org or www.collegescholarships.org/disabilities.htm. The last site is for individuals with all disabilities. One site to check for student aid is: www.studentaid. ed.gov. Another one that might be helpful is www.fafsa.ed.gov. This is the site of the United States Department of Education and the application is called the Free Application for Federal Student Aid. Organizations, such as University Women, PEN Women, and other groups, give some scholarships and these would also be worthwhile to research.

RESEARCHING AND HIRING AIDES

To become independent and no longer live at home, a teen with special needs who requires an aide must learn how to find, interview, and hire this individual. This takes considerable practice, but is an important part of becoming independent for some teens.

I had one lovely patient who became an emancipated minor at age sixteen. She had no idea how to hire an aide, so I had her sit at my office desk and stayed with her as she made the necessary phone calls. She had been living with a friend's family, but was ready to go off to college. It took considerable effort for her to feel comfortable making the calls, but she did a great job and I was very proud of her. She has now graduated from college, is employed, and has many friends; an amazing young woman. She still loves life, despite marked muscle weakness and limited ability to get around in an electric wheelchair.

Grandparents who have the time to help with the details of finding, hiring, and firing aides can make a great contribution. Mothers often want to act as an aide, as their teens gets older, but this is unwise. Young men need a male attendant and mothers or grandmothers should allow them to hire someone they like who might become a friend, as well as an aide. Face-to-face interviews are important and are a learned skill. Parents and grandparents can act as the applicant, so a teen can have some practice with interviewing.

An aide's background must be carefully researched by checking the driving record and credit history to be sure there are no red flags. The U.S. Web site at www.familywatchdog.us gives details about the most serious sex offenders. These are the so-called Level Two or Level Three offenders. The less dangerous ones are not given on the site. The U.S. Department of Justice has guidelines for screening individuals who care for kids. They also suggest getting a credit report and checking an individual's driving license.

HEALTH CARE

Once teens with special needs have outgrown their school clinics and pediatric care, it can be very difficult for them to find on-going medical care. In the United States, few physicians are willing to care for patients with special needs because of the time involved and minimal or no payment.

Coordinating the medical care of patients with special needs takes an enormous amount of time. This can become a real financial burden if a physician cares for many patients with disabilities or special needs. Reimbursement by most state programs in the United States takes much paperwork and often even then there is no payment. Insurance companies do everything possible to keep from paying physicians for this type of care.

There are free clinics run by non-profit groups, but these are generally staffed by volunteers or over-worked staff physicians. Many of these doctors have not had special training with patients having spina bifida, cerebral palsy, autism, neuromuscular disorders, developmental delay, or other special needs. Illnesses or medical problems are often thought to be related to the underlying diagnosis, so much can be overlooked.

There are specific tests that should be done if, for example, a patient has spina bifida or a spinal cord injury. A urological review should be done at least every two years to be sure no kidney or other problems are developing. Urine cultures must be done if there is increased urinary frequency, leaking, or bad odor. The question of maintenance antibiotics needs to be discussed with the urologist and fluid intake should be carefully monitored. Patients often decrease their fluid intake so that less frequent catheterization is needed if they do not use a collecting bag.

If self-catheterization has not been started at an early age or is not successful later on, a ureostomy may be the best answer. This is a surgical procedure where the ureter is brought to the surface to empty into a collecting bag. Having an adult show his or her collecting bag or ostomy to an older teenager is often helpful to both.

A bowel program should begin when a child is two or three years old to have it be successful by the school years. There is nothing more difficult than being around a child with an obvious fecal smell. The kids can be severely ostracized by their classmates and others if there is a constant odor.

I had one patient with spina bifida who had to be frequently hospitalized because of fecal impactions. She would not eat a good diet or follow a bowel plan and her foster parents were too involved with other problems to pay much attention to her. This became a very difficult problem because the hospitalizations seemed to be her way to get a lot of attention and the doctors and nurses became her "real" family. She refused counseling, but ultimately had to have a colostomy because the bowel problems became so severe. She was bright and pretty, but I have always had great concern about her future.

Diapers in older kids can be emotionally devastating and every effort should be made to get rid of them. An individual's self-image can be severely damaged if diapers are still worn. A diet high in fiber and protein, adequate fluid, and the proper use of stool softeners or suppositories should allow a good bowel plan to be developed. If this doesn't work, there are enterostomy specialists who can be consulted. Usually these individuals are connected with a rehabilitation unit.

The onset of menstruation can be a great problem for teenage girls, as well as their parents and grandparents. Every effort should be made to teach teenage girls how to care for themselves during menstruation. If there is not a regular change of pads, tampons, and/or clothing, a most unpleasant odor can occur which will keep others at a distance. Periods can be regulated or even stopped with appropriate medications and this should be discussed with a knowledgeable gynecologist, as soon as signs of puberty begin to develop. The medical means used to control menstrual periods are birth control pills, Depo-Provera, endometrial ablation, and, now rarely possible, a hysterectomy.

Birth control pills cause uncomfortable side-effects in some women with weight gain and irritability. Depo-Provera is given as an injection every three months. Some minor spotting of blood may still occur, but regular periods will cease. Endometrial ablation is a surgical procedure that requires a general anesthetic and is not in common use. Hysterectomies were allowed in the past, but now they take a court order and much documentation before surgery would be allowed.

The possibility of early, unwanted pregnancies is a real fear for girls with disabilities, particularly if they are developmentally delayed. Every effort should be made to safeguard girls who are unable to evaluate situations or people and may feel flattered by having a male seem to be interested in them. Discussion about preventive measures with the physician in charge is important and should be done in the early teen years. This is of particular concern if the girls are in foster or group homes. The home's policy about dating should be carefully researched and questions asked about how they screen their male attendants and staff members.

Masturbation can be a problem if kids are unable to understand this is not something they should do in a public place. If masturbation occurs in a girl, you want to be sure that a vaginal discharge is not the cause. Sometimes this can cause considerable itching, particularly if there is a problem with monilia or a fungus infection. Another reason kids rub themselves in the area between their legs is due to pinworms.

I had one girl as a new patient who had been seeing a child psychologist because she was constantly rubbing herself between her legs. The skin around her rectum and on her labia was quite red, so I asked the mother to check for pinworms that night. (Fifty percent of children will have pinworms at some time when they are little.) There is a special tape that can be placed next to the rectum to catch the pinworms as they emerge at night from the bowel, but you can also take a flashlight and look around the anus, once a child is asleep. This mother saw many pinworms that evening and was horrified. Treatment for these quickly stopped the girl from scratching and rubbing against objects. She no longer needed to see the child psychologist!

Anorexia and bulimia are serious problems today with many teenagers, both girls and boys. The highest incidence is in girls. Many young girls start dieting at a young age, because their mothers may be constantly dieting and the media places such a strong emphasis on beautiful, extremely thin models and movie stars. There are several Web sites supporting anorexia in teenage girls. If you detect that a teenager is not eating adequately or going to the bathroom after eating a meal to vomit up the food, then it may be time to consult the teen's physician or a physician who specializes in eating disorders.

Counseling can make a great difference in a teen's life if he or she has considerable anger or fear about getting out into the big world and living independently. Support groups can also make a great difference. The choice of a counselor is an important one and should be someone who either has worked with many individuals with disabilities or has some type of disability. I have referred patients to some excellent counselors, who themselves had a disability. They were wonderful role models and could understand the fear and poor self-image that plague many kids with special needs.

COLLEGE EDUCATION

A college education is very important in today's world if a teen is interested or has the ability to go on to college. Fortunately, most big universities and even smaller colleges have programs for students with special needs. These should be carefully investigated and grandparents can play an important part in this investigation. If colleges can be visited, that is even better.

I would want to find out several things if a grandchild is thinking of a particular college. This would include what arrangements can be made if special accommodations are needed, accessibility of buildings and classrooms, accessibility of the library, and if special technical aids or equipment are available in case they are needed.

One thing that parents and grandparents often forget to find out about is the college student health service. If there is a problem, such as a convulsion or seizure, are physicians immediately available on-campus and if not who sees the students? Medical care by someone other than a physician would not be a good choice for most college students with special needs. If there is a medical problem, your grandchild's physician should send a letter to the student health service giving details about the problem. A letter should also be given to your grandchild to keep and show to doctors, as needed.

If there has been a problem with depression or a diagnosis of mental illness in the high school or teen years, it would be extremely important for your grandchild's psychiatrist to be involved in both the choice of a college and finding a good psychiatrist in the college or university town. Student health services in most colleges and universities are not well equipped to handle emotional or psychiatric problems in my experience, so a local physician would be important for a student to see for regular visits. A college student who is away from home for the first time may feel very alone and if there is difficulty with socialization and relationships, severe depression may result.

One young man told me that he had "too much freedom as a freshman in college and didn't know how to handle it." He got involved with drugs to help numb the pain and make him feel better. Finally, he did see a psychiatrist, but didn't take the medications the doctor prescribed and subsequently dropped out of school. He then tried to end his life, but failed, and became a paraplegic.

On-going contact with a local psychiatrist, a college counselor, or someone in the student health service would have been important, as would have continued contact with his family, family doctor, or pediatrician.

I have always advised parents or the grandparents-in-charge to find a physician in the community who could be called in case the student health service is inadequate. Your physician or your grandchild's physician should be able to call a physician in the city where your grandchild will be in college and obtain one or two names. I have done this many times for patients.

Immunizations need to be brought up to date prior to entering college and all students must have a meningococcal vaccine before starting college. Meningococcal meningitis can be rapidly fatal, so it is very important that grandchildren be protected.

I have had to be fairly aggressive about contacting colleges in other cities and states, in order to find adequate medical care for college students, who were former patients. I even had to make a trip to a dormitory in another city late on a Friday evening, to see a student who had been diagnosed by a nurse practitioner as having tonsillitis. The teenager was in her dorm alone and was having difficulty swallowing because of enormous tonsils. I thought the young woman most likely had infectious mononucleosis, not tonsillitis, and immediately called an ambulance. Fortunately, the girl got to the hospital before her very big tonsils caused her to stop breathing by obstructing her airway. She did have mononucleosis and had a difficult time recuperating.

Another thing to check on, if you are the college student's legal guardian, is health insurance. Many insurance policies are no longer in effect after a young person turns eighteen. Also, a few colleges will require a student to buy their health plans. Aetna is one of the companies that have health plans for college students.

Before students graduate from college, it is wise to check their health insurance coverage to be sure their policy will still be in effect until a job is found or the decision is made to go on for more education. A policy to cover the post-college time is called a "Bridge policy."

There is insurance called GradMed that covers college graduates and their Web site is: www.gradmed.com. Unfortunately, the insurance does not cover pre-existing conditions, so this probably would not be helpful. However, COBRA insurance is an option and should be investigated. There is something called "High-Risk" insurance that could help a student who needs insurance after graduating from college and getting out into the work world. Not all states have this insurance and it can be expensive, but some kind of coverage is important, particularly when there is a pre-existing problem. A list of the states that offer High-Risk insurance is given in the Appendix.

EMPLOYMENT

Before employment can be found, career counseling or coaching and job training are usually necessary. A job is critical in fostering a healthy self-image, developing independence, and having a source of income. If the individual has a college degree or has attended even one or two years of college, the chance to find good employment is much better than just having a high school diploma. Every effort should be made by parents and grandparents to help a young person with special needs graduate from college or receive special training to help them become employable. Computer skills are particularly valuable if this area is of interest and attainable for a teen.

When a student is ready to find employment, there are several traditional sources of employment that can be investigated. The Department of Vocational Rehabilitation should provide counseling and other help. Other resources are the Goodwill Industries, St. Vincent's, and the Salvation Army. Some cities have non-profit organizations that help people find jobs, whatever their special need. Individuals who are not going to be able to work full-time or need a sheltered workshop may be eligible for special financial assistance or SSI. This is given for "marked and severe functional limitations present for more than twelve months."

Some of the disabilities for which SSI can be received are: HIV infection, total blindness, total deafness, cerebral palsy, Down syndrome, muscular dystrophy, severe "mental retardation" for a child age seven or older, and a birth weight below two pounds, ten ounces. A youth can not earn more than $940 each month to receive this financial assistance.

To receive this financial assistance, reports will be needed from doctors, teachers and others who have knowledge of an applicant. In addition, a birth certificate and social security number will be needed and family income will be considered. It takes usually three to five months for a review to be done and once the payments are granted, a repeat review is done every three years. In some states, Medicaid comes automatically with SSI, but in other states it is necessary to apply for this financial help. The number to call for Social Security is 1-800-772-1213.

Mary Korpi (2008, p.127), author of *Guiding Your Teenager with Special Needs through the Transition from School to Adult Life*, suggests that "It can be helpful to meet with a vocational rehabilitation counselor one to two years prior to the anticipated date of graduation in order to determine eligibility and relevant support services."[16] This is wise advice.

The American with Disabilities Act or ADA was passed "to provide a clear and comprehensive national mandate for the elimination of discrimination against individuals with disabilities." Thus, the act seeks to provide the same opportunities that would be offered to an able-bodied individual. The key word, I am told by a special education attorney, is "opportunity." The act is organized into five sections: employment, public services, public accommodations, telecommunications services, and miscellaneous provisions. It takes an attorney to understand all the language of the act, but some familiarity with it is wise if a grandchild will be actively seeking employment. Some information is also provided on the Equal Employment Opportunity Commission Web site at: www.eeoc.gov.

Grandparents can play an important part by offering advice about researching possible avenues of employment, needed accommodations, and any financial help. These all can involve a great many telephone calls and much paperwork, so any help you can give should be much appreciated.

Grandparents could also suggest that their grandchild organize a support network of other teens who are job hunting. By sharing information with instant messaging, e-mail, or by telephone, the teens can be a great help to each other.

One of the most important gifts parents and grandparents can give teens is instilling a sense of their own self-worth. If the young people can learn to tackle life's problems and see road blocks as challenges and not obstacles, they will be very fortunate.

It is easy to become depressed with the many problems that can arise when you are a teen with special needs, but if your grandchild can find some fun, laughter, and balance in his or her life, the transition from being a dependent teenager to a competent adult will be a much easier and successful one.

LIVING INDEPENDENTLY

If your grandchild wants to live independently and is able to do so with or without an aide, there are many ways to ensure his or her safety. One of the most important ways to relieve your anxiety is for your grandchild to have a personal alert device that is worn around the neck and can be pressed if a fall or other emergency occurs. A central monitoring station will be alerted and help will be given. In the U.K., many communities provide monitoring as do some private companies. Information about these monitoring systems can be found at www.telecareaware.com.

The Telecare Services Association has a list of suppliers of special equipment and alarms. Their Web site is www.asap-uk.org and their number is 01625 520320.

The Disabled Living Foundation at www.dlf.org.uk has a wealth of ideas for other ways an elderly or disabled individual can live independently. Sensors can be placed in a house or apartment to remind the inhabitant to perform certain tasks, such as taking medication or monitoring vital signs (heart rate and respiratory rate), or to automatically shut off gas if gas is detected in the home. A bath alarm is available that hangs down into the bathtub and sounds an alarm if the water reaches it. Also there is a way for a drain to be activated if the water level gets too high.

If an individual gets out of bed at night and there is a risk of falling, disorientation, or wandering, a sensor pad is available that will be activated. With so much new, wonderful technology, individuals who previously had to live in a group home or a special care facility are now able to live with an aide or independently.

DAY PROGRAMS

If a teen has emotional problems and needs on-going counseling or psychiatric help, day programs are available in most communities. Your grandchild's psychiatrist should be able to give you information about these and social workers connected with community agencies or your local hospital should also be able to help. They generally have a wealth of information at their fingertips. It will take considerable energy to find all the available resources, but if you ask a lot of questions and don't give up, the answers should be there.

NURSING HOMES (SKILLED NURSING FACILITIES)

Some grandchildren may need to be placed in nursing homes if they have a progressive disorder or a disability that requires care twenty-four hours a day. It is estimated that there are about thirty thousand individuals between the ages of eighteen and thirty who reside in nursing homes.[17] Some of these individuals had been cared for in long-term care facilities connected with hospitals, but once they reach the age of eighteen, many hospitals and rehab units will no longer care for them. If the family cannot care for a young person at home, then nursing homes are often the only option.

The medical care in U.S. nursing homes often leaves a great deal to be desired. Nurses and aides in these homes have told me that the patients' medical care is left almost entirely up to them, because *most states allow doctors to visit their patients just once a month.*

If your grandchild is going to be transferred to a nursing home, there are several things you can do to be sure the best nursing home will be chosen. In the U.S., the Medicare Web site gives comparisons of nursing homes and it is: www.medicare.gov/NHcompare. There is also another Web site at www.nccnhr.org that is maintained by The National Citizens' Coalition for Nursing Home Reform. This organization provides a guide for choosing a nursing home. All of the nursing homes are supposed to be subject to state and federal regulations, but often there is very little overseeing. You want to first be sure that the nursing home is accredited and that it is the best one available. There is an Assisted Living Federation at: www.alfa.org and their telephone number is: 1-703-894-1805. They can offer suggestions about how the best plans can be made.

If a nursing home has been chosen and you grandchild has been transferred to it, you will want to make frequent visits, if this is possible. If you are concerned about the care your grandchild is receiving, there are several things you can do. The first thing is to speak with the doctor in charge of your grandchild's care. If he or she seems uninterested or too busy to speak with you, I would suggest you make an appointment with the director of the nursing home.

You will want to check what orders have been written for your grandchild. For example, it should be stated how often and for how long a period your grandchild should be up and dressed during the day, if that is possible. Also, the amount of PT or OT or other services should be clearly stated, as should type and dosages of medications and other medical necessities. If you make the director aware that you and several others will be making frequent visits to check on your grandchild's care and that you intend to constantly monitor what is going on, your grandchild will receive much better care.

Special services such as physical and occupational therapy should always be available, but will take an order from the doctor. Blood counts should be checked periodically, as should urines. Constipation is a major problem when patients are inactive, so you will want to be sure that regular bowel movements are occurring. If a patient is constipated, the possibility of having an associated urinary tract infection is much greater. If a special diet is needed, it would be a good idea to make an appointment with the dietitian to discuss this.

If your grandchild has screaming fits, terrible emotional outbursts, or other kinds of disruptive behavior, heavy sedation or anti-psychotic medication may be used. Some of these medications can make the behavior much worse and if a psychiatrist or doctor does not carefully monitor your grandchild's reaction to a drug or drugs, the results can be disastrous.

Any patient should always be given the lowest possible dose of a drug and this is particularly true of anti-psychotic drugs. It has been found in studies of nursing home patients that if they are kept up during the day, have planned activities, and lots of attention, they fare much better. Many new drugs can also cause weight gain and diabetes.

Much can be accomplished if you constantly check with the nursing and other staff members. I have visited nursing homes where the odor is overwhelming, the patients are lying apathetically in their beds, and the staff doesn't really seem to care and may be chatting on the phone or reading magazines. Other nursing homes have excellent staff, but little medical supervision. Nursing homes generally pay their aides and other employees the lowest possible hourly wage, so usually their employees are not well trained and may not have much interest in doing a good job. Some of the staff members will, it is hoped, have genuine concern for patients, but if they have little support from the physicians, their job can be a very difficult one.

It is a sad day when a grandchild has to spend time in a nursing home, but by visiting as much as you can, sending cards or small gifts, if this is appropriate, you can make your grandchild's days much brighter. If you can arrange for some outings for your grandchild, that would be special. In addition, some nursing homes allow patients to have overnight stays in the family's home. This would be something to ask about if you are able to handle your grandchild for an overnight visit. Having friends and relatives visit will also help and make the days pass much more quickly for your grandchild.

Section III

MEDICAL AND LEGAL ISSUES

Chapter Fourteen

Finding the Best Medical Care

Much of the care of children with special needs in the U.S. is done in big centers or clinics. Unfortunately, this type of care can result in many things being overlooked. In the U.K., each child usually has a primary physician who can refer to big clinics or centers. Every child, with and without special needs, should have a physician responsible for his or her care and one who can have a long-term relationship with that child. Often if something comes up that has no relation to a particular disability, it is automatically assumed the problem is caused by the disability. Much can be overlooked that way, including hearing, vision, blood counts, urinalyses, tuberculin skin tests, and immunizations. These should be checked yearly in every child.

In the U.S., due to the amount of time it takes to care for children with special challenges and the poor payment received, most physicians are unwilling to see these kids. In addition, few doctors have specialized training in caring for children with unusual problems. Clinics are usually staffed by interns or residents with an attending doctor available just to answer questions. Most of the young doctors have had little experience with special needs kids and often little patience with their problems. In addition, they are limited in the time they can spend with patients, so they rarely take a complete history or do a thorough physical examination. If possible, every child needs a physician who can be contacted when there is a routine medical problem. It is hoped that he or she will look at the child and not the disability.

In the Center for Handicapped Children I founded and directed in San Francisco, I found that I needed to do considerable general pediatrics instead of just doing consultations. The local family doctors and pediatricians were often uncomfortable seeing children with special needs and overlooked: chronic constipation, congenital urinary tract abnormalities, severe allergy problems, ear infections, and many other common child-hood disorders. I even found two children with active tuberculosis!

FINDING A GOOD PHYSICIAN

For U.S. grandparents, the best way to find a good pediatrician or family doctor, if you are in charge, is to talk to other parents and grandparents of special needs kids. They can tell you who will take the time and has the training for your grandchild's particular problem. It is unwise to look in the Yellow Pages for names or to call your local medical society. The staff can give you doctors' names, but no information about credentials, experience, or how the individual relates to children.

An agency specializing in your grandchild's particular diagnosis can be a good resource most of the time. I unfortunately found one agency director who referred to a specific doctor. He did not relate to kids and was not well trained in that particular disorder. I was never sure just why the agency director recommended him. So you do have to be careful and check with two or three different people about a referral.

It is possible to check the Internet for information on doctors in the U.S.: their medical experience, any malpractice claims, the date an M.D. was received, and similar things. Remember though that some malpractice suits are settled by very good doctors because they don't have the time or energy to go into court.

HEALTH PROFESSIONALS YOU MAY ENCOUNTER

Allergist: A physician with specialized training in the treatment of allergies in adults or children.

Anesthesiologist: An M.D. with several years of additional training giving anesthetics for surgical procedures. Some specialize in pain treatment.

Audiologist: A health professional, not a physician, with training in detecting and aiding those with hearing loss.

Cardiologist: A physician with specific training in diseases of the heart. Pediatric cardiologists have training in children's heart disorders. These doctors are not surgeons.

Dermatologist: A doctor with special training in diseases of the skin. There are pediatric dermatologists with training in skin diseases of children.

Dietitian: An individual with special training in diets and specific nutritional needs of the body. Dietitians are generally connected with hospitals, but some work independently.

Endocrinologist: A medical doctor with special training in treating endocrine diseases of children and adults. Endocrine glands are those concerned with hormones such as insulin, which relates to diabetes, and the production of thyroid hormones, which relate to growth and many other important functions of the body.

Family Practitioner: A physician who has had training in many specialties and sees both children and adults. He or she has often had more years of training than a general practitioner.

Gastroenterologist: A medical doctor with additional training in diseases of the gastrointestinal tract. Pediatric gastroenterologists are usually found in large cities or connected with children's hospitals.

General Practitioner: A medical doctor who treats both children and adults. These doctors are not required to have specialized training after an internship.

Geneticist: A physician who may have pediatric training and additional genetic training. There are also genetic counselors, who may be nurses or other paramedical people. (*When a genetic condition in suspected, the diagnosis should be established, if possible, before a genetic counselor is seen. Counseling is difficult to give unless the exact type of disorder is known.*)

Geriatrician: A medical doctor with training in internal medicine who cares only for elderly individuals.

Gynecologist: A physician who specializes in treatment of problems with women's reproductive organs.

Hematologist: A medical doctor who may have either a pediatric or internal medicine background. Hematologists treat disorders of the blood. Pediatric hematologists treat children with leukemia, anemia, sickle-cell disease, and any blood-related problems.

Hospitalist: These are medical doctors who are usually internists. They work only in the hospital. Some make no contact with the family or the family physician and do not review the medical records. Many doctors in practice no longer see their patients when they are hospitalized, but leave their care to hospitalists or intensive care doctors.

Immunologist: A medical doctor with special training in disorders of the immune system. The immune system is responsible for how our bodies react to foreign substances, viruses or bacteria.

Internist: A medical doctor with additional training in adult disorders. Many internists have subspecialty training in gastroenterology (diseases of the stomach and intestines) or rheumatology (diseases of the joints and related disorders). They generally see adults, but some see teenagers.

Neonatologist: A pediatrician with additional training in the care of premature and newborn babies. They work in hospital nurseries.

Nephrologist: A physician who specializes in diseases of the kidneys.

Neurologist: A medical doctor with pediatric or adult training in disorders of the brain and nervous system.

Neuromuscular Specialist: These are physicians with specialized training in neuromuscular diseases of children and adults.

Nurse Practitioner: A registered nurse with additional training, allowing him or her to do certain examinations and procedures that registered nurses are not licensed to do.

Obstetrician: A physician who sees women during pregnancy and is responsible for delivery and immediate postnatal care. Obstetricians are also trained in gynecology, so they can provide ongoing care involving the female reproductive system.

Occupational Therapist (OT): An individual with specific training in the function of the musculoskeletal system, particularly the upper extremities. OTs are involved in the developmental problems of children and also concerned with activities of daily living, such as dressing and eating, upper extremity strength, and how to adapt the environment to make it more workable for a disabled person.

Oncologist: A medical doctor who treats patients with tumors, both benign and malignant (cancers). Pediatric oncologists have had special training in caring for children's cancers.

Ophthalmologist: A medical doctor with several years of additional training in examining and treating disorders of the eyes. An ophthalmologist is a licensed surgeon and does eye surgery.

Optometrist: A doctor of optometry does not have a medical degree and is not licensed to issue or prescribe drugs. Optometrists can prescribe glasses, eye exercises, and contact lenses.

Orthopedic Surgeon: A physician with several years of postgraduate training in disorders of bones and joints. An orthopedist can perform surgical procedures on the back and extremities. There are subspecialties of orthopedics: hand surgery, back surgery, and children's orthopedics.

Osteopath: An individual who has graduated from a school of osteopathy. Some states allow osteopaths to qualify for an M.D. degree. Their scope of treatment varies according to the school from which they graduated, but many are licensed to do almost the same things medical doctors do.

Otolaryngologist: A medical doctor with additional training in treating diseases of the ears, nose, and throat. There are some who see only ear problems. Some see children; others see both children and adults.

Pathologist: A medical doctor who is trained to make diagnoses by looking at microscopic sections and studying tumors or tissues that have been surgically removed.

Pediatrician: An M.D. with additional training in normal childhood development and the treatment of childhood diseases.

Pediatric Allergist: An allergist who treats children with allergic problems: food allergies, eczema, asthma, and hay fever.

Pediatric Cardiologist: A cardiologist who specializes in children's heart problems.

Pediatric Dermatologist: A dermatologist who specializes in children's skin diseases.

Pediatric Endocrinologist: An endocrinologist who specializes in endocrine disorders of childhood.

Pediatric Neurologist: A neurologist who treats seizures and other childhood disorders of the brain and spinal cord.

Pediatric Orthopedist: An orthopedic surgeon who treats children's diseases of the bones and joints.

Pediatric Rheumatologist: A rheumatologist who treats rheumatoid arthritis and similar disorders in children.

Pharmacist: A drug information specialist. All practicing pharmacists are registered (R.Ph.s) by their particular state board of pharmacy. All pharmacy schools now issue Doctor of Pharmacy degrees (Pharm.D.) and most graduates participate in a host of clinical residency programs in both inpatient (hospital) and outpatient (ambulatory care) settings.

Physiatrist: A medical doctor with additional training in rehabilitation or non-surgical treatment of post-accident victims, back injuries, polio, and neuromuscular diseases.

Physical Therapist (PT): An individual with training in the function of joints and muscles. Physical therapists evaluate and treat children and adults who have problems of the musculoskeletal system. They do this by teaching strengthening exercises, massage, or working with specific equipment to help strengthen muscles. A doctor's prescription is usually required for them to give therapy. There are a few states that allow "Direct access" care. For this, you don't need a doctor's prescription, but you pay the costs, not an insurance company.

Physical Therapy Aide: This individual may have no medical training but is trained by the therapists.

Physical Therapy Assistant: Someone who is licensed to do everything except evaluate a patient. They have had some physical therapy training.

Physical Therapy Technician: These individuals are not licensed and are trained on the job. Some training is available in different states.

Plastic Surgeon: A surgeon with additional training in repair of facial problems or cosmetic surgery.

Podiatrist: A health professional who has graduated from a four-year college of podiatry. They specialize in the care of foot and leg problems and are trained to do surgical procedures on problems below the knees. They are doctors of podiatry.

Psychiatrist: A medical doctor who has had additional training in mental and emotional disorders. There are pediatric psychiatrists, with a background in childhood disorders, and adult psychiatrists. Some psychiatrists see children just in hospitals; others practice only outpatient psychiatry.

Psychologist: An individual who has either a masters degree (M.A.) or a doctorate (Ph.D.) in psychology. Psychologists have had variable kinds of training in working with children and adults. Some do testing and therapy, others do just therapy. There are many different schools of psychology, as well as specialties.

Pulmonologist: An M.D. with additional training in diseases of the lungs. There are both adult and children's pulmonologists.

Radiologist: A radiologist is a medical doctor who has had additional training in diagnosing conditions by X-ray, CAT scan, and MRI. Many radiologists do therapy on cancer patients.

Registered Nurse: An individual who has had nursing school training and works under the supervision of a physician. Now many nurses get additional training so they can do other types of procedures or examinations.

Rheumatologist: A physician who treats either children or adults. Rheumatologists have additional training, beyond pediatrics or internal medicine, in diseases involving the joints, for example, juvenile rheumatoid arthritis, and collagen or connective tissue diseases, such as lupus erythematosus.

Social Worker: An individual with special training in counseling and finding resources for children and adults. Social workers have either a medical social worker (M.S.W.) or licensed clinical social worker (L.C.S.W.) degree.

Speech Pathologist: A professional with postgraduate training in diagnosing and treating speech and language disorders.

Urologist: A surgeon with specialized training in treating disorders and diseases of the urinary tract and kidneys. There are both pediatric and adult specialists.

ABBREVIATIONS YOU MAY ENCOUNTER

M.D.: Medical doctor–An individual who has had four years training in an accredited medical school. To be awarded an M.D., specific tests must be passed. Before practicing, an additional training period or internship is required. To specialize in a branch of medicine, three or more years of additional training or residency are required and tests, called boards, must be passed.

D.O.: Osteopath–An individual who graduated from a four-year school of osteopathy. Some states allow D.O.s to receive a doctor of medicine degree, if tests are taken and passed. The D.O. can then apply to a program for additional training or residency in a medical school to complete board requirements in a specific field of medicine.

Ph.D.: Doctor of philosophy–These individuals may teach in a college or university and may be licensed psychologists.

Board Certified: Specific tests in a specialty have been passed after the required training in a particular field of medicine has been completed.

Board Eligible: Specialized training has been received, but board examinations have not been taken or passed.

D.C.: Doctor of chiropractic (chiropractor)–These individuals specialize in joint and spinal alignment.

P.A.: Physician's Assistant–To be certified as a P.A., the individual must have had a training course and pass certain tests. They are not nurses.

N.P.: Nurse Practitioner–Is a registered nurse with additional training of variable length.

R.N.: Registered Nurse–May have a college degree, but this is not necessary for some nursing programs.

A.P.R.N.: Registered nurses with additional education. Many have a master's degree. The group includes: certified nurse practitioner, certified nurse mid-wife, and certified nurse anesthetist.

L.P.N. or **L.V.N.:** Licensed Practical Nurse or Licensed Vocational Nurse. They must have a high school education, plus a twelve to fourteen month course on basic nursing care. A licensing exam must be passed.

C.N.A.: Certified Nursing Assistant. These individuals receive training to provide non-medical care: bathing, dressing, and helping with bathroom needs.

O.D.: Optometrist–Can prescribe glasses, but not do surgery. The individual must have graduated from an accredited school of optometry.

O.T.: Optician–May have no training or just a few weeks in an eye doctor's office.

D.D.S.: Dentist–There are different types of dentists. Some have special training in diseases of the gum (peridontist) and others in straightening teeth (orthodontist).

M.F.C.C.: Marriage and Family Therapist–These individuals have postgraduate training in counseling and can work in clinics or have their own private practice.

M.F.T.: Marriage and Family Therapist–These are new initials for an M.F.C.C.

L.C.S.W.: Licensed Clinical Social Worker–These professionals have additional training beyond their degree in social work. They are licensed to see patients without the supervision of a physician.

M.S.W.: Medical Social Worker–These are individuals who have graduated from an accredited school of social work. They find solutions for complex family and social problems and are experts at finding community resources for patients. They are attached to clinics or hospitals.

F.A.C.S.: Fellow of the American College of Surgeons. This means a surgeon has completed a prescribed course of training and passed specific board examinations.

F.A.A.P.: Fellow of the American Academy of Pediatrics.

F.A.S.A.: Fellow of the American Society of Anesthesiologists.

F.A.C.O.: Fellow of the American College of Otolaryngology.

F.A.C.O.S.: Fellow of the American College of Orthopedic Surgeons.

F.A.C.P.: Fellow of the American College of Physicians.

F.A.P.A.: Fellow of the American Psychiatric Association.

R.P.T.: Registered Physical Therapist (also P.T.)–An individual with training in the structure and function of joints and muscles. They do evaluations and provide treatments for musculoskeletal problems. Specific prescriptions should be provided by an attending physician.

O.T.R.: Occupational Therapist Registered (also O.T.)–These are individuals who have training in the function and structure, particularly of the upper extremities. They teach activities of daily living (ADL) and work with children who have upper extremity problems or developmental delay.

WHAT CONSTITUTES A GOOD PHYSICAL EXAMINATION?

In the United States today, the usual amount of time HMOs and insurance companies allot physicians to spend with a patient is 8.5 minutes. It is rare for a child to have a complete history and physical, so if there is a disability or chronic illness, you probably will need to find several different doctors. Specialists need to relate to a child and not just look at their area of interest, as for example a curvature of the spine, a wandering eye, or other problem.

I've seen doctors walk into an examining room, never speak to the child, who is the patient, and look only at his or her back, hand, ears, or skin. This is unacceptable and is not a doctor who should be seeing patients, particularly children.

If you have made an appointment for a complete physical and the doctor doesn't want your grandchild undressed, it is time to find another physician. To do a good physical examination, a child must be undressed down to their shorts or underpants with a gown for girls and boys, if they want one.

It is important that the doctor talk to the child if he or she is able to answer questions. Many times the adult in charge wants to answer the questions, but please bite your tongue and let your grandchild talk as much as possible. It is his or her examination and it is important that your grandchild be able to communicate with the physician if he or she is able to do so.

In addition to a complete history and physical examination, a child needs a yearly eye check, hearing test, blood count, and urinalysis. Immunizations should be brought up to date and a tuberculin skin test done. In the U.S. many doctors are overlooking these things, particularly if they are pressed for time. You may have to be fairly aggressive to have them done, as I have had to be with my own grandchildren.

Some doctors want to do a tuberculin test only every other year or every few years, but if an active case of TB is allowed to go on when a yearly test could pick it out, that makes little sense. With the ease of airline travel these days, more and more diseases are traveling from country to country. There is still much active tuberculosis in Mexico and the Far East.

If parents do not have their children immunized because of the fear of autism, there are going to be more and more outbreaks of communicable diseases and probably some deaths. There have been excellent independent studies that show there is no relationship between receiving immunizations and autism. Many parents refuse to accept this and do not allow their children to be immunized or allow the siblings of their autistic child to have immunizations. They, then, become possible candidates for communicable diseases which can be spread to other children who have not been immunized.

CHANGING DOCTORS

Some people are uncomfortable about changing doctors despite their unhappiness with the physician they have. In the U.S., it is not that difficult to change physicians, even if you are in an HMO. No one should ever put up with inadequate or bad medicine or an unpleasant physician. There is an art to good medicine and a doctor should make you feel that he or she cares about you and listens to what you or your grandchild says. A good doctor will sit down and talk with you and your grandchild. Dictating in front of a patient is unprofessional and something I would not accept.

One grandmother makes a duplicate list of the questions that she wants to have answered and gives one to the doctor. That way he or she will know that a quick visit is not on the cards. She says she always gets her questions answered that way. If she doesn't, she finds a different physician.

Another grandmother, a physician, told the story that she took her grandson to see a specialist about a particular problem. A young resident came into the examining room and when she started to ask questions, the grandmother said, "I'm sorry, but we are here to see Dr. X and that is who we will wait to see." The resident wasn't happy, but did go out and brought the staff doctor. He did a five minute cursory exam before there was a knock on the door and he left to answer a phone call. He never returned!

Later, the physician grandfather took his grandson to see a former classmate in another city. This doctor spent considerable time with the boy and when he and his grandfather left, the youth said, "Wow! He was a real doctor. I've never had one like that before."

If you need to find another physician, ask doctor friends, other grandparents and parents of special needs kids. When you've found the one you want, send a written request to the first doctor's office and request that your grandchild's records or a summary of the records be sent to the new doctor. There should not be a charge for this. It is important to follow up with a phone call in a week or so to be sure your letter has been received and the records have been sent to the new doctor. It may take two or three calls to be sure the records have been transferred to the new doctor.

HOW TO GET THE BEST CARE FOR YOUR GRANDCHILD

Once you have found a good pediatrician or family doctor you like and trust, there are ways to ensure your grandchild will have the best care.

1. Being polite and courteous to the office staff and learning their names is important. Some people forget they are a vital part of the medical team. They can misfile records, not let you speak with the physician, and generally cause havoc if they dislike you or your grandchild.

2. Paying your bills on time if you are in the U.S. and not bouncing checks will make you a favorite. Usually doctors are paid last and since pediatricians and family doctors are at the bottom of the pay scale that makes a difference.

3. Keeping appointments and being on time will make you stand out. It is also discourteous to sit in a waiting room and talk on a cell phone. I've been in waiting rooms where a sign is posted asking patients not to speak on their cell phones and yet people are having long, chatty conversations. This always amazes me.

4. If you make unusual demands on the office staff's time or the doctor's time, you are less likely to receive good care.

5. Saying "thank you" is important and an occasional thank you note, holiday card, or even a small gift will be greatly appreciated. *One of my favorite grandmothers always brought a cake warm from the oven. We always looked forward to her visits with her cute grandchild, who was paralyzed on one side from an accident.*

6. Try not to bring other grandchildren with you to the appointment for your special needs grandchild. If this is unavoidable, be sure the other kids have books, games or something to occupy them, so the office staff doesn't have to act as babysitters. (*One mother brought a DVD player that one child watched while I looked at her sibling.*)

7. If the doctor is delayed or seems unusually tired, try to be understanding. If this happens at every appointment then you may need to think about changing doctors. Tired, overworked doctors can more easily make mistakes.

8. Listen to what the doctor has to say. If you have questions, try to make them as short and clear as possible. Try to remember all your questions so you don't need to call back and speak with the doctor again. Having a written list of your questions will help greatly.

9. Have your notebook or file with you to answer the doctor's questions about previous medications, immunizations, hospital visits, etc.

RECOMMENDED IMMUNIZATION SCHEDULES

In the United Kingdom, the following immunizations are recommended:

- DTaP/PV/Hib–Ages 2, 3, 4 months old

- Pneumococcal–Ages 2 and 4 months and around 13 months

- Men C (Meningococcal)–Age 3 to 4 months

- Td/IPV–Age 13–18 years

- HPV–Girls 12–13 years (to prevent cervical cancer)

For special cases:

- BCG–If infants may come into contact with tuberculosis
- Flu–For at risk people with decreased resistance.

Further details are available at: www.immunisation.nhs.uk/Vaccines.

The recommended childhood immunization schedule in the United States is shown in Table 14.1 on p.138.

SPECIAL NEEDS CLINICS

In the U.S. each state has free clinics for special needs kids. There are both advantages and disadvantages to these clinics. One good thing is that you can meet other parents and other grandparents. Also, there is usually a social worker, a physical therapist, and a team of physicians. The down side of these clinics is that there is not time for a complete examination, so if you depend on the clinics for all the medical care your grandchild gets, much can be missed.

Most medical schools and university medical centers have specialty clinics that are a good resource for a particular disability or chronic illness, but they are not designed for general care. Also, these are generally staffed by interns and residents with an attending staff doctor to answer questions. If you can find a physician in private practice with expertise in your grandchild's disorder, you may receive more consistent and on-going care.

RETAIL CLINICS–URGENT CARE

Retail Clinics have now been established across the United States in Target stores, big drug stores, and other large, low-cost stores. These are staffed by nurse practitioners who have not had pediatric training. There are no physicians on-site and one doctor may be responsible for many clinics. These clinics charge smaller fees than do physicians and advertise quick in and out care.

The American Academy of Pediatrics has come out strongly against these clinics for children and they are trying to have some stringent guidelines set up for them. *No child with special needs should ever be seen in one of these clinics.* Nurse practitioners do not have the training or experience to diagnose and treat children and particularly when a child has a chronic disease or other disability. The old saying that "You get what you pay for" is certainly true with these clinics.

Doctors in urgent care clinics and emergency rooms also are not pediatricians and often have had little pediatric training. Having a primary doctor is extremely important. Otherwise, a crucial diagnosis may be missed and there will be great fragmentation of care.

EMERGENCIES

Emergencies are not easy for anyone to handle, unless you are an ER physician. If a grandchild has an emergency, that can be very frightening. Thinking through what you would do in an emergency situation, having first-aid equipment on hand, and a knowledge of CPR, can take away some of the anxiety. Posting emergency numbers in a prominent place or having them accessible on a cell phone is also important.

It is important to check if your local hospital is equipped to care for children. Not all hospitals have pediatric equipment especially in the emergency rooms. They also might not have a pediatric anesthesiologist on the staff.

If a grandchild has a bee sting or other serious allergy, it is important to have an EpiPen at home and in your car. (This is a syringe filled with epinephrine.) Your grandchild's doctor or his or her nurse can show you how to use it. It would be wise, too, to have some pediatric Benadryl liquid or capsules on hand for allergic grandchildren. The American Red Cross and some local hospitals give first-aid courses and one could be very helpful.

True emergencies are:

- severe, uncontrolled bleeding

- choking on a peanut, hard candy, or foreign object

- severe asthma attack with difficulty breathing

- croup with difficulty breathing

- stiff neck with fever and headache

- drug or poison ingestion

- ingestion of a poisonous plant

- severe allergic reaction to bees or food

- loss of consciousness

- fracture of an arm, leg or any serious break

- severe or prolonged vomiting or diarrhea

- severe burns

- eye injury.

MEDICAL CARE IN HMOS

Many HMOs are not interested in caring for special needs kids or do not have the necessary specialists. *I had one sweet child with fused joints who was denied care in an HMO, even though the rest of the family was covered. I called the medical director and he actually said, "We are not responsible for the medical care of kids with disabilities. That is up to the schools and the community."*

The parents could have appealed the man's decision, but both worked long hours and had limited financial resources. I continued to care for the child and did not charge them. I was appalled that a medical director would make a statement like that.

To make an appeal if your grandchild is denied coverage or denied the opportunity to see an outside specialist, you can file a first-level appeal. Each HMO has specific guidelines about how to do this, as do insurance companies. If your grandchild has already seen an outside specialist, be sure to save all your medical bills and any correspondence you have had with the HMO. Keeping a telephone sheet is also a good idea to record the date, time, and name of the individuals with whom you have spoken.

If a first-level appeal is denied, try to find out the name of the individual who denied it. The next step would be to file a second-level appeal. There are organizations that will advocate for you and one of the best I have found is: The National Disability Rights Network. Their Web site is: www.ndrn.org. The organization has offices all over the United States and they have attorneys on their staff who can help. Another agency that might be able to help is Patient Advocate at www.patientadvocate.org. Family Voices has offices all over the U.S. and they are an excellent resource for advocacy and many other things. Their number is 1-888-835-5669 and their Web site is www.familyvoices.org.

If you can have medical coverage outside an HMO, it will be much easier for your grandchild to have the specialist care that he or she may need. HMOs are primarily interested in caring for healthy patients, because they can make more money that way for their doctors and shareholders.

SOME IMPORTANT TERMINOLOGY TO KNOW IN DEALING WITH HMOS

IPA (Independent Practice Association): A group of physicians who practice in their own offices but who agree to abide by the payment plan and rules of an HMO. Each physician is paid a specified amount per patient in his or her care. The doctor receives this amount of money even though a patient needs no care. Individuals with chronic illness or multiple medical problems are not sought out as HMO members. Instead, an attempt is made to recruit a healthy group of patients.

PPO (Preferred Provider Organization): Physicians who belong to a specific group. If you are a member of their group, you receive discounted fees. If you seek care from an "outside" physician, you will be responsible for a large part of his or her fee. In addition, you may find that a referral to an outside specialist will not be covered.

PCP (Primary Care Provider): A physician who is responsible for your health care needs. He or she should make referrals to specialists as needed. Many are reluctant to make referrals as it may reduce their own pay. A "report card" is kept by many HMOs indicating how many referrals each physician makes. Referrals cost the HMO and physicians more and thus are greatly discouraged.

Capitation: This is the amount of money an HMO pays a physician for every patient he or she is expected to see. The doctor makes more money, if the patients are not seen, tests are not requested, and referrals are not made to specialists.

Co-payment: This is the amount of money you are asked to pay at each doctor's visit. The amount is variable according to the individual plan.

Preadmission Certification: Hospital admission for surgery or medical care has to be pre-approved by a representative from the HMO or insurance company. Nurses do this in most cases but your physician can insist on speaking with the Medical Director, if approval is not given. The doctor's office staff or the physician should arrange for a hospital admission.

DOING MEDICAL RESEARCH

Most parents and grandparents, who are comfortable doing research on the Internet, will immediately start searching for information as soon as they are told there is a problem with a grandchild. There is some excellent information on the Internet, *but a great deal that is not valid or up-to-date*. So it is important to check with your grandchild's doctor about any information you find.

One excellent source for rare diseases is NORD or the National Organization of Rare Diseases. They are a unique resource for anyone in the U.K. or the U.S. Their Web site is: www.rarediseases.org and their number is 1-800-999-NORD. They will send information if you give them a call or e-mail them and their staff is most helpful.

I have had three special grandmothers from other countries and states contact me about their grandchildren. Fortunately, I was able to give them the names of the specialists their grandchildren needed to see and all were very grateful. The parents of two of the children had given up looking for an accurate diagnosis and were over-burdened with their work and family responsibilities. The three grandmothers made a great difference in their grandchildren's lives.

One grandchild in a European country had hypotonia, or muscle weakness, but no diagnosis was given despite many tests. The parents and grandparents were greatly concerned. The grandmother e-mailed me and I made arrangements for the child to be seen by Professor Victor Dubowitz in London, the world's expert in pediatric neuromuscular disorders. He diagnosed a genetic, non-fatal, and non-progressive disorder and the child continues to do well. The family couldn't have been happier or more relieved.

OBTAINING A SECOND OPINION

If your grandchild has been diagnosed with an unusual or potentially fatal disease, it is wise to always get a second opinion unless the specialist is one of the experts in that particular disease or disorder.

The best example of this is when one of my children was diagnosed with a brain tumor by a radiologist in a university medical school. I knew the head of the radiology department in another hospital and asked if he would review my daughter's X-rays. This doctor was the author of several radiology textbooks and one of the experts in the field. He looked at the X-rays and said, "I don't see a tumor or any other abnormality!" I thanked him profusely and breathed a great sigh of relief.

Later, I was talking with a friend, who was pathologist in the university medical school, and told her she looked tired. She said, "I've been working overtime because there have been several 'brain tumors' removed recently and all were normal. I just kept checking and re-checking my findings. I don't understand what is going on. Why are so many patients being operated on with no positive findings?" Yes, one of those patients could have been my daughter if I had not sought a second opinion.

It is particularly important to have any biopsy reviewed by an expert in that particular disease. No general pathologist can be an expert in every disease or disorder. I have always reviewed the muscle biopsy slides on patients with whom I consulted. Most of the muscle biopsy slides that I received, even from large medical schools, were not adequately prepared. Many were entirely unreadable and had to be re-done. Patients who have biopsies performed in Europe and other countries where there are excellent neuromuscular centers: England, Italy, Turkey, Australia, Canada, Tunisia, and Japan, are extremely fortunate because the biopsies will be properly prepared and will be interpreted by experts in the field.

Before proper treatment can be prescribed, a physician must know that the biopsy results are accurate. If the opinion of just one pathologist is relied on, there are often mistakes. A good pathologist will send the slides for review such as to the Armed Forces Institute of Pathology in Washington D.C. or other centers where they have specialists who specialize in a particular problem. If a second opinion is not sought, unnecessary fear, anxiety, surgery, and treatments may result.

GENETIC CONSULTATIONS

When children have an undiagnosed disorder, many physicians send them immediately to a geneticist. If a combination of signs or symptoms are present, this could be appropriate to see if the symptoms fit into a particular syndrome. Unfortunately, when some doctors are baffled they use a geneticist without first doing appropriate tests. It is very important to establish a diagnosis, if this is possible, before asking a geneticist's opinion. The role of a geneticist would then be to give statistics about the possibility of recurrence in another child or how other family members would be affected.

In the U.K., there are Regional Genetic Centres. Their Web site at: www.gig.org.uk/services.htm gives lists of publications, useful addresses, patterns of inheritance, and considerable other information.

ALTERNATIVE AND COMPLEMENTARY MEDICINE

Many individuals in the U.S. are turning to alternative and complementary medicine because health care has become so expensive and so fragmented. Acupuncture may be helpful and can often relieve symptoms of pain or spasm. If the individual inserting the needles is also an M.D. that could make you feel a little more confident. Massage may also help a child who is in pain, but you would want to carefully research the credentials of anyone who treats your grandchild.

I would offer a word of caution about giving children herbal medications. They can cause great harm and even death. Herbal medicines will also interact with some medications and cause untoward side-effects. In the U.S., these are not tested and approved by the U.S. Federal Drug Administration. In the U.K., some herbal medicines are licensed. These have an identifying code with a nine number product license (PL) code. There are other herbal medicines registered under the Traditional Herbal Registration act. A third category of herbal medicines is not regulated, but by April 2011 will be required to have one of the above two registrations.

COMMON MEDICAL TERMS

BE: Barium enema is an X-ray taken of the lower part of the bowel after a special enema preparation has been given.

BID: Instructions on a prescription indicating the medicine should be taken twice a day.

BiPap and CPAP: These are terms for night-time ventilation.

Biopsy: A piece of tissue removed from the body for the purpose of diagnosis. The tissue should be examined by a specialist. A muscle biopsy should always be done using a local anesthetic because of the possibility of Malignant Hyperthermia.

Chest Physiotherapy: This is a specific way of inducing mucus and secretions to be brought up by a patient.

Cholesterol: A substance found in the blood and cells of the body. Two types are present: LDL is low-density lipoprotein, which can block arteries, and HDL is high-density lipoprotein, which is believed to help protect arteries from blockage. Increased blood pressure (hypertension), heart attacks, and stroke can result from high cholesterol levels.

Collagen diseases: Included in this group are: rheumatoid arthritis, scleroderma, periarteritis nodosa, and lupus erythematosus. Rheumatologists are the specialists who usually treat these diseases.

Colonoscopy: Direct visualization of the lower bowel performed under anesthetic.

CT scan: Special detailed X-ray study. The initials stand for computerized tomography.

DNR: Do not resuscitate is an order placed on a hospital chart at the patient's request.

EEG (electroencephalogram): Electrical recording of the brain waves.

EKG (electrocardiogram): Recording of electrical impulses from the heart.

EMG (electromyogram): Electrical impulses recorded from muscle.

Endocrine glands: Organs in the body that regulate various body functions: thyroid gland, pituitary, pancreas, adrenal glands, and parathyroid.

Exudate: A fluid or pus-containing substance that can be seen on tonsils with some sore throats or coming from a part of the body.

False negative: A blood test result found to be negative, when a repeat test is positive. This may be due to laboratory error or improper handling of the specimen.

False positive: Errors can occur when blood tests are performed. Also, certain conditions can occur which cause inaccurate results. For example, the CPK blood test, which can help check for muscle disease, can be unusually high if the patient has been very active prior to the test being taken. Blood sugars can be abnormally high, if a heavy intake of sugar containing foods has been ingested prior to the test.

Fibromyalgia: Patients have diffuse muscle aches and pains. Regular exercise, decreasing stress, and injection of "trigger spots" can cause improvement. Trigger spots are painful points in muscles from which pain radiates. (President Kennedy was treated for fibromyalgia by his White House physician, Dr. Janet Travell.)

Flat plate: An X-ray of the abdomen taken without the injection of any contrast substance.

Gastrostomy: An opening into the stomach so fluids can be introduced.

Generic: This term is used for medications that are not licensed by a specific drug company or advertised and promoted by them. *If your doctor orders the generic brand of a drug, it will be much less expensive.* Every drug does not have a generic form and the drug companies try hard to keep drugs from having generic, cheaper forms.

Hospitalist: This is a physician who works solely in a hospital. There can be a problem with fragmentation of care if the doctor does not contact the family, the family doctor or pediatrician, or does not review previous medical records.

HS: Instructions on a prescription indicating that the medicine should be taken at the hour of sleep.

Hyperthyroid: Increased function of the thyroid gland manifested by a rapid pulse, sweating and nervousness. Prominent eyes or exopthalmos can also occur.

Hypertrophy: Enlargement of an organ or extremity.

Hypothyroid: Decreased function of the thyroid gland manifested by dry skin, constipation and lethargy.

ICU: Intensive care unit.

IM: An injection given into the muscle (intramuscular).

IPPB: Intermittent positive pressure breathing given to patients.

Irritable Bowel Syndrome: Cardinal signs are intermittent abdominal pain and loose bowel movements alternating with constipation.

IV: Fluid or a drug injected directly into the vein (intravenous).

IVP: Kidney X-rays taken after an injection of a dye into a vein.

Malignant Hyperthermia: A genetic disorder that occurs with the use of some anesthetics. It has a particular relationship to some of the muscle diseases. A high fever, tightness of the jaw and death can occur, if certain anesthetic agents are used. Succinylcholine and halothane are two of the principal anesthetic agents to be avoided for patients who have or might have this disorder.

MICU: Medical intensive care unit.

MRI (magnetic resonance imaging): A highly magnified X-ray study.

Nerve conduction times: Electrical impulses recorded from nerves.

NICU: Newborn intensive care unit.

NPO: Nothing by mouth after midnight. This is important prior to an anesthetic or some procedures and blood tests.

PICU: Pediatric intensive care unit.

Peritonitis: A serious infection in the abdomen. (A word ending in "itis" means infection.)

Placebo: A pill containing nothing but a substance such as sugar. It is used in drug trials to see if a new drug is effective or acts the same as the fake one.

Sepsis: Infection in the blood stream, which can be extremely serious.

Table 14.1 Recommended Childhood Immunization Schedule in United States

Vaccine	Birth –2 months	4 months	6 months	12 months	15 months	18 months	24 months	4–6 yrs	11–12 yrs	14–18 yrs
Hepatitis B	Hep. B 1 #1	Hep. B 2	Hep. B 3				Hep. B Series			
Rotavirus	Rota	Rota	Rota							
Diphtheria, tetanus, pertussis	DtaP	DtaP	DtaP		DTaP			DtaP	Td	
H influenzae type B	Hib	Hib	Hib	Hib		Hib				
Polio	IPV	IPV	IPV					IPV		
Pneumococcal	PCV	PCV	PCV	PCV			PCV		PPV	
Measles, mumps, rubella				MMR #1				MMR #2		
Varicella				Varicella			Varicella			
Hepatitis A							Hepatitis A Series			
Meningococcal										

SICU: Surgical intensive care unit.

SMA-6, 12, 25: Special blood panel studies.

STAT: This means a procedure, lab test, or drug must be done or given immediately.

TID: Instructions on a prescription that the medicine should be taken three times a day.

Upper GI: X-rays taken of the upper part of the gastrointestinal tract.

Vital signs: Blood pressure, pulse, respiratory rate, and temperature.

SPECIALIZED HOSPITALS IN THE UNITED STATES

Medicine has become so specialized in the United States that children with certain disabilities will have the most up-to-date treatment and care in hospitals designated for their special problems. The four Shriners hospitals that care for seriously burned children are good examples of this type of specialty hospitals. The four hospitals are located in Boston, Massachusetts; Cincinnati, Ohio; Galveston, Texas; and Sacramento, California. The Shriners' Web site is www.shrinershq.org and the main number is: 1-800-237-5055. Any child under the age of eighteen, regardless of income or insurance, can be admitted to a Shriners hospital if the hospital staff decides the child can profit from surgery or treatment in their specific program. The Shriners International headquarters are in Tampa, Florida. The number there is 1-813-281-0300.

Most of the Shriners hospitals are for children who need orthopedic surgery and post-op care. However, they have three hospitals for spinal cord injury patients and these are located in Chicago, Illinois; Philadelphia, Pennsylvania; and Sacramento, California. A hospital that specializes in cleft lip and palate repair is in Chicago, Illinois.

There are also other hospitals and programs that have a special interest in a particular syndrome or disability. The Carrie Tingley Hospital for children in Albuquerque, New Mexico, has an excellent program for children with orthopedic and other disabilities and I have referred many patients to them.

HOSPITALIZATIONS AND ANESTHETICS

Many children with special needs will have one or more hospital stays as they grow up. These may be for illnesses, special tests, therapies, or surgery. When a grandchild is to be hospitalized and you are in charge, there are several questions you want to ask. First, you want to check out the hospital and be sure it has good facilities and has treated many children. To do this I would first ask your grandchild's doctor about how many children your local hospital cares for and also if they have pediatric anesthesiologists on their staff. Many hospitals do not have doctors with special training in giving anesthetics to little children. In an emergency, this would be an important doctor to have if your grandchild is an infant or little one.

The National Association of Children's Hospitals has a Web site at: www.childrenshospitals.net that gives information about hospitals. In addition, it lists several excellent questions to have answered before a grandchild is admitted to a hospital for a non-emergency stay. The group suggests checking if a hospital has been accredited by the Joint Commission on Accreditation of Healthcare Organizations. A Web site at: www.qualitycheck.org gives information about the hospitals that are accredited.

If a particular specialist is needed for your grandchild, you want to be sure he or she is board-certified. I would find out, too, if your grandchild's primary physician has privileges in the hospital you choose and will he or she make hospital visits or turn your grandchild's care over to a physician you have not met. In addition, will it be possible for you or other family members to stay with your grandchild? The National Association of Children's Hospitals Web site at: www.childrenshospitals.net also gives many other questions to ask and is worth reviewing.

If the hospital is a medical school teaching hospital, you want to be sure that you will be able to speak with and keep in touch with the staff doctor in charge of your grandchild's care. Teaching hospitals have the advantage of always having a doctor on-call in the hospital. The drawback of teaching hospitals is that there will be interns and residents assigned to your grandchild's care. This means several doctors-in-training will examine and treat your grandchild and some may have had little experience with your grandchild's particular problem.

It is important that young doctors-in-training learn, but you will want to have someone constantly at your grandchild's bedside to be sure the young doctors are pleasant, relate well to your grandchild, and seem to know how to do any necessary procedures, such as giving intravenous fluids or other invasive tasks. If you are uncomfortable about what an intern or resident is doing, don't be shy about speaking up.

You should have a daily briefing about what is taking place with your grandchild and what tests or other things are being planned. It would be wise to try and arrange a time with your grandchild's primary staff doctor to find out what the best time would be to speak with him or her.

For any hospital admission, you need to be sure you have a pre-authorization for the admission and that you have with you all the necessary legal documents and medical information needed to answer questions about your grandchild. The information might include a record of past illnesses, hospitalizations, surgeries, medications, immunizations, and most importantly a document giving you the legal right to make decisions about your grandchild's medical care.

If surgery is planned, you will want to meet the surgeon and be sure he or she is someone with whom you and your grandchild feel comfortable. You will, I am sure, already have checked on the doctor's training, credentials, and experience. Meeting the anesthesiologist is also important. I would be sure the doctor is a pediatric anesthesiologist if your grandchild is an infant or small child. It may be that the hospital does not have any pediatric anesthesiologists on their staff. *I would not want a nurse anesthetist to give a grandchild an anesthetic.* Their training is about half the number of years as a U.S. board-certified anesthesiologist.

In U.S. hospitals today, there is such a shortage of nurses that much of the care is left to untrained aides. Around the clock vigilance by the family is sadly needed, so if you are unable to find friends or relatives to help around-the-clock, it would be wise to hire a private duty nurse if this is financially possible. This is now quite a common procedure if there is money to pay for these nurses. The nurses can be obtained from a nurses' registry and your grandchild's doctor or the staff in the hospital nursing office can help you make arrangements for one. It could make the difference in your grandchild's life.

If there are financial problems, I am told that many hospitals, both large and small, as well as some doctors' groups have charity clauses. This allows them to help patients who have financial problems. Payment plans are also possible in some situations. Thus, if your grandchild needs an admission for a medical or surgical problem and money is a problem, it would be wise to inquire about these funds.

SURGERY AND ANESTHETICS IN PRIVATE OFFICES

More and more procedures are being done in private offices in the United States, because of the cost of hospitalizations and also for the doctors' convenience. If a child has any kind of a procedure in a doctor's office requiring an anesthetic, you want to be absolutely sure that a board-certified anesthesiologist will be giving the anesthetic. You will also want to ask what anesthetics will be used. This is particularly important if your grandchild has a muscle disease, because of the risk of Malignant Hyperthermia. If the question makes the anesthesiologist or the doctor doing the procedure uncomfortable, I would think about changing physicians. Some offices do not have enough of the preventive medicine, Dantrolene, on hand to adequately treat Malignant Hyperthermia if it occurs. This medication is expensive and if it is not available or not enough is available, deaths have resulted.

Another question you want to ask is does the office have adequate equipment and the necessary preparations to treat an emergency? Also, how close is the nearest hospital that treats children, in case something happens that makes it necessary for your grandchild to be transported to a hospital? Remember that not every hospital is equipped to handle children. You may have to be a bit pushy to get answers, but using your honeyed voice first may get you the information you need. If not, you may have to put the procedure on hold until you get satisfactory answers.

DENTAL CARE

Many kids with special needs are unable to sit quietly in a dental chair and will need an anesthetic either in the dentist's office or in a hospital. If an anesthetic is not needed, it may help if a child is able to watch a DVD while in the dentist's chair or have on headphones to hear some favorite music.

There are fortunately dentists who specialize in the care of kids with special challenges. Some of these dentists are connected with children's hospitals and some dental schools have special needs programs. I have referred many patients to the excellent program at the University of Pacific Dental School in San Francisco and found their staff always to be caring and professional.

A question to ask the dentist if your grandchild needs an anesthetic and has muscle weakness is, will there be a problem with Malignant Hyperthermia? If the dentist is unsure about the association with this disorder and the anesthetic that is to be used and is in the U.S., he or she can call the Malignant Hyperthermia Hotline at: 1-800-644-9737. Their staff will immediately get in touch with the doctor on-call. This physician usually quickly returns the call with an answer. If the dentist is unwilling to make this call, he or she is definitely not the dentist you want treating your grandchild.

In the U.K., the British Malignant Hyperthermia Association can be contacted at www.bmha.co.uk.

SPECIAL DENTAL PROGRAMS

There are some special organizations that can be helpful if you are having a difficult time finding accessible dental care for your grandchild. One of these is the National Foundation of Dentistry for the Handicapped. Their Web site is www.nfdh.org and their telephone number is 303-534-5360. They have volunteer dentists in some states who care for the dental needs of individuals with disabilities. You can call them or check the Internet for your state to see if this free care is available.

There is also another organization, the Academy of Dentistry for Persons with Disabilities. Their number is 312-527-6764. Some state programs for children with disabilities in the United States will cover the cost of dental care if it fits under the umbrella of their services and extensive care is needed.

In the U.K., the National Health Service will cover many dental problems, so it is wise to check with your grandchild's primary physician about what can be covered.

Chapter Fifteen

Special Medical Problems and Treatments

Some grandchildren have medical problems in addition to their underlying disability. Being knowledgeable about these is important if you have care of a grandchild for even a few hours.

SEIZURES OR CONVULSIONS

One of the scariest problems for caretakers is seizures or convulsions. If your grandchild has cerebral palsy, autism, or hydrocephalus, with or without spina bifida, a seizure may occur. There are also some other rare conditions that can be accompanied by seizures. Twenty-five percent of children with cerebral palsy have seizures and about thirty percent of children with autism have them. A small child may have a febrile seizure, so it is important to know what to do in case a convulsion or seizure occurs. If your grandchild is at risk for seizures, it would be wise to take a CPR course. Knowing what to do in an emergency should give you confidence to handle an emergency situation. In the United States, some hospitals, the Red Cross, and various private agencies give CPR courses. In the U.K., CPR help is available at www.safekids.co.uk/CPRChildren.html.

There are several different kinds of seizures. The most frightening kind is a grand mal seizure where a child loses consciousness, has jerking movements of the arms and legs, may lose bladder or bowel control, and the eyes roll up or to the side. Grand mal seizures are now called tonic-clonic seizures.

The treatment for this type of seizure is to be sure the child has a clear airway and doesn't have a piece of food or something else stuck in the throat. I would immediately call 911 because oxygen may be needed and hospitalization. It is always important to know that a child is not febrile and that the seizure is not a febrile seizure. (These usually occur in smaller children.) When a child has a grand mal seizure you should not try and restrain him or her, but be sure to check that nothing sharp is in the way of the jerking movements. Usually, the seizure will not last more than two or so minutes.

Other types of seizures are: Generalized absence seizures (formerly called petit mal), complex partial seizure (psychomotor), simple partial seizure (focal or Jacksonian), myoclonic seizures, atonic or drop seizures, and photosensitive seizures. Each of these has specific characteristics. If a seizure does not respond after about five minutes, a child may be developing what is called status epilepticus. This is when the seizures continue and emergency care, medication, and hospitalization will be needed.

If a febrile seizure is accompanied by a stiff neck, a spinal tap should always be done. Meningitis can occur in any child and prompt treatment with antibiotics is important. A spinal tap in a child is a simple procedure if the doctor is experienced.

An electroencephalogram is indicated after a few days following a first seizure. If a child has difficulty staying still during the procedure, sedation may be necessary. The best EEG results are obtained when a child is sleep-deprived. A CT scan or MRI may also be done to rule out a brain tumor or malformation of the brain.

There are several medications to treat seizures and a pediatric neurologist should be the one to prescribe these drugs. There are side-effects to many of the drugs, so this would be an important question to ask the neurologist. In addition, some of the drugs that control seizures interact with other drugs, so this is another important question to ask.

CEREBRAL PALSY

The spasticity that occurs with cerebral palsy is now treated in some centers with botox injections. If a child has lower extremity spasticity with a scissor-like gait, a surgery procedure called a posterior rhizotomy is done in special centers. I have seen some excellent results in a few patients who had this surgery. Some patients with cerebral palsy are treated with oral baclofen, valium, clonidine, or dantrolene. Baclofen is given, in some cases, intrathecally which means into a specific space in the back.

KIDNEY INFECTIONS OR PYELONEPHRITIS

Children with paraplegia, quadriplegia, and spina bifida are at risk for developing kidney failure and they also have an increased risk of serious kidney infections. (See section on spina bifida for more information.) The first symptom of such an infection may be a high, spiking fever. The children may have pain, but if there is a marked loss of sensation, pain may not be a factor. The best thing to do is to obtain a urine specimen by catheterization and then take it to a laboratory for a urinalysis and urine culture.

All kids with paraplegia, quadriplegia, and spina bifida should have urines checked on a regular basis and certainly at least once a year. Urinary studies, including abdominal ultrasounds, CT scans or other tests should be done about every two years to be sure no kidney damage is occurring. Some kids have a low-grade bladder infection and often are placed on a single, daily dose of antibiotic. This is called a maintenance dose and is something that should be discussed with your grandchild's pediatric urologist if there is an on-going problem with urinary infections. All of these kids should also be encouraged to drink a lot of fluids. They can carry a small plastic bottle or a folding drinking cup.

Children with incomplete or mild paraplegia and spina bifida should be taught to empty their bladder every two hours. Others will have to use a catheter (small plastic tube) to empty the bladder. Children who catheterize themselves often have bacteria in their urine, but if the bacteria are not causing problems they may not need treatment.

I have had little girls, who were patients, learn to catheterize themselves as young as five years of age. Pediatric urologists who treat these kids now also have boys catheterize themselves. In the past, boys were fitted with a snug bag over the penis that was connected to a leg bag. These are not much in use today.

If a child is school age, it is important that the school personnel be aware of the urinary problems. Sometimes, there is little understanding of the difficulties these kids have and I have known of children who were punished for wanting to go frequently to the bathroom or soiling their underclothes.

When a child starts a new school or has a new teacher, it is important to have a discussion with the teacher and school nurse, if there is one, about the bladder and bowel problems. The questions I would ask are:

- Is there one individual who will help with my grandchild's bladder and bowel problems?

- Where will the leg bag or diapers be changed?

- How often will there be a change?

- How difficult is it for my grandchild to get water in the school?

- Is my grandchild the only child with bowel or bladder problems and will this be a problem with the teacher or other children?

- Has the school ever had a child with this special problem?

If your grandchild has an aide, you will want to work with him or her to be sure all problems are worked out. It would be best if your grandchild's pediatric urologist could send a note to the school or speak with the school nurse. It is always helpful to have a team approach with children who have these special problems. Your grandchild's pediatrician or family doctor should also be willing to send a note or letter.

MUSCLE DISEASES

The most important treatment for muscle diseases at this time is to keep the kids active. Muscles that are not used will get weaker. The best way to keep the muscles as strong as possible is to have a grandchild involved with a swimming program or for the child to swim with someone in attendance in a pool.

I saw Molly, a little two-year-old, at an HMO facility for a consultation. After the muscle biopsy was done, I diagnosed intermediate spinal atrophy. I did not see the child again until she was eight years old and was most unhappy at the amount of muscle weakness she had developed. Molly was also in long-leg heavy metal braces. I wrote a new prescription for light-weight plastic braces and suggested to the parents that the little girl be enrolled in a swim program.

A few months later, I saw an entirely different child. Molly was much more active and was walking quite well in her light-weight braces (calipers). The father told me that he took the child swimming every day and insisted she spend a certain amount of time swimming. The swim program continued as the child grew up and Molly is now living and working independently and getting around quite well. This father was one of the best I have ever had. He made a commitment to Molly and never veered from it. What a great difference he made in Molly's life.

Dr. Paul Vignos set the standard for the treatment of kids with muscle diseases many years ago.[18] He showed that keeping the kids active with good exercise programs, physical therapy, appropriate orthopedic surgeries, and stand tables could keep even boys with Duchenne muscular dystrophy walking much longer. Stand tables can be used at home or in the school classrooms. Parents and grandparents can help by stretching contractures. These develop over a period of years at the back of the legs (the heel cords), the hips, the knees and the wrists and the elbows. The families who do stretching exercises on a regular basis make a great difference in their children's lives.

It is important that children with muscle disease not be allowed to become overweight. If they do, it makes it much more difficult for them to get around. Sometimes these kids get depressed because of their muscle weakness and want to stay in the house and watch TV or play games on the computer. It is hard to be a tough parent or grandparent, but unless the children get up and get moving, their lives can be shortened and multiple problems can develop.

Heart problems can accompany Duchenne muscular dystrophy, Becker muscular dystrophy and Emery-Dreifuss muscular dystrophy. As the kids get into their early teens, a careful review of the cardiac status should be done by the principal doctor or by a pediatric cardiologist. Medication may need to be prescribed and can make a difference. Heart transplants have also been successful with some Becker dystrophy patients. Boys with Emery-Dreifuss muscular dystrophy will most likely need a pacemaker in their early teens and if their cardiac status is not carefully watched, death can occur suddenly. Some of the other neuromuscular disorders may also have associated heart problems, so this is a question to ask the specialist caring for your grandchild.

If children with muscle diseases have orthopedic surgery of any kind, they should be given physical therapy as soon as possible. Usually the therapy should start the day following surgery. As soon as possible, even after back surgery, a child should be upright and move as much as possible. There are orthopedists who insist a child lie flat in bed after spinal surgery, but this can cause great difficulties.

An orthopedist, who had had little experience with children with muscle diseases, did a spinal fusion on a child with intermediate spinal atrophy. He insisted she lie flat in bed for over a month and it changed the girl's life. She became depressed, very weak, and was never able to walk again.

Another orthopedist performed an operation on a child's hips and did not order physical therapy following the surgery. The child never walked again and died in her teens.

If you find a grandchild, who has a muscle disease, lying in bed following orthopedic surgery, I would immediately talk to the orthopedic surgeon. If this does not result in an order for physical therapy, I would talk to the head of the physical therapy department or seek a second orthopedic opinion. However, if a second orthopedist has not had experience with children with muscle diseases, it may not be helpful.

Many pediatric orthopedists have had extensive training and experience with cerebral palsy and other more common conditions, but muscle diseases in children don't get the same amount of attention in U.S. teaching programs as they do in the U.K. and many other countries, where they have excellent pediatric neuromuscular centers. Thus, you may have to be a bit aggressive to see that your grandchild has the proper physical and/or occupational therapy following orthopedic surgery.

MUSCLE BIOPSIES

If your grandchild has muscle weakness and a muscle biopsy is planned, it is not wise to have one done in a small local hospital unless the pathologist plans to send the frozen muscle to a large medical center where there is a technician trained to do the latest, up-to-date stains and techniques on biopsies. Very few hospitals in the U.S., even big medical centers, have the personnel or facilities to do the studies that are routine in countries where there are large neuromuscular centers. Patients who live in England, France, Italy, Turkey, Tunisia, Australia, and Japan are very fortunate because these countries have neuromuscular centers that have been in existence for a long time and do the latest techniques and studies on muscle biopsies.

Every child with a muscle disease who may be at risk for Malignant Hyperthermia should wear a Medic Alert bracelet. Thus, if there is an accident at school or an accident in a friend's car, the treating physicians will be alert to the risk of using anesthetics such as halothane or succinylcholine.

I have always given a special letter about Malignant Hyperthermia precautions to the parents or grandparents of my muscle disease patients. This way if their child or grandchild has emergency or other surgery, the precautions can be discussed with the anesthesiologist. One important point that might be overlooked by an anesthesiologist is that the anesthetic machine to be used for the surgery should be flushed several hours prior to use or overnight with ten liters of air or oxygen for twenty minutes. The drugs that can cause problems are: succinycholine, halothane, enflurance, isoflurance, and sevoflurance. If these drugs are avoided, then prophylaxis with the drug Dantrolene is not recommended. However, if there has been a previous episode of Malignant Hyperthermia then Dantrolene should be used. There are five centers in the U.S. that can test to see if a patient is susceptible to Malignant Hyperthermia. However, the test requires traveling a distance and a muscle biopsy that has to be done under a general anesthetic.

JUVENILE RHEUMATOID ARTHRITIS (JRA)

It often takes a long time for a primary physician, orthopedist, or neurologist to realize that a little child has juvenile rheumatoid arthritis (now called juvenile idiopathic arthritis by some). This disorder does not appear to be a subject that is given much emphasis in U.S. medical schools or pediatric training programs. There are three types of JRA: pauciarticular or involvement of a single joint, polyarticular or involvement of several joints, and systemic arthritis where there is widespread joint pain accompanied by fever and rash. A pediatric rheumatologist is the specialist who should always initially see and then follow a child with JRA.

I was recently called by a doctor friend about the grandchild of one of her friends. The little boy had pain in his one ankle and one hip and the doctors were calling it Osgood-Schlatter's disease. With migratory arthritis in a child, you have to think of juvenile rheumatoid arthritis.

The parents liked their doctors and didn't want to hurt their feelings by consulting a specialist outside their health plan. Both my friend and I agreed that the most likely diagnosis was JRA. My friend told the boy's grandmother of my thoughts and the specialist I suggested seeing in another city. I knew this doctor was an expert in the diagnosing and treating of JRA. It took many weeks of pushing by my friend and the grandmother before the parents finally took the little boy to see the specialist. The specialist agreed with the diagnosis of JRA and gave the parents a treatment plan.

Doctors often do blood tests for rheumatoid arthritis and if these are negative, they think JRA is not the correct diagnosis. Unfortunately, the tests that are positive in adults are frequently not positive in children. This can be very misleading to a physician who has not had training or experience in the diagnosis of arthritis in children.

If a child is having joint pains and intermittent swelling of one or more joints, the first step is to see a pediatric rheumatologist and then a pediatric ophthalmologist or eye doctor. It is particularly important that the diagnosis of JRA be made as soon as possible because the eyes can be seriously damaged. *I saw a child in our arthritis clinic who was blind because her JRA was not diagnosed early on, so no treatment was started until considerable time had elapsed.* This should never, ever happen. If there is a diagnosis of JRA, it is important that an eye doctor or pediatric ophthalmologist check your grandchild every three to six months to look for eye problems. The eye doctor should do what is called a slit-lamp examination because there can be inflammation in the eyes that is only picked up by this examination.

It should be noted that JRA occurs much more frequently in girls. With aggressive, early treatment, most of the kids will, in time, be free of pain and any joint deformities. So anything you can do to get an early diagnosis and proper treatment will make all the difference in your grandchild's life.

Several years ago I visited a hospital in England for children with rheumatoid arthritis. The medical director told me that the only children she saw for early diagnosis of rheumatoid arthritis and treatment were doctors' children. The children who had marked delay in their diagnosis and treatment had a life-time of pain and crippling deformities.

I was working in a neuromuscular unit in a big U.S. hospital for a few months when the director of the program asked if I would see a sweet little seven-year-old who was complaining of pain in her hip. Her pediatrician referred her to the neuromuscular unit because she was limping and seemed to be hurting. Her blood tests had all been within normal limits. However, when I tried to move her right hip, there was limited motion and obvious pain. I told the head doctor that I thought the child may have juvenile rheumatoid arthritis. The man didn't believe me and proceeded to do a muscle biopsy and other tests related to neuromuscular diseases.

A year later when I had taken a position in another hospital, I was speaking to the director of the previous program and he asked if I remembered the little girl with the painful hip. "Yes," I said. "Well," he said. "You were right. They finally diagnosed juvenile rheumatoid arthritis. It took them a year."

CELIAC DISEASE

The diagnosis of celiac disease is often delayed both in children and adults even though this genetic disorder is found in 1:150 individuals. A child may have a protuberant abdomen, poor growth, diarrhea or constipation, listlessness, lack of interest in food, and sometimes forceful vomiting. The children are sensitive to gluten, a protein found in wheat, rye, oats, and barley. These days, gluten seems to be contained in almost everything, so labels need to be carefully read before a food is given to a gluten-sensitive child. Two good Web sites to check are: www.glutenfree.com and www.gfcfdiet.com. See the Appendix at the back of this book for a list of other Celiac Disease organizations.

There is also an excellent book by Danna Korn (2001), *Kids with Celiac Disease*, that lists multiple resources, including foods that contain gluten, where to buy gluten-free foods, and much other information.[19] It is important that a doctor sends a child's blood specimen to laboratories that have had experience with the required tests and these are also listed in Danna Korn's book. As with any other special disorder if a laboratory is not equipped and experienced in doing a particular test, the results may be erroneous. A small intestine biopsy performed by a pediatric gastroenterologist would confirm the diagnosis. This is a life-long condition and if a gluten-free diet is not given to a child who has celiac disease, there can be serious consequences later in life.

ALLERGIES

If you have a strong family history of allergy and are concerned that your grandchild might be allergic, some of the symptoms could be:

- Spitting up, crying excessively, and colic in a small baby could be signs of a milk or other allergies. (This can happen even in a breast-fed baby because of the allergens transmitted through the mother's breast milk.)

- Many loose, possibly bloody bowel movements.

- A little child who dislikes certain foods could have food allergies.

- If you notice dark circles under your grandchild's eyes and the child gets plenty of sleep, these could indicate an allergic child.

- A so-called "allergic salute" that occurs frequently. The "salute" is when an allergic child flips or rubs a hand against the nose.

- Frequent runny nose or rhinitis.

- Frequent coughing or wheezing.

- Frequent illnesses.

- Hives.

- Irritability and unusual fatigability.

- Scaly skin patches which could be eczema.

- Migraine headaches can have an allergic basis in some individuals.

A pediatric allergist spoke one morning at a pediatric grand rounds and I was amazed at what he said. The doctor showed pictures of five children he had treated for severe asthma. None of the children had been referred to a pediatric allergist prior to seeing him and none had been tried on an elimination diet. The allergist found all five to be highly allergic to milk and milk products. Once these were removed from the children's diets, their asthma was no longer a problem. It was hard to believe that their pediatricians or family doctors had not tried elimination diets or made an early referral to a pediatric allergist.

Asthma can be a very serious problem with children and can lead to emphysema with a barrel chest, difficulty breathing, poor growth, and frequent illnesses. Emphysema develops when there is trapping of air in the chest due to disease in the lungs. Smoking around a child or in the same house can greatly aggravate asthma and increase the risk of emphysema.

One of the most vivid memories of my pediatric residency was a pale, asthmatic child, gasping for breath, being carried into the hospital emergency room on the shoulder of her doctor father. I was not involved with her care, but was heart-broken to learn the next morning that the child had not lasted through the night. I have never understood why she was not hospitalized sooner.

If you suspect your grandchild is allergic, there are many things you can do if you are in charge. The most important step is to make an immediate appointment with a pediatric allergist. Many family doctors and pediatricians think a referral is unnecessary and try to manage allergic children themselves. However, they have not had the specialized training an allergist has had, so seeing this specialist is important. If it will be some time before you can get an appointment there are some immediate things that can be done. These are:

- No smoking should ever occur in the house or around your grandchild.
- Keep your grandchild's room as dust-free as possible.
- Eliminate any heavy drapes or other dust catchers in your grandchild's room.
- Wash fuzzy toys often and eliminate as many as possible.
- Wash sheets and pillow cases in hot water as often as possible.
- Keep any animals out of your grandchild's room and wash the animals weekly.
- Cover mattresses and pillows with special allergen-free covers.
- Use cotton sheets and bedding.
- Wash throw-rugs weekly.
- Don't use feather pillows or comforters.
- Wet mop tile, hardwood, or linoleum floors frequently.
- Consider installing a room air cleaner with a special filter.
- Eliminate as much as possible from the closet in your grandchild's room.

- Keep windows closed in your grandchild's room.

- Put toys and other dust collectors in an enclosed area or space.

- Use allergy-free soaps both in bathing and in washing a grandchild's clothes.

- Cotton clothing is best for allergic children who have skin problems.

- Skin lotions, cosmetics, shampoos, and anything else that touches the skin can cause allergic reactions in some individuals.

- Start eliminating allergenic foods one at a time for at least a week. The main offenders are: milk, eggs, citrus, nuts, wheat, chocolate, fish, and shellfish. Some children are allergic to soy products.

A good resource for further information is the Food Allergy and Anaphylaxis Network. Their Web site is www.foodallergy.org and their telephone number is 1-800-929-4040. They have a wealth of information that can be downloaded including tips about handling allergic kids in schools, camps, and even on bus trips. Remember that food intolerance is not the same thing as a food allergy. The first may cause pain and physical symptoms, but not be potentially life-threatening.

Not only can foods, dust mites, and pets cause allergic reactions in some children, but your yard can also be a source of allergens. Some of these are: weeds, mold, oak, elm, pecan, and maple trees. In Rochester, New York, there is such a problem with pollens around the time schools start that the schools were closed, when we lived there, if the pollen count was too high. A daily pollen count was reported in the local newspaper.

A pediatric allergist should give you or your grandchild's parents brochures and information about local allergens. Allergy injections can make a difference in a child's life, as can making a child's environment as allergen-free as possible.

SPINA BIFIDA

If your grandchild has spina bifida, there are several things to watch for and about which to be cautious. The most important one, if a shunt is in place because of hydrocephalus, is to watch for: severe headaches, vomiting, sudden loss of consciousness, a fever, or stiff neck. These could be signs of shunt failure. Sometimes the shunt needs to be replaced and ongoing contact with a pediatric neurosurgeon is needed.

Another concern is the possibility of a bladder infection or severe constipation. A child can be put on a daily or maintenance dose of antibiotic if there are recurrent bladder infections. (Usually, it is possible to detect a bad odor when there is an infection.) A workable bowel plan is important for all children with spina bifida. Often constipation and urinary tract infections go hand in hand.

Because of the frequent, necessary use of rubber gloves, catheters and other things containing latex, kids with spina bifida can develop an allergy to latex. It is wise to always put medical personnel on notice about the use of latex if a grandchild has spina bifida. In addition, latex is found in pacifiers, baby bottle nipples, and balloons, so these can be sources of trouble.

Another concern with a grandchild who has spina bifida is to be very cautious about bathing or allowing any objects to touch the lower part of the body that could cause burns. This is because children with loss of sensation will not feel the pain like other kids. Bath water should always be carefully tested and old houses may need a hot water regulator to be sure a burn does not occur. Healing after a cut on the legs may be delayed and infection should be watched for if there has been a pressure sore or laceration in the lower extremities.

Another worrisome concern is that twenty to thirty percent of children with spina bifida have seizures. A single seizure can occur or there can be multiple seizures. Usually seizures occur in the children with hydrocephalus who have a shunt in place. Kids who do not have shunts are at much less risk for seizures. Knowing CPR and having all the emergency numbers posted can reduce some of the anxiety about a grandchild's seizure disorder.

A non-medical problem which can be overlooked is that children with spina bifida often have moderately severe learning disabilities. There also may be some developmental delay. A good psychoeducational assessment should pick up difficulties that need special help and these should be noted in a child's IEP (see Chapter Twelve).

Despite all these concerns, many children with spina bifida lead full lives. *One of my favorite patients married, had a baby, and now runs her own company with her very supportive husband. It is always special to hear from her. She did have a tethered spinal cord that had to be released, but the surgery went smoothly and the young woman gets around quite well.*

HEARING

A baby who is not making sounds by three months should immediately have his or her hearing checked in a pediatric hearing center. Many times parents and others think a baby is just being very good if there isn't any crying or other sounds. The majority of the states now in the United States do check hearing in the newborn nursery. However, remember that no test is one hundred percent reliable, so if you have any questions about a baby's or child's hearing, it should be redone. In the U.K., infant hearing testing is available soon after birth through the National Health Service.

Some doctors in the United States don't take time to clean out a child's ear canal if there is a lot of wax and frequently miss diagnosing an ear infection. Pediatricians have actually told me that they were not taught how to clean out a child's ear canal, so they don't do it! I find this to be scary, because frequent untreated ear infections can scar the eardrums which can then result in a loss of hearing.

Little children and some with developmental delay will put almost anything in their ears and noses. I have removed bread crumbs from a child's nose, a dead bee from another child's ear, and a bead and a little metal ball from others. The bead had been there for several months and a previous doctor had given the child repeated courses of antibiotics because pus was oozing out of the ear canal. He apparently didn't make any attempt to see the ear drum or realize that something was obstructing the ear canal.

If you are concerned about a hearing problem in your grandchild it is important to remember that most children say at least five short words by one year of age. By two, they should be putting several words together. If there is a speech delay, it can be for reasons other than a loss of hearing, but that would be the first thing to have checked. *One mother told me that everyone thought her son was unusually good, but when she saw him "talk" on his play phone using just his lips and not making any sound she knew there was something definitely wrong.*

I have seen three children in a family all with congenital deafness. The first child was not diagnosed as deaf until quite late, but fortunately the other two were picked up right away.

According to the National Institute of Deafness, twelve thousand babies are born yearly with some hearing loss.[20] In addition, seventeen of each one thousand children under age eighteen have a degree of hearing loss. When ear infections are not properly treated or there are multiple ear infections, there can be some loss of hearing. Another cause of hearing loss is the extremely loud music played and listened to by young people.

There is still some dispute about the insertion of cochlear implants even though they have been found to be successful in multiple cases. Some in the Deaf community have strong feelings against these. *I spoke to a young woman at a college one day who had them inserted and she said they made the difference in her life.*

It has been found that there is an increased risk of meningitis after the insertion of cochlear implants, but this is a treatable disease if it is diagnosed right away. If there is a hearing loss, it would be important to talk to a pediatric otologist or ear doctor who has had considerable experience with cochlear implants. In the U.S., the Cochlear Implant Awareness Foundation can be found at www.ciafonline.org. They will provide much good information and have many resources. There is also a Children's Hearing Institute at: 212-614-8380. In the U.K., I would check with your grandchild's primary physician and also look at the Web site www.nciua. org.uk for information.

SLEEP PROBLEMS

When an infant or child has trouble sleeping, it can lead to tired, unhappy parents or grandparents. Sleep problems can be related to obesity, central nervous system problems, or sometimes medications that have been prescribed. Anyone can react badly to a medication, but little children often react in exactly the opposite way to what would be expected. For example, Phenobarbital, which is a sedative, may act like a stimulant and Dexedrine or Ritalin can act as a depressant or a stimulant. For some children and teens, Benadryl helps induce sleep and I have used Valium with good success in patients with severe cerebral palsy.

If a new medication is prescribed for hyperactivity, seizures, asthma, or anything else, the drug could cause sleep problems. If after a day or two of a new medication, sleep problems are occurring, I would suggest calling your grandchild's doctor. If you are having problems reaching the physician, you could talk to a pharmacist.

If a child has prescriptions from more than one doctor, there could be some interaction or interference between the drugs that might cause unwanted effects. Often busy doctors are not aware that another physician has prescribed a medication or they don't want to take the time to check with a pharmacist to see if two drugs can be given together.

If your grandchild's sleep problems are not related to drugs, I would try old-fashioned tried and true methods to help a child get to sleep. Some suggestions would be:

- Establish a regular routine for bedtime with a soothing bath, drink, story, and toileting. (If baths are a problem, these could be given at a different time during the day.)

- Fit the size and type of bed to the child's age and special need.

- Have a nightlight in the room.

- Be sure there are not too many or too few covers.

- Be sure a loud TV, radio, or loud conversations cannot be heard.

- The room should be comfortable and not too hot or too cold.

- A child's pajamas or nighttime clothing should not be too much or too little.

- Extra diapers or pull-ups may be needed if a child has poor bladder control and gets soaked during the night.

- A child with croup or breathing problems may need a cool mist vaporizer.

- An asthmatic child should have a dust-free room and non-allergenic blankets, pillows, and mattress. Dust-catchers should be removed, as should fuzzy stuffed animals. If a child is allergic to pets, they should not be allowed in the child's room. Heavy curtains can catch dust and should be replaced by cotton, washable drapes or curtains.

- A CD player with a bedtime story can often help a child go to sleep.

- A story read by a parent that has been recorded on a tape recorder may help.

- Soft music helps some children sleep.

- A child must not be allowed to climb in and out of a grandparent's bed.

- A "dream-catcher" hung over a child's bed may help. The hanging can be combined with a story about the significance of these and there is a beautiful book for children about dream-catchers. *Dreamcatcher* by Audrey Osofsky (New York: Scholastic, 1992).

- No scary TV or movies should be watched before bedtime.

- If a child snores, enlarged tonsils and adenoids could be the problem and can cause difficulty sleeping soundly.

It can be helpful to talk over special problems with other grandparents and your grandchild's doctor. Chat rooms and some books can provide new approaches, but the old-fashioned methods often still work the best.

If your grandchild is a sleep-walker, it is best, the experts say, not to try waking the child, but just gently lead the child back to bed. Sleep-walking occurs in as many as twenty percent of children, usually when the child is anxious or overly tired. The average age for sleep-walking is between four and twelve and by the teenage years, it usually is no longer a problem. *One father and mother started a ritual when their children were small of pretending to place a magic circle around their child's bed. The child had been quite fearful of going to sleep and this seemed to keep the "monsters" away.*

As my children were growing up and each one was in bed for the night, I would sit on the edge of the bed and talk about the day's activities or problems. This seemed to make it easier for the kids to settle down and it gave us some good one-to-one time together.

TREATMENTS FOR PAIN

Many times the pain of a disability is the major problem parents and grand-parents have to handle. Pain management is not a high priority in many medical teaching programs, so you may have to do some research and networking to find the right answers to a grandchild's severe pain. You want to be sure that a thorough physical examination has been done before seeking other resources for pain management. Also, it is a good idea to have your grandchild's principal doctor check blood potassium and other blood chemistry levels, especially if the pain occurs intermittently or spas-modically. A basic blood count, blood panels, urinalysis, and chest X-ray should be done if there is on-going pain without a good reason.

There are many ways that severe pain can be controlled. One good resource that many people do not know about is a doctor who specializes in pain treatment. In the United States, these doctors are usually board-certified anesthesiologists. Some work out of their own offices, while others are connected with hospitals. There are also major hospitals that offer pain clinics.

There are a variety of other modalities for pain control. Some are more invasive than others. Massage and biofeedback can be helpful and there are many ways that acupuncture can treat pain. Codeine is a drug that is not a good choice for children. It can be constipating, nauseating, cause depression, and be addicting. Some orthopedists prescribe it after they have done a surgical procedure and don't realize that codeine is not a drug that children tolerate very well. In extreme cases, pain specialists can insert a catheter into your grandchild's back that will allow a slow drip of a pain medication.

Over-the-counter drugs such as aspirin and Tylenol can be dangerous if they are not given in the prescribed pediatric doses. Aspirin should never be given to a child without a doctor's prescription because of the risk of a serious condition called Reye's Syndrome. Also, Tylenol can cause liver failure if it is used in excessive doses. If a child has a very low pain tolerance, sometimes just giving a sugar coated pill or placebo can take away the pain. I would talk this over with your grandchild's doctor if you decide to treat mild pain this way.

Some children have a high pain tolerance or just don't want to keep asking for pain medication. Other kids don't understand their pain and may not be able to tell you that it is occurring. Head banging could be an indication of pain, as could extreme irritability. Knowing how your grandchild handles pain is important and can help you and the treating doctors know which is the best pain management method to use.

SIGNS AND SYMPTOMS OF COMMON CHILDHOOD DISEASES

Roseola Infantum (Exanthema Subitum)
This can be a frightening disease for parents. An infant or small child will have a high fever for one to five days with almost no other symptoms. Then the fever falls suddenly after the fourth or fifth day and a tiny, flat, small rash appears all over the body. The rash starts and is mostly seen on the baby's trunk. Some children are irritable and may have enlarged lymph nodes at the base of their skulls. The major complication is that convulsions or seizures can occur, if the temperature is not kept down by cooling measures and Tylenol. (Note side-effects of Tylenol on previous page.) It is important for a child to be seen by a pediatrician or family doctor when the fever persists to be sure there are no other problems, as an ear infection, meningitis or other illness.

Chicken Pox (Varicella)
This childhood disease is very contagious with an incubation period of twelve to twenty-one days. For the first twenty-four hours an infant or child may just have a slight fever, decreased appetite, and less energy. Then small red, blister-like spots or lesions are seen usually first on the trunk, then the chest, and back. The blisters come in bunches and cause quite

severe itching. It is important to keep a child from scratching, so there will not be scarring or secondary infection. A child's finger nails should be kept short and cotton gloves or socks can be put over the hands. Antihistamines and cooling baths will help the itching. A child is contagious until the lesions have crusts on them. Encephalitis or an infection in the brain is a rare complication, but should be watched for. A few mild cases of chicken pox are occurring despite the immunization for this disease. However, the immunization is an important one for a child to receive.

Whooping Cough (Pertussis)
The incubation period for this disease is seven to ten days. Fortunately, not too many cases are seen each year in the U.S. because of the DPT immunization (D = diptheria, P = pertussis, and T = tetanus). Initially, a child will have a cough, runny nose, and mild fever. In about two weeks, the cough will become severe and frequent with a "whoop" at the end of a cough. The coughing may last for several weeks. Antibiotics may help prevent secondary complications. Severe complications can occur. These can affect the lung causing pneumonia, or other problems. Convulsions and brain hemorrhage can also develop. Small infants should be closely watched in a hospital.

Measles (Rubeola)
This disease has an incubation period of eight to fourteen days. The first symptoms are usually fever, sore throat, cough, and runny nose. Red eyes (conjunctivitis) are a common accompanying symptom. The rash is usually seen about the fifth day and starts on the face, behind the ears, then to the chest, abdomen, and lastly the extremities. The rash gradually turns into large, red patches. Complications are ear infections, pneumonia, or encephalitis (an infection of the brain). A dark room may help because light often bothers a child. Itching can occur and can be treated with antihistamines or cool baths. A child should be kept as quiet as possible until there is no longer an elevated temperature.

Streptococcal Infections (Streptococcosis)
Group A streptococcus can cause severe disease if it is not recognized and treated. The incubation period for a strep throat infection (pharyngitis) is two to five days. A child will suddenly develop a fever, have a loss of appetite, red cheeks, and a severe sore throat. There may be white matter (exudates) on the tonsils and these can be quite large. There are usually big, boggy glands or lymph nodes under the chin at the angle of the jaw. A throat culture is important to have done prior to treatment with penicillin.

A follow-up throat culture should be done after ten days of treatment with penicillin to be sure the strep has been completely eliminated. Untreated strep throat can lead to kidney disease (glomerulonephritis), rheumatic fever, or scarlet fever. Ear infections may also occur.

Impetigo is a strep infection of the skin. The crusty, yellowish skin lesions are usually around the nose, ears, on the face, and shins. Other sites may also be infected. Treatment is cleansing frequently and antibiotics.

Mumps (Epidemic Parotitis)

The incubation period for mumps is twelve to twenty-four days. The onset is usually an elevated temperature followed by a loss of appetite and pain on chewing or behind the ears. Swelling occurs in the glands at the angle of the jaw extending to the face. A child should be kept in the house and quiet until the fever and swelling have subsided. A severe infection in the mouth or a tooth infection can mimic mumps. There are some serious complications of mumps, so the immunization is important for all children to receive.

Viral Infections

Coxsackie and other viruses cause infections in children. These are quite common in the summer and fall months. The treatment is generally keeping the temperature under control, being sure enough liquids are taken, and keeping a child as quiet as possible. This is important because, otherwise, complications can occur.

Pneumococcal Disease

Pneumococcal disease is caused by the bacteria, *Streptococcus pneumoniae*. People with the disease can spread it by sneezing or coughing. Children with low resistance or chronic lung disease are at risk. Ear infections, sinusitis, pneumonia, eye infections, and meningitis can result in susceptible patients. Children under five years of age are particularly at risk.

Rotavirus Infections

Rotavirus infection generally affects infants and children between the ages of three months and two years. The symptoms are diarrhea, fever, nausea, and vomiting. The most important thing is to be sure a child takes enough fluids to keep up with the diarrhea and the fever is kept under control. If a child is not urinating adequately and seems dehydrated, hospitalization may be necessary. It is important to keep in touch with the child's doctor during the illness. The incubation period is two to three days and the virus is very contagious. Usually the fever and vomiting will stop after two to three days, but the diarrhea may last for several more days. A stool culture may be necessary to look for ova and parasites. It would be important to be sure there is no accompanying ear infection.

SIDE-EFFECTS OF SOME MEDICINES

There are well known side-effects to some of the medicines widely used in rheumatoid arthritis, asthma, muscular dystrophy, and seizures or convulsions. It is important to be aware of these and ask questions of your grandchild's doctor if one is prescribed.

Cortisone or prednisone (steroids) is a medicine used to treat arthritis, dermatomyositis, polymyositis, Duchenne dystrophy, and asthma. Often very large doses are initially prescribed. If this is the case, it is important that the dose be decreased as quickly as possible with careful monitoring.

Prednisone can cause a large weight gain, increased blood pressure, hyperactivity in some children, make bones weaker, increase the risk of diabetes and heart disease, and also suppress growth and signs of infection. A low salt diet can help with the weight gain, as can watching a child's caloric intake.

I was consulted one afternoon about a boy with Duchenne dystrophy. The ten-year-old had been started on high doses of prednisone by a neurologist who primarily cared for adult patients. There had been no follow-up. The boy's blood pressure was high and he had gained an enormous amount of weight. I was appalled that the physician had not seen the boy on a weekly or bi-weekly basis, as I would have done. So, as a grandparent-in-charge, if something like this happens to a grandchild on steroids, please make a visit to the child's doctor.

Some of the drugs used to treat convulsions or seizures can cause changes in liver studies and blood counts. If a child is on seizure medication, I would ask your grandchild's doctor if there is any need to monitor blood counts or liver function tests on a regular basis.

Codeine can cause constipation, nausea, depression, and it is also addicting.

Tylenol given in excessive doses can cause liver failure, so it is important to carefully check the prescribed dose and not give more than indicated.

If you have any questions about the safety of a drug or whether it can react with another medication, I would ask your grandchild's physician and also a pharmacist if you are still worried.

TIPS ON GIVING MEDICINE TO GRANDCHILDREN

There are quite a few creative or sneaky ways that children can be convinced to take medicine. One way is to put the medicine in a little Coca-Cola, if this is something a child likes. Another is to mix it in a little chocolate syrup, honey, jelly, jam, or peanut butter, as long as a child can have those. A medicine dropper can be used or even a small syringe to squirt the medicine into your grandchild's mouth. With the syringe, it is best to squirt the medicine into the side of the mouth. That way it is not so easily spit out. Tablets can be crushed and capsules can be opened and the medicine mixed with something palatable. Also, a pharmacist can mix a medication in a good tasting cherry or other syrup. If a child is vomiting, there are suppositories that can be used to stop the vomiting. These are by prescription, so you would need to call your grandchild's doctor.

As you remember from your own children, one of the most important things in caring for an ill child is tender loving care and attention. Yes, the child may need a visit to the doctor and some special medicine, but being confined to bed and feeling ill are probably the worst things. *I have fond memories of a neighbor who came each afternoon to read to me when I was sick and in bed with the measles. In those days, children had to lie quietly in a darkened room with their eyes closed. For a five-year-old active, book-loving child, this was terrible punishment. I looked forward to the neighbor's visits and remember her with great affection.* Your grandchild will probably have similar memories of you during times of pain or illness.

Chapter Sixteen

Finding Resources for Specialized Services

Most kids with physical disabilities will need to be evaluated by a host of specialists. It is important to know where and how to find the best ones if you are the one doing the research. Children with emotional problems or chronic illness will probably also need different specialists, so considerable research and networking will be necessary. Grandparents can play an important role in finding the right specialists because it can be very time consuming. It is hoped that your grandchild's principal doctor will be a good resource, but you want to be sure that he or she doesn't just refer to friends, golf, or health club buddies who may not be the best.

If the specialists are connected with a clinic, there probably isn't a choice. However, if you are uncomfortable about either the care your grandchild is receiving or the way the specialist relates to your grandchild, don't be shy about speaking up or seeking a second opinion.

SPECIAL EQUIPMENT

If special equipment is needed, you want to be sure you are not sold something more expensive than is required. A wheelchair needs to be measured to fit your grandchild and not have a lot of fancy, unnecessary extras. Remember that you may be the one to get a wheelchair on or into a car, so try to buy or rent a chair that is sturdy, but as lightweight as possible. A child should be measured to be sure a wheelchair is the right size. The other important things to think about are: detachable arm rests, detachable leg rests, a firm back rest, and firm cushion. There are padded boards that can be slipped behind a child to increase the firmness of the back. In addition, many different types of wheelchair cushions are available. The right cushion is particularly important for a child who has decreased or absent sensation in the legs because of the concern about pressure sores. Head supports and extended backs are important for children who have weak necks or poor head control and a seat belt in the wheelchair is a wise addition to be used when a child is in a van or bus.

Occupational therapists can be very helpful in being sure that you select the right equipment. They also can measure your grandchild if a wheelchair is needed. Some will make home visits to see how things can be made easier for you and your grandchild. They can also show you the best way to lift a child or teenager. If you hurt your back lifting, it could cause on-going problems and who would be there to care for your grandchild?

In the bathroom, raised toilet seats with or without side supports can be helpful for some children, as can bath safety bars and bath seats. These can make toileting and bathing much easier and offer stability to a child. *One step-father designed and installed an overhead lift in the bathroom so he could lift his step-son from his wheelchair and settle him safely in the bathtub. This special man also helped install these for other parents.* You can purchase lifts that are attached to ceiling tracks for use in a bathroom or small space.

Braces (AFOs and KAFOs) or calipers, as they are called in the U.K., must be made by a licensed orthotist or brace maker. He or she will need to make careful measurements to be sure they will fit properly. If not they may cause pressure sores and be very uncomfortable. Then they will end up in a closet or garage. Braces should be lightweight and fit under the legs of pants.

Back braces can be very uncomfortable, so you need to be sure that the individual making the brace has a great deal of experience. All braces should be prescribed by a children's orthopedist and made by a licensed orthotist. Many of my patients traveled long distances to come to the excellent orthotist we used in San Francisco.

Walkers, tray tables for wheel chairs, cushions, and special aids can be found online, so you can make some comparison of prices. In the U.K., a good source is: www.ableize.com. The National Health Service provides some equipment, so it would be a good idea to check with your grandchild's therapist, doctor, health visitor, or a knowledgeable individual in a child health clinic if special equipment is needed.

Some U.S. insurance policies pay for specific types of equipment as do the Muscular Dystrophy Association at www.mda.org and the Muscular Dystrophy Family Foundation at www.mdff.org. It would be worthwhile to check with your insurance carrier first and then see if your grandchild's disability comes under the umbrella of disorders that the two muscle disease organizations serve.

In general, it is better to try and rent equipment before you buy it. Then you can determine if it is really necessary or if it will just be one more thing with which to hassle. If equipment is not carefully researched before it is purchased, it frequently ends up in a closet or the garage.

SOME OTHER HELPFUL DEVICES

There are some devices that have been around for many years and some newer ones that rely on computer technology. All of these can make life easier for individuals with mobility problems or muscle weakness. In the U.K., the Disabled Living Foundation at www.dlf.org.uk has a very comprehensive list of aids for individuals with disabilities. Their contact number is 0845 130 9177.

There are many available devices to make life easier for anyone with a special need. Some of these are:

- *Butler-in-a-Box*–A small voice-activated unit that acts like a butler. The device can be programmed to turn on lights, appliances, stereos, and TVs, among other things.

- *Eating Aids*–Useful for those with limited hand strength, function, or spasticity. Eating utensils are available that have built-up or longer handles. Plastic rims or guards around the rims of plates help food from being scattered. Specialized cups that won't tip and cups with built-up rims can all be ordered from special catalogs or online.

- *Dressing Aids*–Button hooks, dressing aids and other dressing helps are available. The Sammons-Preston catalog is a good resource and they will send a catalog at no cost. Their number is 1-800-323-5547.

- *Telephone Aids*–Telephone companies have special devices and services for those who need help. In the United States, there should be a number on your telephone bill you can call to speak with a representative or you can find the number in your local telephone book. Special speaker boxes are available, as is equipment for individuals who are deaf. Braille dials and other aids are also available and there is usually no charge for these special pieces of equipment.

- *Electronic On/Off Switches*–Lights can be turned on or off by small devices that can be purchased fairly inexpensively in electronic stores.

- *Ramps*–There are now lightweight ramps that can be rolled up and can be purchased in three, five, and eight foot lengths. They are called "Roller ramps." They are convenient to use if building a solid ramp is too expensive or not possible. In the U.K., ramps are available at www.raalloy.co.uk.

- *Lifts*–A good mechanical lift can save a caretaker's back and is more comfortable for the individual who needs to be moved. The Hoyer lift has been in use for many years, but the wide base makes it difficult to use in a small bathroom or where there is limited space. They do have a ceiling lift and the Hoyer lift can be operated manually or by a battery. These lifts work well in bigger spaces. The CindyLift has a smaller base and can be used, it is said, by individuals who do not have a lot of muscle strength. Lifts can be used at the bed side or attached to a bathtub and there are also car top lifts. Several companies make different types of lifts. In the U.K., bath lifts are available at www.bathtimemobility.co.uk.

- *Pony or Scooter*–A child or teenager who needs a wheelchair may be able to use a pony or scooter instead. These are much more socially acceptable for most kids and can be more fun. Also, many kids feel a wheelchair sets them apart from other kids and limits their independence and they prefer a pony or scooter.

- *Bathroom Aids*–Side bars can be attached to toilet seats or the side of a bathtub and wheelchairs are made that can go into a roll-in shower.

- *Transfer Boards*–These are good to easily transfer a child from a bed to wheelchair or elsewhere. There are different types that can be ordered at medical supply houses or from a specialized catalog. One good source is Mobility Transfer Systems and their number is 1-888-593-0377.

- *Medical Alert Buttons*–These are connected with an answering service that will alert medical personnel in case of an emergency. A patient can wear a cord around the neck to which one of these buttons is attached. There are also small hand-held devices that can be activated in case of an emergency. In the U.K., medical alert buttons are available at www.medicalert.org.uk. The different companies in the United States that provide this service can be found on the Internet or in your local telephone book or Yellow Pages. The heading would be "Medical Alert System" or "Home Medical Alert System."

- *Automatic Door Opener*–These can be life-saving. They can be obtained from Power Access and the number is 1-800-344-0088.

- *Reachers*–can be very helpful for individuals in a wheelchair to reach objects at a distance or they can be used to access objects in high places.

- *Page Turners*–are helpful to individuals with limited hand strength or spasticity.

- *Swing Clear Hinges*–These can add two inches to a doorway and can be obtained from Accessible Environments. Their number is 1-800-776-1461.

Another good source for specialized equipment in the U.S. is the Independent Living Aids Catalog at 1-800-537-2118 and at the Web site: www.independentliving.com.

SPECIAL TESTING

It takes very skilled and specially trained educational psychologists to do the tests necessary to identify emotional problems, attention deficit disorders, learning disabilities, developmental delay, or disorders in the autism spectrum, also called pervasive developmental disorders. The kids don't need a Stanford-Binet or IQ test, but a battery of tests that will give what is called a psychometric profile. A child's strengths and weaknesses will be detected by these tests, so the optimum help can be received.

It is important to remember that children with Duchenne muscular dystrophy and spina bifida have a high incidence of learning disabilities. *A cousin of one of my patients had Duchenne muscular dystrophy and he sat in the same classroom with the same teacher for eleven years, was never tested, and never learned to read. Astounding, but true and this was in a school in a large city.*

Kids who exhibit problems early on should be tested as soon as possible so they can receive the best help. If a child starts school before a diagnosis of a problem is made, the school psychologist may be the one asked to do the testing. In my experience, many school psychologists in the United States do not have the necessary training to accurately diagnose some of the more difficult learning or emotional problems. If possible, a child should always have an assessment by a private educational psychologist, who is both experienced and well-trained.

The other problem about relying on the school psychologist's report is that they often have limited time in which to do an assessment. It can sometimes take two or three days to do adequate testing because some children can't sit still long enough for the testing to be completed or they cannot concentrate for more than short periods at a time.

Some psychologists in the U.S., unfortunately, are influenced by their administrator's concern that every child who is diagnosed with a special need will cost the school district extra money. This is sad, but true as many teachers have told me. *Two teachers were told they could only have two children a year identified with special problems.*

Once a child is diagnosed as needing special help or a special class, a psychologist's report must be heard and adhered to in an IEP. This Individualized Education Program is required for every U.S. special needs child. (See Chapter Twelve for further information about IEPs.)

COUNSELING RESOURCES

If you have full-time care and decide some counseling is needed for your grandchild, it is important to carefully check on a counselor's credentials. It may take considerable research and talking to other parents and grandparents before you find just the right one. I would start with your grandchild's primary doctor, but then you can do some research on your own. Often agencies that specialize in your grandchild's special disability can be helpful. Remember there are different kinds of counselors with quite different training. In the U.S., these include:

- Licensed clinical social workers (L.C.S.W.) can work in clinics or have their own offices.

- Marriage and Family Counselors (M.F.C.C) may or may not have special training with kids.

- Psychologists (Ph.D.)–Some are trained to counsel children and some just see adults.

- Psychiatrists–are medical doctors (M.D.) with several more years of training in psychiatry. They are not usually needed for most childhood problems. If the problem is more serious, a child psychiatrist would be needed.

ART, MUSIC AND DANCE THERAPY

I have seen some wonderful changes happen in kids when they have the luxury of spending time in art, music, or dance therapy. A physical therapist in San Francisco started the Center for Movement Therapy using dance as therapy. Several of my patients were able to take part and they made friends, developed confidence, and had fun. It was an outstanding program and there are probably similar programs in other communities or perhaps you could convince a physical therapist to start one. The rewards are great.

Art therapy is used in some hospital child psychiatric units and there are also private art therapists. In the U.K., the National Health Service will provide art therapy in some situations, so this is a good question to ask. In the U.S., because so many schools have removed art from their programs, a way for kids to express themselves is even more critical for those with special needs. Having some art supplies on hand that a grandchild can use in your home can be both therapeutic and fun.

I had one teenage patient who used a wheelchair because of severe disability from spina bifida. He was very angry and I wanted him to have counseling. However, he said that he didn't need counseling and he wasn't angry. I handed him a large art tablet and a red crayon and asked him to draw what he was feeling. The youth pressed so hard on my desk that I thought he was going through to the floor. He drew volcanoes with large amounts of lava spouting out and flowing down the sides. His anger came out clearly and dramatically in the drawing and both he and his parents finally agreed to counseling.

Music therapy can be excellent for kids who scream a lot or get greatly excited. We convinced our local state office of the California Regional Center to pay for music therapy for one boy and it completely changed his moods. It also made it possible for his single parent mother to control him because before the music therapy, she was at her wit's end about how to manage the boy.

In the U.K., information about music therapy can be obtained at (020) 7267 4496 or www.musictherapy.org.uk. In the U.S., the Music Therapy Association can be contacted to find out if there is a licensed music therapist in your local area. They are located in Silver Springs, Maryland, but can be reached at at: 301-589-3300 or by e-mail at: info@musictherapy.org.

The benefits of music therapy that they list on their Web site (www. musictherapy.org) are: to "promote wellness, manage stress, alleviate pain, express feelings, enhance memory, improve communication and promote physical rehabilitation."

ASSISTIVE TECHNOLOGY

Every child with and without special needs should have access to a computer if they will profit from the use of one. In the U.K., help is available for assistive technology at www.alt.ac.uk. This is the Web site for the Association for Learning Technology.

There are ways that pictures or symbols can be used to facilitate communication and a consultant trained in assistive technology needs to do an assessment and make recommendations for any necessary adaptations to a computer to fit your grandchild's particular needs.

You will want to find out what type of computer is suggested and if adaptations will be needed. In addition, it is good to ask what specific software programs will provide the best help for your grandchild. Kids can control their computers with a light on a head band that can be moved to click on the keyboard; keys can be extended or enlarged and something called "sticky keys" will make writing much easier. There is also a keyboard that can be adapted, so seven keys take care of the entire function. Software is available, too, that will speed up the typing or it can predict the words if just the first few letters are typed in. With a computer, a child can communicate, have pen pals, do assignments, play games, and learn about the world.

It may take a little help from an advocate or a special education attorney to have assistive technology written into the IEP, but every child who needs help with a computer should have it. (In some states, as California, the phrase "limited use funds" should be written into the IEP. Otherwise, the school may say they do not have adequate funds to purchase a computer.)

Both the exact amount of time a computer is to be used during the day and the number of days it is to be used each week must be written into the IEP. If there is a need for a pocket-size communicator or a computer with touch symbols these should also be noted. I have visited classrooms where daily use of a computer was written into an IEP, but the computer sat in the closet for many months until this was discovered. So parents and grandparents have to constantly monitor the use of a computer if one is needed.

The Center for Assistive Technology in Berkeley, California, is a great resource and there are other assistive technology centers all across the United States. The Center in Berkeley can be contacted at info1@cforat.org and their Web site is www.cforat.org. I have visited the Center and been most impressed about the help they give kids with special needs and their experience and knowledge. The Web site for the National Technical Assistance Center is www.taalliance.org and they will also provide you with a wealth of information and assistance. The telephone number of this Center is: 1-888-248-0822.

In the U.K., help can be found from the Foundation for Assistive Technology. Their Web site is www.fastuk.org.

Chapter Seventeen

Medical Questions and Answers

1. **Question:** Our three-year-old grandson still isn't talking. He gets very frustrated and hits his little sister. What do you suggest?

   Answer: My first answer would be that he must not be allowed to hit his sister. I would put him in his room for longer and longer periods each time he hits. Before you do that, I would say a very firm "No" and mean it. Next, I would want to be sure your grandchild's hearing is checked in a pediatric hearing center. If the hearing is normal, an appointment with a speech pathologist is the next step to be sure there is not a problem with **aphasia** or **apraxia**. If that is not helpful, the next step would be to have an evaluation by a pediatric neuro- or educational psychologist. There could be neurological or learning problems.

2. **Question:** My grandson's doctor wants him to have a **muscle biopsy** at our local hospital because he has muscle weakness. I am concerned that they don't have much experience doing muscle biopsies and wonder if we shouldn't take him to a big medical center?

   Answer: You are right to be concerned. I would not have a muscle biopsy done at a local hospital. In the United States, even most of the big medical centers and hospitals do not have personnel trained to do adequate, up-to-date staining and processing of muscle biopsies. There are many new techniques that should be used, but because money is short in most hospitals, this is not a priority. There are very few hospitals or even big medical centers in the U.S. where I would have a biopsy done. If you live in England, France, Italy, Turkey, Tunisia, Japan, or Australia, there are outstanding pediatric neuromuscular centers. Unfortunately, this is not true of the U.S.

Also, most surgeons in the United States hospitals insist that a child have a general anesthetic when a muscle biopsy is to be done. This is not necessary or wise in the usual case. A muscle biopsy should be done on an out-patient basis with the use of a local anesthetic. This way the risk of Malignant Hyperthermia, if a general anesthetic is given, is greatly reduced.

3. **Question:** My granddaughter has **Down Syndrome** and is now having seizures. My daughter and I are both exhausted trying to take care of her. Do you have any suggestions?

   Answer: Has your grandchild been seen by a pediatric neurologist and also had a good physical examination, blood count, and urinalysis? If the seizures continue, I would want a second opinion about the child's medicines from another pediatric neurologist. There are many new medicines to control seizures. Also, I would arrange for some help or apply for some respite help. If you or your daughter get ill or have an accident because you are too tired and stressed, there could be some bad results.

4. **Question:** My grandchild has **myotonic dystrophy** and **drools** badly. Is there anything that can be done about that? His doctor wants him to have surgery on the salivary glands in his mouth. Is that wise?

   Answer: There are medications that can control drooling and are generally quite successful. My favorite is Cogentin. This drug has been widely used for many years and I have prescribed it with great success in quite a few patients. The dose has to be tailored or titrated to a child's size and the amount of drooling that occurs. Your doctor could talk to a pharmacist about the drug. Surgery on salivary glands is not successful in my experience. It also requires a general anesthetic which should be avoided in a child, particularly with a muscle disease.

5. **Question:** My teenage granddaughter has been diagnosed as having **cerebral palsy**. She has a funny gait and some mild weakness in her legs. Also, the back of her legs (her calves) are very thin. We have a very hard time buying her shoes because her arches are so high. I have read up about cerebral palsy and don't feel that her symptoms fit this diagnosis. We live in a small town and have limited pediatric specialists. I hope you can help us.

   Answer: It sounds as if your granddaughter has a very classical picture of **Charcot-Marie-Tooth** disease. Individuals with this disorder generally have quite a typical or "steppage" gait, high arches, great difficulty in buying shoes, thin calves, called "stork-legs," weakness in the lower extremities and often then in the hands. I would suggest that your granddaughter see a neurologist and have nerve conduction times done. It may be that other family members also have mild Charcot-Marie-Tooth disease or just decreased nerve conduction times. This is usually an inherited disorder.

6. **Question:** Our great-granddaughter has been weak since birth and has been diagnosed as having "**congenital benign hypotonia**." Could you tell us about this diagnosis?

   Answer: This diagnosis no longer exists. It was discarded many years ago by physicians who treat children with muscle weakness. Now we know that there are many different disorders that cause a baby or child to be weak. Some of the reasons babies are floppy or weak is that they may have a muscle disease. One cause could be a Congenital Myopathy. In this group are several different disorders: **Central Core Disease, Myotubular Myopathy, Minicore Myopathy** and **Nemaline Rod Myopathy** to name a few. Specific genetic abnormalities have been found in some of these. **Spinal muscular atrophy** is another disorder that causes babies to be weak. Your great-grandchild needs to be seen by a pediatric neuromuscular specialist to ensure the correct diagnosis is made. Most likely a muscle biopsy will be needed and it should definitely be done using a local anesthetic, not a general anesthetic. Children with Central Core Disease are particularly prone to having Malignant Hyperthermia and the necessary precautions should be taken.

7. **Question:** My step-grandson has just been diagnosed with an **atrial septal defect**. He is six years old. He has been slow to grow and an X-ray of his hands shows that he is missing three bones in one hand and four bones in the other. He can't keep up with other kids and is getting very frustrated and unhappy. What are your thoughts?

   Answer: I discussed your question with my favorite geneticist and he says that there are many syndromes that have a combination of atrial septal defect, abnormalities of the limbs, and growth retardation. A pediatric geneticist should be consulted and a chromosome test done.

8. **Question:** Our three-month-old grandson has been diagnosed with **hemi-hypertrophy**. Could you please tell us more about this? What is the cause, the short- and long-term effects, and if there is anything, treatment or something else, we should be doing?

Answer: In most cases, the cause of hemi-hypertrophy is not known. However, we do know there can be an association with abnormalities of the urinary tract and Wilms' tumor. Studies need to be done at some point to look for these. As your grandson grows, there will be a difference in the size of the arms and legs, if one half of his body is involved. Sometimes, just a leg is involved. A pediatric orthopedist should be seen yearly to watch your grandson's back to be sure a curvature of the spine or scoliosis does not develop.

9. **Question:** My granddaughter has been seen by a group of professionals and her parents have been told that she has a problem with "**decoding**." None of us in the family have any idea what that means and we were not given a good explanation. We are at a loss about what to do next or what resources are available to help her.

   Answer: "Decoding" means there is difficulty with reading skills. I would urge your granddaughter's parents to take a written request for a special education assessment to the district office for special education. I would either send it certified or deliver it in person. They should keep a copy of the letter. The office staff should give them a brochure listing how many days it will take for an assessment to be done and what the next steps will be to have an IEP or meeting for an Individualized Education Program.

   If it is financially possible, I would look for the best educational psychologist you can find and pay for a private assessment. This testing should be introduced at the IEP meeting. Your granddaughter's pediatrician should be able to give you the name of a good educational psychologist. It would be important to keep track of the number of days the special education department has to complete the testing. They often need a little prodding! Private tutors are available for kids with reading problems and some communities have reading clinics available to kids with difficulty reading and decoding.

10. **Question:** My grandson is having trouble with kids **bullying** him at school. He uses a wheelchair and we don't know how to help him. One day, one of the kids stuck a block in the spokes of his wheelchair, so it wouldn't move. Another time, my grandson left his wheelchair outside the classroom door. He wanted to be like the other kids, so he transferred to a regular chair and desk. Several kids took the wheelchair out for a spin and damaged it. What do you suggest?

    Answer: Kids can be very mean. One of my patients had a very creative way to handle a bullying problem. He was on the student council and they sponsored a "Wheelchair Day." The group borrowed wheelchairs from different places and checked them out to students in a class that had several bullies. The kids had to use them for the whole day and that solved the problem. The kids found out that it was not easy being in a wheelchair and the bullying stopped.

One thing I have done is to talk to classes about disabilities. There are also organizations that give "Disability Awareness Programs." One group of disabled adults, who are all actors, do skits for groups and schools. You might check to see if there is anything similar in your area. In addition, I would certainly let the teacher and principal know about the bullying.

11. **Question:** My granddaughter, who is three months old, has a **congenital torticollis**, which we think happened because of her traumatic birth. She also has a **broken clavicle** and some **facial asymmetry**. We have been stretching her neck now for two and a half months and there is no improvement. What is our next course of action and what can be the long-term effects of this?

    Answer: I think it would be important for your grandchild to see a pediatric surgeon. Often a simple release of the tight sterno-cleido-mastoid muscle, which is causing the torticollis, will correct or help the problem. If surgery is not done, long-term facial asymmetry can occur.

12. **Question:** My three-year-old grandson was having some soiling and the doctor thinks he may have a partial **sacral agenesis**. What does this mean and what can be done?

    Answer: If there is a true sacral agenesis or absence of the sacrum, then a child can have a problem controlling his urine and may get repeated bladder infections. In addition, there may be a problem with constipation and sensation in the legs may also be affected. If there is just a partial sacral agenesis, the cause of the soiling may be something else. There is something called psychogenic megacolon where a child is unusually stressed, gets constipated, and soils around a fecal impaction. It would be important for an MRI of the sacrum to be done, as well as a rectal examination to see if there is good rectal sphincter tone.

13. **Question:** My step-grandson is **developmentally delayed** and when we put him down for a nap, he often has a bowel movement in the bed. He smears the bowel movement around and we are desperate for a solution. What can we do?

Answer: The trick that has worked well is at nap-time to put a gentle restraint around the child's elbows, so he can't bend his arms. You can use a magazine or a lightweight splint you can buy in a drugstore. Try to get him on a regular bowel plan, so he has a bowel movement before you put him down for a nap. The use of suppositories may be helpful and your grandchild's doctor should be able to work out a good bowel plan for your grandchild. There is also a helpful book by Maria Wheeler about toilet training.[21]

14. **Question:** My grandson is five years old. We recently had him in the hospital because he was so filled with feces. He has always had a major problem with constipation. A specialist did a barium enema because he thought the diagnosis was **Hirschsprungs'** disease. My grandson is small for his age and always has a distended abdomen. However, then a rectal biopsy was just done and showed that Hirschsprungs' disease was not the diagnosis. Can you help us? His doctor does not have an answer.

Answer: I am wondering if the diagnosis of **Celiac Disease** has been considered? You are describing a typical case. These children can have either diarrhea or constipation. I would immediately see a pediatric gastroenterologist. The doctor should do a special blood test and if that is positive, a small intestine biopsy will need to be done. Both of these should be performed before you eliminate gluten from the little boy's diet. There are some good cookbooks for wheat-free diets that can be obtained from the Celiac organizations. Danna Korn's book, *Kids with Celiac Disease* (2001), also should be very helpful.[22] She lists acceptable and unacceptable foods.

15. **Question:** I am concerned about my six-month-old granddaughter. A few weeks ago, her parents and I noticed that she wasn't closing one eye as well as the other. Now we notice that one side of her face seems to droop. Our family doctor was not any help, but referred us to an eye doctor. We can't get an appointment for a month. What can we do? We are very worried.

Answer: You are describing facial weakness or a **Bell's palsy**. I would immediately see a pediatric neurologist. It may be something that will go away in a few weeks, but an MRI of the head would be important to look for something more serious, such as a tumor. This could be a treatable problem if it is found early. (On follow-up, a treatable brain tumor was found.)

16. **Question:** My two-year-old granddaughter has a fairly big **blood tumor** or **hemangioma** on the side of her face. A doctor wants to operate and remove it. Should we allow this? I'm not sure she has had much experience with these.

    Answer: You are quite right to be concerned. The usual treatment for these is to allow time for them to decrease in size. Surgery can cause ugly scarring and sometimes other serious complications. I would suggest you find a dermatologist who has had extensive experience with hemangiomas. This may be a pediatric dermatologist in private practice or could be one who is connected with a medical school. Your primary physician should be able to make some calls and find just the right specialist for your granddaughter.

17. **Question:** Our thirteen-year-old granddaughter has **Turner's Syndrome** and gets very lonely. She likes to use the Internet, but we are uncomfortable with her making connections with someone on the Internet who could become a pen pal. Is there a safer way for her to find a friend or pen pal? We have tried to get her involved in different activities, but at this time we have not found a good fit since she is very shy and uncomfortable about her appearance.

    Answer: I would suggest two ways a friend or pen pal might be found that should be safe. The first would be to have you or your granddaughter write a letter to the Editor of the *Exceptional Parent* magazine. They often publish letters from someone looking for a pen pal. You could also contact the Turner's Syndrome agency (see Appendix) to see if they could suggest a teenager who has Turner's Syndrome. They should be able to make a request for you since they most likely would not give you a name or address because of privacy issues. I've found that the staff members in most agencies for kids with special needs are very responsive to such requests.

Chapter Eighteen

Handling a Progressive Disease

Having the part-time or full-time care of a grandchild with a progressive disorder must be one of the hardest things a grandparent ever has to do. How do you get through each day without crying and screaming? What is the best way to help your grandchild live as normal a life as possible?

I asked Marjorie, the mother of a favorite Duchenne dystrophy patient, how she coped so well with her son Larry's terrible disease. Larry died at age twenty-one having lived a full and happy life and leaving a host of friends and admirers. I was among them.

Marjorie thought for a few minutes and then said, "Well, we didn't think about the future, but just did the best we could each day. I never let Larry get by with anything, but treated him just like my other children. He was expected to do his chores, his homework, be courteous, and behave. We just got through each day and tried to make that day the best we could."

It was always a pleasure to see Larry in my office or the hospital. I don't think Larry ever felt sorry for himself, but just figured that was the way "the cards were dealt."

It takes an unusual person and family to handle a progressive disease so well and I have always felt great admiration for Marjorie and her family. As grandmothers, we can strive for the same attitude even if we have just a few hours care of a grandchild now and then.

Kids pick up on the way adults handle their lives and I think we owe it to our grandchildren to live the best way we can. By hiding our own pain and fear, we can try to make each day count. Yes, there will be many dark days, but remember to treasure the special moments, reach out to others, and look for different, less stressful ways to do things.

Joyce, the mother of a child with a progressive disease, once remarked to me, "I wish it were all over now. I just can't stand to see Jane get weaker and weaker."

I sat down with the mother and said, "I understand how hard this must be for you. No child should ever have a progressive disease, but remember new medicines and treatments could be found tomorrow. You can't give up hope. Instead, if you try to make each day count, you will be surprised how different life can be."

The last few years of the girl's life brought increased closeness and love between the mother and her daughter. I was proud of Joyce for making such a remarkable turnabout. She now helps other families who have a child with a progressive disorder.

I have found that the families who have a deep faith in some higher power get through the days much better both before and after the loss of a child. I can't think of anything more painful than losing a child. Some parents and grandparents almost cease to function for days, months, and even years. They feel numb and completely cut off from their everyday lives. *One mother of a boy who died in his teens from a progressive disease said she does not remember much that happened in the two or three years following her son's death. She went through the daily motions of living and took care of her family, but that was all. Gradually, this mother came out of her terrible fog and went back to school. Now she does grief counseling for other families in need.*

If a grandparent has medical problems, these may become much worse with the stress of watching a grandchild slowly decline and then die.

Ways must be found to reduce the stress, so the medical problems don't become incapacitating. Exercise, time with good friends, writing in a journal, some therapy, and a treat now and then can help you make it through the days.

HELPING THE SIBLINGS

When a child or teenager dies, if there are brothers or sisters they will also need help with their grief and pain. Often a sibling thinks that he or she had something to do with the death and will feel great guilt. The child may have thought some negative thoughts about his or her sibling and is often sure these were the cause of the brother or sister's demise. Kids need to talk with someone who is close to them to get rid of their feelings of guilt and grief. The help of a counselor who has had special training in helping kids with grief may also be needed. Grades in school can drop precipitously after a sibling's death and stress-related medical problems may occur. Family discussions about what has occurred are greatly needed with lots of hugs, closeness, and awareness of what a brother or sister is feeling. A grandparent may be the one most able to help a child, particularly if the parents seem numb and are not functioning well.

GRIEF COUNSELING FOR GRANDPARENTS

Most cities have grief counseling available in hospitals or privately. A hospital, hospice, or agency social worker should be able to give you a good referral if you want help. No one should be afraid to admit that they are in pain and need help. It is very important to find a good support system of friends or other individuals who can understand your pain and what you are going through.

I have suggested Catherine Marshall's book, *To Live Again,* to many parents, friends, and family members.[23] She said that just getting through each day after her husband's death was extremely difficult for a long, long time. By putting one foot after the other, she slowly found a way to survive. Catherine Marshall went on to become a well-known author and eventually found happiness when she married again.

Sometimes all that any one of us can do is just make it through a day at a time. Remember that with each ending there is a new beginning. Terrible losses are often the basis for important projects and foundations by which many individuals are helped.

Each of us has to find our own way through grief. We cannot bury our pain, but must allow it to surface, so we can grieve and eventually find ways to make our lives work for us. The pain and feelings of loss will always be there, but if you can try to remember the good times you had with your grandchild and the joy he or she brought, you will get back on the long road to recovery and life will again seem worth living.

Chapter Nineteen

Legal and Financial Resources

It has been estimated that the care of a child with special needs can cost many thousands of dollars in the first eighteen years and over a lifetime, the cost can be into the millions. The cost depends on the nature of the disability and the amount of extra services which parents or grandparents are able and willing to provide. In the U.S., there is some state and federal help, but it is often an on-going fight to get any assistance. If you are the one supporting a grandchild with special needs, some help is available depending on your financial status, but it varies from state to state.

There may be some help through the federal Social Security Agency. This would be dependent on whether you have legal custody, your income, and several other things. It would be a good idea to call them and if necessary visit your closest Social Security office.

LEGAL RESOURCES

When you have full-time care of a grandchild with special needs, you need to be sure that you are protected legally. There are different kinds of custody: *legal, shared,* and *physical.* If grandparents are going to be the ones to make all the decisions on behalf of their grandchild, *legal custody* must be awarded. Some grandparents have *shared custody* with one or both of the parents. This might become tricky depending on the parent or parents and the circumstances. You would want to be sure that all of your legal rights are spelled out and clearly documented, so there can be no cause for any misunderstanding and you are protected.

The third kind of custody is *physical custody.* This is probably not the best for you as a grandparent because you have *no* decision making power. You do the work and probably pay a lot of the expenses, but have no legal authority. In this situation, the advice of a family attorney would be extremely important. To find the best attorney, you need to network with other grandparents and do considerable research.

There are several organizations that can offer help. These are:

In the U.K.

There are several organizations that can offer help:

- **Grandparents Apart**
  - www.grandparentsapart.co.uk/forum/

- **Grandparents' Association**
  - www.grandparents-association.org.uk
  - Helpline: 0845 4349585

In the U.S.:

- **Full Circle of Care**
  - www.fullcirclecare.org

- **Grandparent Caregiver Law Center**
  - 1-518-434-4571
  - www.fullcirclecare.org/grandparents/grandlegal.html

- **Foundation for Grandparenting**
  - 1-805-662-4283
  - www.grandparenting.org

- **Federal Eldercare Locator**
  - 1-800-677-1116
  - www.eldercare.gov

- **Administration on Aging**
  - www.aoa.gov

- **National Committee of Grandparents for Children's Rights**
  - grandparentsforchildren.org

- **Advocates for Grandparent Grandchild Connection**
  - www.grandparentchildconnect.org

If you find that none of the above resources are helpful, then check with an attorney friend, or the attorney friend of a friend, your local Legal Aid Society, agencies, and other grandparents of children with special needs.

Once you have the name of an attorney, it is a wise idea to make an appointment and see how you relate to the individual. There should be no charge for the initial appointment, but be sure to ask about this before you keep the appointment. There are several questions to have answered once you have the initial consultation. They are:

- Find out what experience the attorney has had with custody issues.

- Ask about charges. Does the attorney charge an hourly rate and, if so, how much is it? Is a retainer necessary? What are the charges for copying, photocopying, and routine clerical work?

- How often will you be billed and will the services be itemized?

- Will the attorney continue to represent you or will the case be assigned to a junior, less experienced attorney?

- Will you receive a letter or contract confirming the information you were given?

If you have retained an attorney and after a little while become uncomfortable with what he or she is or is not doing, then I would change attorneys. To do this, you need to first find another attorney and then send a letter to the previous attorney and request that your file be sent to the new lawyer. I would suggest following up in a week to ten days to be sure this has been done. You may need to meet with the first attorney to discuss any money owed or other things that are not clear.

Another reason that you might want to seek the advice of a family attorney is if you have been denied visitation rights with your grandchild. This may be due to family disruptions, remarriages, or other problems. You could start with some of the grandparenting Web sites given above, but if they can't help, a family attorney should be able to find a way for you to see your grandchildren. Family connections are too important for kids not to see their grandparents. We are important to our grandchildren, so I would pursue every possible avenue to be able to see them.

One grandmother had legal custody of her granddaughter for seven years after the father left and the mother was sent to jail for drug use. It was a tragic day when the mother was released from jail and hired an attorney in an attempt to get her daughter back. The judge who handled the case was a young attorney, standing in for a judge. He had no knowledge of the true situation and awarded custody back to the mother. The mother did not allow the grandmother to see her granddaughter.

As the child grew older, she would occasionally call her grandmother if a telephone at school or elsewhere was available. Finally, on her eighteenth birthday, she ran away from her mother's house and appeared on her grandmother's doorstep. She said she had been badly abused by the mother's various boy friends. Drugs had taken over her life and she went down hill from then on, despite the grandmother's great efforts. The young lawyer had changed the girl's life forever. If the grandmother had had the financial means or knowledge about where to get legal help, the granddaughter's life could most likely have been saved.

TAX OR FINANCIAL ASSISTANCE

If you provide either part-time or full-time care of your special needs grandchild, you want to be sure that all possible tax benefits are being received. If you have an accountant or tax person do your tax returns, he or she should be able to ensure you are all right. In the U.S., each state has a CPA Society that you should be able to find on the Internet or from information. Other resources for tax assistance are: AARP if you are a member. Their volunteers will answer tax questions and there is also a "Benefits QuickLink" on the AARP Web site at www.aarp.org. In addition the National Center of Children in Poverty gives rules for each state's child and tax dependent tax credits.

In the United Kingdom, there is a Tax Benefits Helpline at: 0800 88 2200. There is also online tax assistance at www.direct.gov.uk. The Children's Society at 0845 300 1128 or www.childrenssociety.org.uk will also give advice about benefits. It takes considerable time and energy to find the best resources, but considerable help is available if you are willing to do quite a lot of research and make numerous telephone calls.

To have a dependency exemption for your grandchild in the U.S., you must show that you provide more than fifty percent of your qualifying grandchild's financial support and that the grandchild lives with you more than half the year. The grandchild must be under nineteen by the end of the year and not be paying more than half of his or her own support. The grandchild could also be a full-time student until the age of twenty-four or permanently or totally disabled.

You are allowed to deduct medical expenses that you pay for your grandchild, if you have provided more than half of the living expenses. If you have some extra money, you can put away some yearly for your grandchild's education. This can go into an Education Savings Account or ESA. Each year you are allowed to put $2000 away for a grandchild and the money can be used for kindergarten through higher education. Any distributions from an ESA are tax-free if they are used for qualified educational expenses.

Another way to put money away for higher education is through a 529 plan. You can currently put up to $12,000 in this plan per year without having to pay a gift tax. The money does have to be used for higher education. Again, distributions from 529 plans are tax-free to the extent they are used for qualified education expenses. If you are willing to take on the care of a grandchild, you should not have to pay a financial price, particularly if you are on a fixed income. It will take quite a lot of telephoning or using the Internet to get answers, but the answers are there if you ask the right questions and are persistent.

There is considerable assistance from state programs depending on your income and whether you have full-time care. If you need help, it would be worthwhile to check with a social worker in the Child Care Aware program at 1-800-424-2246. You may be eligible for child care financial assistance. The organization has a brochure they will send and there is also information on their Web site at: www.childcareaware.org. Medicaid or California Medi-cal or the Temporary Assistance to Needy Families program (TANF) may provide some help. In addition SSI or Social Security Supplemental Income may be available.

A parent was kind enough to e-mail about a source of financial help of which I was unaware. She said that some states have what is called a "Deeming Waiver." This is also called a Katie Beckett Waiver and Medicaid also has a waiver. Unless you know to use these special terms when asking a state agency about financial help, no one will probably mention it. (The states like to give you as little of their money as possible!)

These waivers are for parents or caretaking grandparents to help the purchase of medical equipment and other necessary items. The Deeming Waiver does not look at the family's income, but instead considers the income or assets of your grandchild. The waiver can be applied for even if a grandchild is covered by private insurance. This is because most insurance policies either don't cover medical equipment and similar needs or they have a limit on the amount of coverage. The Waiver can act as secondary insurance to cover expenses not covered by other means. There are specific eligibility requirements for a Deeming Waiver. These are:

- a grandchild must be under eighteen years of age

- must meet Social Security disability requirements

- must not be eligible for SSI (Supplemental Security Income)

- must meet nursing home placement criteria. (This is puzzling because it does not mean a child has to be placed in a nursing home, but just has to meet a state's requirements for a nursing home.)

An adult Medicaid worker in your local Department of Family and Children's Services is the one to contact for a Deeming Waiver. Of course, many documents will be required, but it could save you a tremendous amount of money according to the parent who kindly sent me the information.

Some grandparents set up a trust so a grandchild will be protected. This can be done with the help of an estate attorney. Big insurance companies also will help set up these trusts. Money could be placed in the trust to be used for special services or needs not covered by any of the state programs if you are no longer alive.

HEALTH INSURANCE

Another thing to think about, if you have full-time care of a grandchild, is health insurance. In the U.S., if you are the legal guardian, you may be able to add your grandchild to your own health insurance. There are also different programs for children with special needs which should be investigated. The amount of coverage and services vary state by state, but in many states you should be able to get help from the SCHIP or state children's health insurance program and/or the programs that specifically cover children with disabilities (see Appendix). Low income grandparents may qualify for Medicaid or Medi-Cal in California. A social worker at the local office of your state agency for children with special needs should be able to answer your questions. You can also call someone in your state capital's office for children with special needs and the numbers are listed in the Appendix.

To ensure your grandchild has some basic living expenses when you die, an additional life insurance policy in your grandchild's name is a good investment. Many of us who thought our child-rearing days were over find that is not so. But always remember the time you spend with a grandchild and the energy you put into the relationship will pay off a thousand-fold for both you and your lucky grandchild.

ESTATE PLANNING

All of us need to have plans outlined for when we are no longer alive. This is particularly true if you have a grandchild with special needs and want to be sure that some provisions are made for the child. Planning should never be put off. Most people don't like to think about the end of life, but unless we make provisions about our estate, someone else may take over and make sure everything goes into their bank account. This happens far too often and may be by someone who has had no real involvement with you, but sees an opportunity to steal from your estate.

The questions below will help you start getting things in order if you have not already done so.

1. Do you have a will that is up-to-date, signed and witnessed?

2. Have you made financial provisions for each of your grandchildren and particularly your special needs grandchild?

3. Have you designated an executor?

4. Does someone close to you know where you keep your important papers?

5. Is the location of your safe deposit known, if you have one?

6. Do you have life insurance payable to your grandchild or grandchildren?

7. Is money immediately available for your grandchild on your death if he or she lives with you?

8. Do you have a guardian designated for your grandchild if this is necessary?

9. Do family members or someone close to you know where you keep your bank account or accounts?

10. Do you have a family member's name on your bank account along with yours?

11. Do you have a notarized Living Will and Advance Medical Directive?

12. Are your papers in good order, so they can be easily accessed?

13. Do you have a list of credit cards, your social security number, and other financial information in a special place?

14. Have you made provisions for someone to take over the care of your grandchild if this will be necessary?

An easy way to put things in order is to use a three-ring notebook that has dividers. Each divider can have a different label as: Will, insurance papers, trust papers, numbers to call, list of credit cards to be cancelled, location of bank account or accounts, and any other important information your executor or heirs will need.

If you have done all of these things, you can relax and know that you have done the very best you can in the event of your death. If an estate attorney has helped with your estate plans, then this individual will be able to offer invaluable help to your children and grandchildren. I am sure they will be extremely grateful that you have done your best to leave things in good condition. Those of us who have had to spend many hours sorting through a family member's papers would salute you for a job well done. A relative's death is hard enough to handle without the added problems of having to sort through stacks of messy legal and other papers.

Section IV

YOU NEED TIME TOO

Chapter Twenty

Time Out for Grandparents

If you are responsible for your grandchild for a few hours, a few days each week, or have full-time care, your own needs may get pushed aside. How do you establish right from the start that you are important and that your needs must be taken into consideration?

One grandmother became so stressed by the care of a grandchild with multiple disabilities that she backed her car out of the garage and didn't check to be sure the back car doors were both firmly closed. One car door was not quite shut and as the grandmother backed out of the garage, it swung open and was severely damaged. A tow-truck had to be called to take the car in for expensive repairs. The grandmother told me she was extremely tired, was worried about her grandchild and hadn't been paying attention. She said she learned a good lesson from that stressful, expensive experience and didn't let herself get that tired again.

WEEKLY APPOINTMENTS

I have always advised caretaking parents and grandparents to make weekly appointments with themselves in order to have time away from caring for their homes, kids, and grandchildren. A good idea is to find a special place to go as for a cup of coffee or tea, browse in a bookstore, sit in a beautiful park, visit a historical area, walk on a beach, or window shop on a fun street.

If you take along a thermos of coffee or tea, a book, some paints, or knitting, you might find just being alone in a quiet, beautiful place can recharge your batteries and put life back in a better perspective. You could also meet a good friend for a movie, lunch, coffee, or a walk.

MEDICAL CARE

There are several things that grandparents may not think about if they are leading stressful lives. Physicians, too, can be at fault for not knowing how stressed a grandparent might be and not make recommendations for good preventive health measures.

Shingles is something you certainly don't want to get and a vaccine is available to prevent this painful and often prolonged illness that occurs in fifty percent of the cases. The vaccine can also lessen the intense pain of shingles. The vaccine is called Zostavax in the U.S. and is made by Merck pharmaceutical company. Only individuals who have had chicken pox can get shingles and you can't catch it from someone else. The accurate name for shingles is Herpes Zoster. Shingles can cause headache, chills, sometimes pneumonia, hearing problems, and encephalitis. This vaccine is expensive, but is offered by some U.S. pharmacies and your doctor may be able to give it to you. I have been told that some insurance companies will pay for the vaccine, so that would be worthwhile to check.

A **Pneumonia** shot is also important for older grandparents, particularly those with respiratory or breathing problems. The injection has to be repeated every five years, but many pharmacists now give them, so they are easy to obtain and don't require a doctor's prescription.

Regular yearly checkups are important and should include a flu shot, basic blood work, and a urinalysis. A yearly chest X-ray is a good idea for smokers and women should have yearly mammograms. Older men should have a PSA blood test regularly to screen for prostate cancer. Eye examinations on a regular basis are important for older grandparents. If there is a question of hearing loss, many cities have centers where hearing can be checked at little expense. Hearing aids are also available, often at little cost, through special hearing centers.

Diabetes and hypertension (increased blood pressure) should be carefully monitored. If you have a family history of either of these, it is wise to be even more careful if unusual symptoms develop.

For older grandparents who do not want to develop cataracts, my excellent ophthalmologist tells me that it is important for us to always wear a hat and sunglasses when we are outdoors. He said that the ultra-violet rays help cataracts to develop. This was new information to me and is worth remembering.

NUTRITION

Because increased weight gain can result in difficulty with backs, hips and knees, it is important to watch your diet as you get older. If you are on an unpalatable, restricted diet, you may find yourself wanting to have a special treat now and then. It would be wise to check with your doctor about what you can have. You could also check with a dietitian at your local hospital.

There is such a major problem with obesity these days in the United States that careful watch of your calorie intake is important. If you develop health problems because of overeating, you are not going to be able to take care of your grandchild. How you eat can also reflect on how you feed a grandchild. You may need to re-learn some of your cooking skills or even take a cooking class. I am told that there are also some good cooking programs on television that could be helpful.

EXERCISE

Swimming or walking are the best to provide good exercise. *One grandmother was concerned about her rapid weight gain and started walking forty minutes twice a day. She lost twenty-five pounds and felt better, looked better, and lowered her blood pressure.*

Health clubs and some big hotels have swimming pools and gyms. In the U.K., a good way to locate a gym or health club is at: www.abouthealthclubs.co.uk. In the U.S., most YWCAs and YMCAs have inexpensive gyms and some have swimming pools.

If you don't like machines, as I don't, then you need to find the kind of exercise that works best for you. Dancing and ballet are fun and work well for some people. A used stationary bicycle can be purchased, so one doesn't have to be too elaborate or expensive.

The most important thing to remember is that you are the one who has to take care of yourself. Getting enough sleep, proper medical care and exercise and finding ways to have fun are all important. Finding a balance in life is hard for everyone, but when you are older and have the care of a special grandchild, it is even more important to take very good care of yourself.

Chapter Twenty-One

Planning for the Future

Once our children became adults, few of us ever envisioned that we could again be in a caretaking role. We thought we would probably have to care for our parents when they became old or other older relatives who needed us, but not a grandchild with special needs. When faced with this reality, plans need to be made both for the grandchild and for ourselves. By thinking and writing about some of the questions below, you can be sure everything possible has been done for you, your children and grandchildren and the grandchild with special needs.

1. Is there anything else I need to do to ensure the well-being of my special needs grandchild?

2. Have I overlooked the needs of any of my grandchildren?

3. Are my papers and finances in order in case I become ill or have an injury?

4. Do I have a good medical support system?

5. Have I been as active as I can be in supporting individuals with special needs? For example, writing, calling, or e-mailing my representatives in Congress about special issues or being an active member of the organization that is specifically interested in my grandchild's problem?

6. Do I have a Living Will and an Advanced Medical Directive?

7. What special memories will my grandchild have of me?

8. Have I done everything I can to help my grandchild be as independent as possible?

9. Have I done all I can to help boost my grandchild's self-esteem?

10. Are there other things I can do to help the parents have a better quality of life, including some time for fun and vacations?

11. Have I planned enough time for myself to have some fun and recreation?

All any of us can do is our best and sometimes the circumstances, our health, finances and other things work against us. But if you offer unconditional love and support to your grandchild and his or her parents, you will have made a tremendous contribution that will long be remembered.

Section V

HELP FROM OTHERS

Chapter Twenty-Two

Questionnaire Answers from Grandparents and Parents

The grandparents of a special needs grandchild and the parents of that child generally have wisdom and advice that is invaluable. Because of this, the director of a special needs agency kindly sent out the questionnaire I devised to see what advice grandparents and parents would offer. The results were informative and I wanted to share some of the replies with readers. All gave excellent answers to my questions.

GRANDPARENTS' REPLIES

One grandmother, who is also a great-grandmother, wrote: *"The hardest thing about being the grandparent of a special needs child is the worry about what will happen to the child after his parents pass away. Also, the realization that our government is not spending enough money on research and help for the education and health of these children."*

❀

Another grandmother, who lives at a distance from her grandchild said, *"After twenty years of having my granddaughter in the family, I think I have accepted her situation, and felt that there was little worrying I could do about her or her future. I know her parents have made provisions for her future."* She also said, *"Having my grandchild being so far away has been difficult for me. When I am with my grand-daughter and her brother, I do find time for one-to-one with both of them."*

A grandmother, who was instrumental in finding the expert who diagnosed her grandchild's problem, sent me some very wise words. She said: *"The news that a child will have special needs, possibly forever, must be met with an instant attitude adjustment. We plan no pity parties. We plan on walking side by side with our grandchild's parents and enjoying our sense of family."*

In answer to my question about any financial plans for their grandchild, she said, *"The Special Needs Trust is something we are looking into at this time, but only in conjunction with the kids* [the parents]. *It will be a single document that is part of our will and perhaps in the form of a specialized trust. Our estate is simple and we trust our son to manage whatever funds may be available."*

A wise grandmother wrote: *"Trying to refrain from fixing everything with my expert advice is the hardest thing about being the grandparent of a child with special needs."* She said she handled the grief and worry about her grandchild by *"Crying and trying to find answers." "My greatest support is from friends at work and we have a network for families with special needs."*

A grandmother, who is her grandchild's primary caretaker during the day, sent me some wise and helpful replies. She wrote: *"Our daughter works full-time, so we are full-time grandparents until she is home from work. Our grandson has breakfast before we take him to school and we help him with his homework after school. When Mom comes home from work, we eat dinner together. So, we feel our help brings security and a sense of stability to his life. This is, of course, with the great guidance our daughter gives him also."*

In answer to my question about how they handle their grief and worry, she said: *"We try to be positive thinkers instead of 'worriers'. So, one of the things we do is keep in constant contact with his teachers."*

The grandmother's advice about how grandparents should take care of themselves when caring for a grandchild with special needs was: *"Rest! Rest! Rest! And keep your minds sharp, for these wonderful, special little ones have many, many very intelligent questions."*

Some wise replies were sent by a grandmother of a boy with cerebral palsy. She noted that *"The hardest thing about being a grandparent* [of a child with special needs] *is to see the child struggle in order to do what we consider simple things of life. My husband and I spend lots of one-to-one time with all three of the grandchildren. Our grandson's sisters are thirteen and fourteen years old. It was not until last year that they began asking questions about what was wrong with our grandson. We spoke openly about him and his condition. They were primarily interested at that time as to why is he the way he is? Our primary concern is will people mistreat or take advantage of him. The only way of handling concerns is through prayer and taking each day at a time—don't look too far into the future."*

In answer to my question about how to take care of themselves or their grandchild, she replied: "[We] *give our grandson the attention he needs to be as normal a child as possible. Let him have experiences that other children his age experience. Go out into the woods and touch trees, get dirty, and play in a pile of sawdust. My husband and I take short trips to get away for a while to refresh."*

How fortunate this mother and grandchildren are to have such loving, wise grandparents.

❀

A grandmother who lives across the United States from her only grandchild said: *"The most difficult aspect of being the grandparent of* ------- *is that she is so far away. I know living in California makes their lives much easier. This makes me feel good for them. But I am sad that it is so difficult for me to be with them, especially on special occasions like holidays, and, recently, my granddaughter's graduation. It is difficult for me to understand my granddaughter over the phone, so we cannot communicate with each other as I would like to be able to do. Another difficulty is not being able to take care of her since I can no longer lift her or support her physically. My granddaughter has never spoken to me about her illness. My heart aches constantly for my daughter and the pain she is suffering."*

❀

When I asked about special memories, a grandmother who is very involved and helpful with her granddaughter and the brother and sister replied: *"My favorite memory is of working with a PT with* [my granddaughter] *when we were trying to get her to sit up. We tried again and again—to no avail. Finally, one day she did it—and Carrie (PT) and I whooped and hollered as if we had won the lottery!"*

A very caring and involved grandmother wrote that she has learned to work the pump for her grandson's feeding tube, even though she is not completely comfortable doing so. (That takes a lot of courage and determination.) In answer to my question if the siblings opened up and talked with her, she wrote, *"Yes,* [my granddaughter], *the five-year-old, finds me a safety valve and asked me many questions that obviously she doesn't want to ask her parents."* What a lucky child! When I asked where the grandmother got her support, she wrote, "I get my support from being a stoic at heart and from my friends and from my daughter with her incredible courage."

PARENTS' REPLIES

One mother wrote: *"My father was supportive and actually came to medical appointments. He also helped us when our daughter was born and we had extensive medical bills and my husband needed a new car. When it became clear that my daughter would never learn to ride a bike, my father got her an adult trike."*

A father answered my questions with many helpful thoughts. He wrote: *"The best way my parents can help is by being hands-on and asking: 'How can we help?' As the parents of a child with autism, my wife and I don't like having to ask for help as often as we must. But yet, many times we have to rely on others. I wish my parents would educate themselves better not only about their grandson's disability, but about children with disabilities in general. I wish they would vote accordingly in state and federal elections and be more outspoken advocates by going to IEP meetings."*

A single parent mother with one child said, *"My father hasn't taken the time to understand the behaviors of autism that causes my son to say or do certain things. He automatically thinks he is being disrespectful, etc. It's understanding the world through their eyes that will help grandparents understand and know how to deal with certain behaviors."*

One mother of several children with special needs said she didn't have time to sit down and write answers to the questionnaire, but asked if I would call her. When I did, she gave me some good insight to the problems of having many kids with special needs. *Her advice to grandparents was that they accept and try to understand their grandchildren with special needs. If they deny there is a problem, they hurt the children and their parents. She added that it is important that one child not be favored over the other, as happens with her children's grandparents. This particular boy is still "spoon fed" by his grandmother, even though he can eat by himself without difficulty.*

The mother feels her parents are embarrassed by having grandchildren with special needs. Also, they often intrude and make comments in front of the kids that are hurtful. She wishes they would spend some real time with the children, such as playing games or having fun with them. Instead, the grandmother is good about babysitting and doing household chores which the mother greatly appreciates, but she feels some fun time with the children would be more important.

Another reply gave important insight to the problem of gifts. This mother wrote that *"Gift certificates were sent to our older sons, ages fifteen and twelve, for $50 each for Best Buy (an electronics store). In an effort to treat our son with special needs 'just the same,' they gave him a $50 gift certificate to Best Buy also. My son with autism is ten years old, but developmentally, he is about three. No three-year-old needs $50 to spend—much less to an electronics store. In a way, purchasing the Best Buy certificate was almost as if they refused to acknowledge their grandson's disability or to pretend it doesn't matter. But that's not something we can easily discuss."*

A mother of a child with multiple disabilities wrote in answer to my question about how a grandparent can help, *"My mother lives close to me and it is fantastic. When my son gets hospitalized, it is rarely with notice. She has been great about having to run and pick up my daughter from school, pack clothes for me, and generally make it so I do not have to worry about my daughter and can focus on my son."* In answer to the question about what she would wish that grandparents not do this mother said, *"My husband's parents try to make it seem like all will be okay despite evidence to the contrary. That is frustrating as I feel they can't be supportive if they are just always trying to make us feel better."* She said that, *"I wish they [the grandparents] called more. They always say they don't want to intrude since they know we have so much going on, but it would be so great for my husband and all of us to talk to them more. They have just recently seemed to figure*

out how stressful it is with all the appointments and therapies and endless hours on the feedings pump and so are more empathic." Her final thoughts were: "We experience isolation from our peers, anger at everything (god, fate, whatever) for this happening and having to become experts in a field you know nothing about. Grandparents are similar. They are grieving for their grandchild, as well as for their child. They see the pain their child is going through and do not know how to help."

A mother of four children, in replying to my question about what she wished grandparents would not do, said: "I do not like it when 'special' treatment is given, i.e. allowing tantrums, getting his way, making brothers/cousins be careful with him, etc. It's not good for my son and it's not good for the rest of the children. They do not fully grasp the situation and I think it's better to treat everybody equally."

A mother of a child with multiple problems made it very clear what an important role grandparents can play. In her situation, one of the grandmothers was very helpful at first, but then when "it became a life-long thing," the grandmother distanced herself and "she became hands off." This grandmother has not seen her lovely granddaughter for several years and it hurts her daughter and granddaughter terribly. Kids are very sensitive to a relative's withdrawal, particularly if it is a grandmother.

In answer to how a grandparent did not help, the mother wrote, "My mother would make reservations at a restaurant for as late as seven o'clock, because she feels it is easier to eat out. We have to take my daughter's food with us, a chair for her to sit in, and it is too late for a kid who needs a lot of sleep. My mother thinks the answer for everything is to get a sitter. She has no idea how difficult it is to get one or travel with our daughter. We do it, but it is tough and there is a lot of planning ahead that needs to happen. We just can't move as quickly as most families."

She added that she hoped if she were ever in the same situation she would put herself in her child's situation and think "How can I help" and do what she was asked to do, rather than what she thought needed to be accomplished. Her final touching statement was "I think the biggest need for me is to be able to get away with my husband. I don't want to leave my daughter with a sitter. If she were staying home with Grandma, it could be special, like their times together when she was younger. I know that can't happen, so I have tried to adjust my expectations of my mother, but when I hear of friends going on a getaway with their husband, I still think about it."

One mother told of their struggles with a daughter who has Angelman Syndrome. She noted that the child is *"completely non-verbal and profoundly mentally retarded. She also has severe epilepsy."* She recalls *"a weekend when the seizures were coming one on top of the other and* [her daughter] *required constant care. As soon as I told my folks, they whisked the other two kids away, so we could take care of our daughter and the other two could have a good time!"* *"She does not sleep well unless she's in an enclosed bed; she's prone to wandering. My in-laws allowed us, with no questions asked, to add hooks for doors and to build a gate for her bottom bunk."* This mother's final thoughts were: *"I do believe one reason things go so smoothly with our parents is that I'm not afraid to ask."* Then she added an important thought, *"Don't talk about the child with a disability in a different tone of voice."* *"All of our children, regardless of whether they have a disability, have special needs (and so do adults)."*

I felt very sad for the parents, the grandparents, and grandchild after reading the reply from one mother. In answer to my questions about the best way grandparents can help with the child with special needs or brothers or sisters, the mother said: *"Frankly, they do so little, I would not even know what the best help would be."* She went on to say that *"I wish and wish they would acknowledge that there are invisible disorders and despite our children's and our best efforts, there will be some limitations. I wish that they would recognize and accept our unique ways of doing things. I have explained again and again that we often can finish the race, but we just have to figure out new ways to actually get there."*

In answer to my question about accepting all the grandchildren or if the child with special needs was treated differently, this mother said, *"Yes, they treat her differently, almost push her away—I believe because they are finally acknowledging her differences, and I believe (shoot, I almost hope) that they are feeling just a tad guilty."* When I asked what she would like the grandparents to offer if they lived at a distance, she said, *"Just to listen—that would be huge."*

In the mother's reply to my question about how the grandparents reacted when they were told of their grandchild's special problem, she wrote, *"They totally ignored it—they actually avoided us and spent more time with other family members—again I am assuming it is a coping-skill—but difficult for us to swallow none the less."*

The mother's final suggestion about how grandparents can offer the best help was: *"Try to reach outside their own learning to step into the world I must learn—it can be lonely."*

Epilogue

A physical, emotional, or developmental disability can make a child feel lonely and isolated. Helping a grandchild develop good self-esteem, while learning to communicate and interact with family and friends, is an important role for grandparents. Parenting a child with special needs can be a daunting task that presents major on-going obstacles. Grandparents can take over or help in many ways. By providing love and support to the parents and grandchild, you can make a world of difference in a family's life.

Grandparents can also provide a sense of history and tradition that gives a grandchild a feeling of rootedness and belonging. Life in some families becomes so fragmented that the children feel they don't matter. When this happens, they look for ways to stand out or be counted by taking drugs or becoming involved in other kinds of destructive behavior. A grandchild who is loved and treasured will be able to overcome many more obstacles than a child who feels unloved and unwanted. A grandparent's love is very special and will be long remembered.

APPENDIX

APPENDIX

Helpful Web Sites

ACCESSIBILITY AND WHEELCHAIR AIDS

Automatic Door Openers
www.power-access.com

Therapeutic Seating Systems
www.ergoair.com (Has an online catalog)

ASSISTIVE TECHNOLOGY

National Technical Assistance Center
www.taalliance.org

BOOKS FOR SPECIAL NEEDS

www.specialneeds.com

CAR SEATS

www.carseat.org
National Highway Traffic Safety
Administration
www.nhtsa.gov

CHILD CARE SITES

Safe Sitter (Information for teen sitters)
www.SafeSitter.org
www.lovingnannies.com
www.naccrra.org

CLOTHING

www.oddshoefinder.com
www.ableapparel.com
www.dignitybydesign.com

DISCIPLINE

www.growingchild.com

EDUCATION

www.naeyc.org

HEAD START

www.nhsa.org

HEALTH RELATED SITES

www.kidshealth.org
www.onhealth.org
www.keepkidshealthy.com
www.healthfinder.gov

Diabetes Information
www.childrenwithdiabetes.com

Allergy and Asthma Information
www.allergynetwork.com
www.allergykids.com

American Academy of Allergy, Asthma,
and Immunology
www.aaaai.org

Information for Overweight Kids
www.kidnetic.com

Health Insurance Comparisons
www.eHealthInsurance.com

HEALTHY EATING

American Dietetic Association
www.eatright.org

IMMUNIZATIONS

www.immunizationinfo.org
www.cdc.gov/vaccines
www.immunisation.nhs.uk

LEARNING DISABILITIES
www.dyslexia-parent.com
www.chadd.org
www.ldonline.org
www.schwablearning.org
www.dyslexia.com
www.texthelp.com

MILITARY FAMILIES
www.militarychild.org

MISSING KIDS
www.missingkids.com

MULTIPLE BIRTHS
www.nomotc.org

NEUROMUSCULAR DISORDERS
Periodic Paralysis
www.periodicparalysis.org

Charcot-Marie-Tooth
www.charcot-marie-tooth.org

Facioscapulohumeral Muscular Dystrophy
www.fshsociety.org

Duchenne Muscular Dystrophy
www.parentprojectmd.org

Spinal Muscular Atrophy
www.fsma.org

Congenital Fiber-Type Disproportion
http://children.webmd.com/fiber-type-disproportion-congenital

Myotubular Myopathy
www.mtmrg.org

Prader-Willi
www.pwsausa.org

Nemaline Rod
www.nemalinefoundation.org

PRODUCT SAFETY
www.cpsc.gov

RECALLS
www.recalls.gov

RESOURCE CENTERS
www.lydc.org

SAFETY
Resource to look for neighborhood sexual predators
www.familywatchdog.us

www.safeteens.com
www.webwisekids.org

SPORTS
National Disability Sports Alliance
www.nscd.org

STEP-FAMILIES
www.stepfamily.org
www.stepfamilyinfo.org
www.stepfamilies.com

TRAVEL INFORMATION
Travel Access for Disabled Travelers
www.access-able.com

U.S. Agencies for Children with Special Needs

Abused Children
Childhelp
2346 Central Ave.
Phoenix, AZ 85004-1329
1-800-4-A-CHILD
www.childhelp.org

Adopted Children
Adopted Families of America, Inc.
P.O. Box 37006
Charlotte, NC 28237-7006
www.spafa.org

Aicardi Syndrome
Aicardi Syndrome Newsletter, Inc.
5115 Troy Urbane Road
Casstown, OH 45312-9711
1-513-339-6033

Amputees
National Amputee Foundation
40 Church St.
Malverne, NY 11565
1-516-887-3600
www.americanamputee.org

Amputee Coalition of America
900 East Hill Ave.
Suite 205
Knoxville, TN 37915-2566
1-888-267-5669
www.amputee-coalition.org

Limbs for Life Foundation
5929 N. Main
Suite 511
Oklahoma City, OK 73112
1-888-235-5462
www.limbsforlife.org

Angelman Syndrome
Angelman Syndrome Foundation

414 Plaza Drive
Suite 209
Westmont, IL 60559
1-800-432-6435
www.angelman.org

Arthritis
Arthritis Foundation
P.O. Box 7669
Atlanta, GA 30357-0669
1-800-283-7800
www.arthritis.org

Arthrogryposis
Arthrogryposis Multiplex Congenita
Support
P.O. Box 1883
Salyersville, KY 41465
www.amcsupport.org

Ataxia
National Ataxia Foundation
2600 Fernbrook lane
Suite 119
Minneapolis, MN 55447
1-763-553-0020
www.ataxia.org

Auditory Processing Disorders
National Coalition on Auditory
Processing Disorders, Inc.
P.O. Box 490
Rockville Centre, NY 1157-9494
www.ncapd.org

Autism
Autism Society of America
7900 Woodmont Ave.
Suite 300
Bethesda, MD 20814-3067
www.autism-society.org

Birth Defects
Association of Birth Defect Children, Inc.
930 Woodcock Road
Suite 225
Orlando, FL 32803
1-407-245-7035
www.independentliving.org

Birth Defects Research for Children, Inc.
800 Celebration Avenue
Suite 225
Celebration, FL 34747
1-407-566-8341
www.birthdefects.org

March of Dimes
1275 Mamaroneck Ave.
White Plains, NY 10605
1-914-997-4488
www.marchofdimes.com

Easter Seals Society
230 W. Monroe St.
Suite 1800 Chicago, IL 60606
1-800-221-6827
www.easterseals.com

Bipolar Disorder
Bipolar Kids Foundation
1000 Skokie Blvd.
Suite 570
Wilmette, IL 60091
1-847-256-8525
www.bpkids.org

Bipolar Support Group
P.O. Box 184
Deer Lodge, TN 37726
www.supportgroup.net/bipolar

Blindness
Helen Keller National Center
141 Middle Neck Road
Sands Point, NY 11050-1218
1-516-944-8900
www.hknc.org

The National Federation of the Blind
1800 Johnson Street
Baltimore, MD 21230
1-410-659-9314
www.blind.net

Recording for the Blind and Dyslexic
20 Rozel Road
Princeton, NJ 08540
1-866-732-3585
www.rfbd.org

Brain Tumors
National Brain Tumor Foundation
22 Battery Street
Suite 612
San Francisco, CA 94111-5520
1-800-934-2873
www.braintumor.org

Cancer
Candlelighters Childhood Cancer
Foundation
P.O. Box 498
Kensington, MD 20895-0498
1-800-355-2223
www.candlelighters.org

Carnitine Deficiency
Assistance for Babies and Children with
Carnitine Deficiency
1010 Jorie Blvd.
Suite 234
Oakbrook, IL 60521
1-800-554-2223

Celiac Disease
Celiac Disease Foundation
13251 Ventura Blvd.
Suite #1
Studio City, CA 91604-1838
1-818-990-2354
www.celiac.org

American Celiac Society
5p Crystal Avenue
West Orange, NJ 07052-4114
1-973-325-8837

Gluten Intolerance Group of North
America
15110 Tenth Avenue
Suite A
Seattle, WA 98166-1820
1-206-246-6652
www.gluten.net

Cerebral Palsy
United Cerebral Palsy
1660 L Street-NW
Suite 700
Washington DC 20036-5602
1-800-872-5827
www.ucp.org

Charcot-Marie-Tooth Syndrome
Charcot-Marie-Tooth Association
2700 Chestnut Street
Chester, PA 19013
1-800-606-2682
www.charcot-marie-tooth.org

CHARGE Syndrome
CHARGE Syndrome Foundation, Inc.
2004 Parkade Blvd.
Columbia, MD 65202-3121
1-800-442-7604
www.chargesyndrome.org

Chromosome Deletions
Chromosome Deletion Outreach, Inc.
P.O. Box 724
Boca Raton, FL 33429-0724
1-561-395-4252
www.chromodisorder.org

Cleft Lip and Palate
Prescription Parents, Inc.
45 Brentwood Circle
Needham, MA 02492
1-617-499-1536
www.samizdat.com/pp1.html

Cleft Palate Foundation
1504 E. Franklin Street
Suite 102
Chapel Hill, NC 27514-2820
1-919-933-9044
www.cleftline.org

Cornelia de Lange Syndrome
Cornelia de Lange Syndrome Foundation
302 West Main Street
Suite 100
Avon, CT 06001
1-800-223-8355
www.cdlsusa.org

Cri-Du-Chat Syndrome
5P- Society
1-888-970-0777
www.fivepminus.org

Cystic Fibrosis
Cystic Fibrosis Foundation
6931 Arlington Rd.
Bethesda, MD 20814
1-800-344-4823
www.cff.org

Deafness
American Society for Deaf Children
3820 Hartzdale Drive
Camp Hill, PA 17011
1-800-942-2732
www.deafchildren.org

National Institute on Deafness & Other
Communication Disorders
NIH Bldg. 31, Room 3C35
Bethesda, MD 20892
1-800-241-1044

John Tracy Clinic
806 West Adams Blvd.
Los Angeles, CA 90007
1-800-522-4582

Dentistry
National Foundation of Dentistry for the
Handicapped
1800 15th St.
Suite 100
Denver, CO 80202
1-303-534-5360
www.nfdh.org

Academy of Dentistry for Persons with
Disabilities
401 N. Michigan Ave.
Suite 2200
Chicago, IL 60611
1-312-527-6764

American Academy of Pediatric Dentistry
211 E. Chicago Ave.–Suite 1700
Chicago, IL 60611-2637

Diabetes
Juvenile Diabetes Research Foundation
International
129 Wall St.
19th Floor
New York, NY 10003
1-800-533-2873
www.ChildrensDiabetesFdn.org

Disabilities
National Parent Network on Disabilities
1727 King Street
Alexandria, VA 22314
1-703-684-6763
e-mail: npnd@cs.com

American Association of People with
Disabilities
1629 K Street NW
Suite 503
Washington DC 20006
1-800-849-8844
www.aapd.com

Down Syndrome
National Down Syndrome Congress
1370 Center Drive
Suite 102
Atlanta, GA 30338
1-800-232-6372
www.ndsccenter.org

National Down Syndrome Society
666 Broadway
New York, NY 10012
1-800-221-4602
www.ndss.org

Dysautonomia
Dysautonomia Foundation
315 W. 39th St.
Suite 701
New York, NY 10018
1-212-279-1066
www.familialdysautonomia.org

Education
Special Education Legal Resources
www.wrightslaw.com

Ehlers-Danlos
Ehlers-Danlos Foundation
3200 Wilshire Blvd.

Suite 1601 South Tower
1-213-368-3800
www.ednf.org

Employment
Equal Opportunity Employment
Commission
1801 L Street NW
Washington DC 20507
1-202-663-4900
1-800-669-4000

Epilepsy
American Epilepsy Society
342 N. Main St.
West Hartford, CT 06117-2507
www.aesnet.org

Epilepsy Foundation
8301 Professional Place
Landover, MD 20785
1-800-332-1000
www.epilepsyfoundation.org

Facial Differences
AboutFace
P.O. Box 93
Limekiln, PA 19535
1-800-225-3223

Children's Craniofacial Association
9441 LBJ Freeway
Suite 115-LB46
Dallas, TX 75243
1-800-535-3643

Fetal Alcohol Syndrome
Fetal Alcohol Support Family Resource
Institute
P.O. Box 2525
Lynwood, WA 98036
1-253-531-2878

Fragile X Syndrome
National Fragile X Foundation
P.O. Box 190488
San Francisco, CA 94119
1-800-688-8765
www.nfxf.org and www.fraxa.org

Galactosemia
Parents of Galactosemic Children, Inc.
P.O. Box 2461
Mandeville, LA
1-855-900-PGC1
www.galactosemia.org

Gaucher Disease
National Gaucher Foundation
11140 Rockville Pike-Suite 101
Rockville, MD 20852-3106
1-800-925-8885

Glycogen Storage Disease
Association of Glycogen Storage Diseases
P.O. Box 896
Durant, IA 52747
1-563-785-6038
www.agsdus.org

Growth Disorders
Little People of America
P.O. Box 750
Hillsboro, OR 97123
1-888-LPA-2001
www.lpaonline.org

Health Resources
Resources for Children with Special
Needs
116 E. Sixteenth Street
New York, NY 10003
1-212-677-0606
www.resourcesnyc.org

Federation for Children with Special
Needs
Tremont Street
Suite 420
Boston, MA 02120
1-800-331-0688
www.fcsn.org

Hearing Disorders
The Children's Hearing Institute
310 East 14th Street
New York, NY 10003
1-212-614-8380

Cochlear Implant Awareness Foundation
3109 Beaver Creek Lane
Springfield, IL 62712
www.ciafonline.org

Hemophilia
National Hemophilia Foundation
116 W.32nd St.
11th Floor
New York, NY 10001
1-800-43-HANDI
www.hemophilia.org

Huntington's Disease
Huntington's Disease Society
505 8th Ave.
Suite 902
New York, NY 10018
1-800-345-4372
www.hdsa.org

Hydrocephalus
Hydrocephalus Association
870 Market St.
Suite 705
San Francisco, CA 94102
1-888-598-3789
www.hydroassoc.org

Independent Living
National Council on Independent Living
1700 Rhode Island Avenue NW
Washington D.C. 20036
1-877-525-3400
www.ncil.org

Kidney Disease
National Kidney Foundation
30 E. 33rd St.
New York, NY 10016
1-800-622-9010
www.kidney.org

Learning Disabilities
National Center for Learning Disabilities
381 Park Ave. S.
Suite 1401
New York, NY 10016
1-888-575-7373
www.ncld.org

Leukemia
Leukemia and Lymphoma Society of
America, Inc.
1311 Manaroneck Ave.
Suite 310
White Plains, NY 10505
1-800-955-4572
www.leukemia.org

Liver Disease
American Liver Foundation
75 Maiden Lane
Suite 603
New York, NY 10038
1-212-668-1000
www.liverfoundation.org

Children's Liver Association
27023 McBean Parkway
Suite 126
Valencia, CA 91355
1-877-679-8256
www.classkids.org

Lupus
Lupus Foundation of America, Inc.
2000 L Street N.W.–Suite 710
Washington DC 20036
1-800-558-0121
www.lupus.org

Malignant Hyperthermia
Malignant Hyperthermia Association of
the United States
11 East State Street
P.O. Box 1069
Sherbourne, NY 13460
1-607-674-7901
www.mhaus.org

Marfan's Syndrome
National Marfan Foundation
22 Manhasset Ave.
Port Washington, NY 11050
1-800-862-7326
www.marfan.org

Mental Illness
National Alliance on Mental Illness
(NAMI)
Colonial Place Three
2107 Wilson Blvd-Suite 300
Arlington, VA 22201-3042
1-888-999-6264
www.nami.org

Muscle Diseases
Muscular Dystrophy Association
3300 E. Sunrise Drive
Tucson, AZ 85718
1-520-529-2000
www.mda.org

Muscular Dystrophy Family Foundation
2330 N. Meridian St.
Indianapolis, IN 462087
1-800-544-1213
www.mdff.org

Myasthenia Gravis
Myasthenia Gravis Foundation
1821 University Avenue West
Suite S256
St. Paul, MN 55104
1-800-541-5454
www.myasthenia.org

Neurofibromatosis
Neurofibromatosis, Inc.
P.O. Box 18246
Minneapolis, MN 55418
1-800-942-6825
www.nfinc.org

Organ Transplants
Children's Organ Transplant Association
2501 West COTA Drive
Bloomington, IN 47403
1-800-366-2682
www.cota.org

Osteogenesis Imperfecta
Osteogenesis Imperfecta Foundation
804 W. Diamond Ave.
Suite 210
Gaithersburg, MD 20878
1-800-981-2663
www.oif.org

Paget's Disease
National Paget's Disease Foundation
120 Wall Street
Suite 1602
New York, NY 10005-4001
1-800-23-PAGET
www.paget.org

Prader-Willi Syndrome
Prader-Willi Syndrome Association
8588 Potter Park Drive
Suite 500
Sarasota, FL 34238
1-800-926-4797
www.pwsausa.org

Premature Infants
American Association of Premature
Infants
P.O. Box 6920
Cincinnati, OH 45206
1-513-956-4331
www.prematurity.org

Rare Diseases
National Association of Rare Diseases
55 Kenosia Ave.
P.O. Box 1968
Danbury, CT 06810
1-800-999-6673
www.rarediseases.org

Retinitis Pigmentosa
National Retinitis Pigmentosa Foundation
11350 McCormick Road
Suite 800
Hunt Valley, MD 21031-1002
1-800-638-5683 (TTY)
www.blindness.org

Rett Syndrome
International Rett Syndrome Association
4600 Devitt Drive
Cincinnati, OH 45246
1-800-818-7388
www.rettsyndrome.org

Scleroderma
United Scleroderma Foundation, Inc.
300 Rosewood Drive
Suite 105
Danvers, MA 01923
1-800-722-4673
www.scleroderma.org

Scoliosis
National Scoliosis Foundation, Inc.
Five Cabot Place
Stoughton, MA 02072
1-800-673-6922
www.scoliosis.org

Short Stature
Little People of America, Inc.
250 El Camino Real
Suite 201
Tustin, CA 92780
1-888-LPA-2001
www.lpaonline.org

Sickle Cell Disease
Sickle Cell Disease Association
231 East Baltimore Street
Suite 800
Baltimore, MD 21202
1-800-421-8453
www.sicklecelldisease.org

Sleep Apnea
American Sleep Apnea Association
1424 K Street NW
Suite 302
Washington DC 20005
1202-293-3650
www.sleepapnea.org

Spina Bifida
Spina Bifida Association
4590 MacArthur Blvd NW
Washington DC 20007
1-800-621-3141
www.sbaa.org

Spinal Atrophy
Families of Spinal Muscular Atrophy
P.O. Box 196
Libertyville, IL 60048-0198
1-800-886-1762
www.fsma.org

Spinal Cord Injury
Christopher Reeve Paralysis Foundation
636 Morris Turnpike
Suite 3 A
Short Hills, NJ 07078
1-800-225-0292
www.christopherreeve.org

Sturge-Weber Syndrome
Sturge-Weber Foundation
P.O. Box 418
Mt. Freedom, NJ 07970-0488
1-800-627-5482
www.sturge-weber.org

Stuttering
Stuttering Foundation
3100 Walnut Grove Road
Suite 603
P.O. Box 11749
Memphis, TN 38111-0749
1-800-992-9392
www.stutteringhelp.org

National Center for Stuttering
200 E. 33rd Street
New York, NY 10016
1-800-221-2483
www.stuttering.co

Sudden Infant Death
American SIDS Institute
509 Augusta Drive
Marietta, GA 30067
1-800-232-SIDS
www.sids.org

Tourette Syndrome
Tourette Syndrome Association, Inc.
42-40 Bell Blvd.
Suite 205
Bayside, NY 11361-2820
1-717-224-2999
www.tsa-usa.org

Trisomy 18 and 13
SOFT USA
2982 South Union Street
Rochester, NY 14624
1-800-716-7683
www.trisomy.org

Turner Syndrome
Turner Syndrome Society
10960 Millridge North Drive
Suite 214A
Houston, TX 77070
1-800-365-9944
www.turnersyndrome.org

Visually Impaired
National Association for Parents of the
Visually Impaired
P.O. Box 317
Watertown, MA 02471
1-800-562-6265
www.spedex.com/napvi

U.K. Agencies for Children with Special Needs

Angelman Syndrome
Angelman Support Group
15 Place Crescent
Waterlooville
Portsmouth, Hampshire PO7 5UR
UK
01705 264224
www.angelman.uk.org

Arthritis
Arthritis Care
18 Stephenson Way
London NW1 2HD
England
020 7380 6500
www.arthritiscare.org.uk

Attention-Deficit Disorder
ADDISS
P.O. Box 340
Edgware
Middlesex HA8 9HL, UK
020 8952 2800
www.addiss.co.uk

Autism Spectrum
National Autistic Society
393 City Road
London EC1V 1NG
UK
020 7833 2299
www.nas.org.uk

Blindness
National Blind Children's Society
Second Floor
Shawton Gouse
792 Hagley Road
Birmington B68 0PJ, UK
01278 764770
www.nbcs.org.uk

Cerebral Palsy
SCOPE
6 Market Road
London N7 9PW
UK
020 7619 7100
www.scope.org.uk

Coeliac Disease
Coeliac Society of the United Kingdom
P.O. Box 220
High Wycombe, Bucks HP11 2HY
England
UK
01494 437278
www.coeliac.org.uk

Deafness
British Deaf Association
13 Wilson Patten Street
Warrington
Cheshire WA1 1PG
01925 41469
UK
www.bda.org.uk

Royal National Institute for the Deaf
19-23 Featherstone Street
London EC1V 8SL
UK
0808 808 0123
www.rnid.org.uk

Disabled Living
Disabled Living Foundation
380-384 Harrow Road
London W9 2HU, UK
020 7289 6111
0845 130 9177
www.dlf.org.uk

Disabled People's Council
0845 130 9177
www.bcodp.org.uk

Down Syndrome
Down Syndrome Association
Langdon Down Centre
2a Langdon Park
Tedding TW11 9PS
0845 230 0372
UK
www.downs-syndrome.org.uk.com

Dyslexia
British Dyslexia Association
Unit 8
Bracknell Beeches
Old Bracknell Lane
Bracknell RG12 7BW
UK
0845 251 9003
www.bdadyslexia.org.uk

Epilepsy
British Epilepsy Association
New Anstey House
Gate Way Drive
Leeds LS19 7XY
UK
0113 210 8800
www.epilepsy.org.uk

Gaucher Disease
Gauchers Association
25 West Cottages
London NW6 1RJ, UK
020 7433 1121
www.gaucher.org.uk

Heart Disease
British Heart Association
14 Fitzhardinge Street
London W1H 6DH
UK
08450 70 80 70
www.bhf.org.uk

Huntington Disease
Huntington Disease Association
Neurosupport Centre
Liverpool L3 8LR
UK
0151 298 3298
www.hda.org.uk

Independent Living
European Network on Independent
Living
www.independentliving.org/docs2/

Liver Disease
Children's Liver Disease Foundation
36 Great Charles Street
Birmingham B3 3JX, UK
0121 212 3839
www.childliverdisease.org

Marfan Syndrome
Marfan Association
Rochester House
5 Aldershot Road
Fleet
Hampshire GU51 3NG
UK
01252 810472
www.marfan-association.org.uk

Mental Health
www.sane.org.uk
www.mentalhealthcare.org.uk

Mobility Equipment
Whizz Kidz
Edward Rudolf House
Margery Street
London WC1X 0JL
UK
020 7798 6118 (or 6116)
www.whizz-kidz.org.uk

Moebius Syndrome
The Moebius Syndrome Support Group
R7 Linskill Centre
North Shields
Tyne and Wear NE30 2AY
UK
0191 296 4050
www.moebiussyndrome.co.uk

Muscle Diseases
Muscular Dystrophy Campaign
61 Southwark Street
London SE1 0HL, UK
0800 652 6352
www.muscular-dystrophy.org

Neurofibromatosis
The Neurofibromatosis Association
Quayside House
38 High Street
Kingston on Thames
Surrey KT1 1HL, UK
020 8439 1234

Nystagmus
Nystagmus Network
13 Tinsley Close
Claypole
Nottinghamshire NG23 5BS
0845 634 2630
www.nystagmusnet.org

Prader-Willi Syndrome
Prader-Willi Syndrome Association
125a London Road
Derby DE1 2QQ
UK
01332 3656756
www.pwsa.co.uk

Special Education
National Association of Special Education
Needs
Nasen House
415 Amber Business Village
Amber Close
Tamworth
Staffordshire B77 4RD
UK
01827 311500
www.nasen.org.uk

Spina Bifida
Association for Spina Bifida and
Hydrocephalus
42 Park Road
Peterborough
PE1 2UO
UK
0845 450 7755
www.asbah.org

Spinal Cord Injuries
Spinal Injuries Association
SIA House
2 Truemand Place
Oldbrook
Milton Keynes MK6 2HH
UK
0845 678 6633
www.spinal.co.uk

Spinal Muscular Atrophy
Jennifer Trust for Spinal Muscular
Atrophy
Elta House
Birmingham Road
Stratford upon Avon
Warwickshire CV37 0AQ
UK
01789 267520
www.jtsma.org.uk

Turner Syndrome
Turner Syndrome Society
13 Simpson Court
11 South Avenue
Clydebank Business Park
Clydebank G81 2NR
UK
0141 952 8006
www.tss.org.uk

Visually Impaired
Reveal
Royal National Institute of Blind People
105 Judd Street
London WC1H 9NE
UK
0845 766 9999
www.revealweb.org.uk

Other Countries' Agencies for Children with Special Needs

CANADA

Aicardi Syndrome
Aicardi Syndrome Awareness Support Group
29 Delavan Avenue
Toronto, Ontario
Canada M5P 1T2
1-416-481-4095

Angelman Syndrome
Canadian Angelman Syndrome Society
P.O. Box 37
Priddis, Alberta TOL 1WO
Canada
1-403-931-2415

Autism
Autism Society Canada
Box 22017
1670 Heron Road
Ottawa, Ontario K1V OC2
Canada
1-866-476-8440
www.autismsocietycanada.ca

Big Brothers and Big Sisters
Big Brothers and Big Sisters of Canada
3228 South Service Road
Suite 113E
Burlington, Ontario L7N 3HB
Canada
1-800-263-9133
www.bigbrothersbigsisters.ca

Blindness
Canadian Council of the Blind
403-396 Cooper Street
Suite 200
Ottawa, Canada K2P 2H7

1-613-567-0311
www.ccbnational.net

Celiac Disease
Canadian Celiac Association (CCA)
5170 Dixie Road
Suite 204
Mississauga, Ontario L4W 1E3
Canada
1-800-363-7269
www.celiac.ca

Communication Devices
Equip Kids International
63 Burrard Road
Toronto, Ontario M9W 3T4
Canada
www.equipkids.org

Cornelia de Lange Syndrome
Cornelia de Lange Association
1258 Pettit Road
Fort Erie, Ontario L2A 5A3
Canada
1-905-994-0499

Cystic Fibrosis
Canadian Cystic Fibrosis Foundation
2221 Yonge Street
Suite 601
Toronto, Ontario M4S 2B4
Canada
1-800-378-2233
www.ccff.ca

Diabetes
Canadian Diabetes Association
1400-522 University Avenue
Toronto, Ontario M5G 2RS
Canada

1-800-226-8464
www.diabetes.ca

Down Syndrome

Canadian Down Syndrome Society
811 14th Street NW
Calgary, Alberta T2N 2A4
Canada
1-800-883-5608
www.cdss.ca

Education

Centre for Inclusive Education
www.edu.uwo.ca/Inclusive_Education

Ehlers-Danlos Syndrome

Canadian Ehlers-Danlos Association
163 Charlton Avenue
Thornhill, Ontario L4J 6E9
Canada
905-761-7552
www.ehlersdanlos.ca/Inclusibe_Education

Epilepsy

Epilepsy Canada
Bureau 745
1470 Rue Peel
Montréal, Quebec H3A 1 T
Canada
1-800-860-5499
www.epilepsy.ca

Canadian Epilepsy Alliance
1-866-374-5377
www.epilepsymatters.com

Facial Differences

AboutFace
99 Crowns Lane
Toronto, Ontario
Canada
1-800-665-3223

Gaucher Disease

National Gaucher Foundation
4100 Yonge Street
Suite 310
North York, Ontario M2P 2B5
Canada
1-416-250-2850

Western Canadian Children's Heart
Network
4 C 2 Walter C. Mackenzie Centre
Edmonton, AB T6G 2 B7
Canada
1-703-407-1522
www.westernchildrensheartnetwork.ca

Hemophilia

Canadian Hemophilia Society
45 Charles Street East
Suite 802
Toronto ON M4Y 1S2
Canada

or

625 President Kennedy Avenue
Suite 505
Montreal, QC H3A 1K2
Canada
1-800-668-2686
www.hemophilia.ca

Independent Living

Canadian Association of Independent
Living
1104-160 Laurier Avenue West
Ottawa, Ontario
Canada K1P 5VS
1-613-563-2581
www.cailc.ca

Learning Disability

Learning Disability of Canada
250 City Centre Avenue
Suite 616
Ottawa, Ontario K1R 6K7
1-877-238-5322
Canada

Liver Disease

Canadian Liver Foundation
1500-2235 Sheppard Avenue East
Toronto, ON M2J 5B5
Canada
1-800-563-5483
www.liver.ca

Marfan Syndrome
Canadian Marfan Association
Centre Plaza Postal Outlet
126 Queen Street South
P.O. Box 42257
Mississauga, Ontario L5M 4ZO
Canada
1-866-722-1722
www.marfan.ca

Neurofibromatosis
Neurofibromatosis 1 & 2 Association
Box 12 Site 10 RR3
Rocky Mountain House
Alberta T4T 2A3
Canada
1-866-939-2263
www.nfcanada.ca/nearyou

Neurologically Impaired
The Association for the Neurologically
Disabled of Canada
The AND Centre
59 Clement Road
Etobicoke, Ontario
Canada M9R 1Y5
1-800-561-1497
www.and.ca

Prader-Willi Syndrome
Ontario Prader-Willi Syndrome
Association
2788 Balhurst Street-Suite 303
Toronto, Ontario M6B 3A3
Canada
1-416-481-8657
http://members/allstream.net/~opwsa

IRELAND
Ehlers-Danlos Syndrome
Ehlers-Danlos Support
24 Wendell Ave.
Portmarnock Co
Dublin
Ireland
01 8460570

Marfan Syndrome
Marfan Support Group
78 Whitehorn Drive
Palmerstown
Dublin 20
Ireland
www.marfan.ie
01 623 9563

Muscle Diseases
Muscular Dystrophy Society of Ireland
Carmichael House
North Brunswick Street
Dublin, 7
Ireland
01 8721501
www.mdi.ie

AUSTRALIA
Angelman Syndrome
Angelman Syndrome Association
P.O. Box 2025
South Plimpton SA 5038
(08) 8371 4255
www.angelmansyndrome.org

Autism and Asperger Syndrome
Asperger Syndrome Support Network
P.O. Box 159
Virginia QLD 4014
Australia
07 3865 2911
www.asperger.asn.au

Autism Aspergers Advocacy Australia
P.O. Box 717
Mawson ACT 2607
Australia
www.a4.org.au

Autism Society Australia
262 Marion Road
Netley SA 5037
P.O. Box 304
Marleston DC SA 5034
Australia
1300 288 476
www.autisms.org.au

Cerebral Palsy

Australia Cerebral Palsy Association
(ACPA)
1300 30 29 20
www.cpaustralia.com.au

The Centre for Cerebral Palsy
P.O. Box 61
Mt. Lawley
Western Australia
618 9443 0211
www.disability-resource.com/cerebral-palsy

Coeliac Disease

Coeliac Society of WSW Inc.
P.O. Box 271
Wahroonga NSW 2076
(02) 9487 5088
www.coeliacsociety.com.au

Coeliac Society of Australia
11 Barlyn Road, Mount Waverley, 3149
P.O. Box 89
Holmesglen, 3148
03 9808-5566
www.coeliac.org.au

Cornelia de Lange Syndrome

Cornelia de Lange Syndrome Association
159 Boddington Crescent
Australian Capital Territory
Kambah 2902
Australia
02 62 31 68 66
www.cdlsaus.org

Cystic Fibrosis

Cystic Fibrosis Australia
51 Wicks Road
North Ryde NSW 2113
Australia
1-800-232-823
www.cysticfibrosis.org.au

Diabetes

Diabetes Australia
GPO Box 3156
Canberra ACT 2501
Australia
02 6232 3850
www.diabetesaustralia.com.au

Juvenile Diabetes Research Foundation
www.jdrf.org.au

Disabilities

Disability Australia
National Disability Abuse and Neglect
Hotline
52 Pitt Street
Redfern WSW
P.O. Box 666
Strawberry Hills NSW 2012
Australia
1-800-880-052
www.pwd.org.au

Down Syndrome

Down Syndrome of South Australia, Inc.
P.O. Box 436
Greenacres, SA 5086
Australia
(08) 8369 1122
www.downssa.asn.au

Ehlers-Danlos Syndrome

Ehlers-Danlos Support Group
P.O. Box 106
Marulan NSW 2579
Australia
0011-61-2-4841-1111
www.edsaus.ning.com

Epilepsy

Epilepsy Action
GPO Box 9878
In Your Capital City
Australia
1300 37 45 37
www.epilepsy.org.au

Gaucher Disease

Gauchers Association
P.O. Box 983
Sunbury
Victoria 3429
(00610) 39740 7203
Australia

Haemophilia

Haemophilia Foundation Australia
1624 High Street
Glen Iris
Victoria 3146
Australia
(03) 9885 7800
www.haemophilia.org.au

Heart Disease
HeartKids Queensland Inc.
P.O. Box 118
Underwood QLD 4119
07 3341 8145
Australia
www.heartkidsqld.org.au

HeartKids of SA Inc.
P.O. Box 364
North Adelaide
South Australia 5006
0406165111
www.heartkidssa.org.au

Learning Disabilities
Learning Difficulties Australia
P.O. Box 349
Carlton South
Victoria 3053
03 9890 6138
www.ldaustralia.org

Liver Disease
www.liver.org.au

Marfan Syndrome
Marfan Association
P.O. Box 294
Summer Park
Queensland Branch
Queensland 4074
Australia
61 7 3376 6160
www.marfan.net.au

Multiple Births
Australian Multiple Birth Association
P.O. Box 105
Coogee NSW 2034
Australia
1300 88 64 99
www.amba.org.au

Muscle Diseases
Muscular Dystrophy Limited
111 Boundary Road North
Melbourne VIC 3051
Australia
61-39320 9555
www.mda.org.au

Neurofibromatosis
Neurofibromatosis Association of
Australia, Inc.
P.O. Box 603
Lindfield NSW 2070
Australia
94166244
www.nfaa.org.au

U.S. State Resources for Children with Special Needs

ALABAMA

Children's Rehabilitation Services
2129 E. South Blvd.
P.O. Box 11586
Montgomery, AL 36111
(205) 288-0220

Special Needs Programs
Division of Vocational Educational
Services
Department of Education
5239 Gordon Persons Bldg.
P.O. Box 302101
Montgomery, AL 36130
(205) 242-9111

Developmental Disabilities Planning
Council
Department of Mental Health and Mental
Retardation
200 Interstates Park Dr.
P.O. Box 3710
Montgomery, AL 36109
(205) 271-9207

Special Education Action Committee
(800) 222-7322
www.iser.com/SEAC-AL.html

Alabama Lifespan Respite
(866) 737-8252
www.alabamarespite.org

ALASKA

Exceptional Children and Youth
Department of Education
801 W. 10th Street
Suite 200
Juneau, AK 99801

(907) 465-2970

Health Care Program for Children with
Special Needs
1231 Gambell Street
Suite 30
Anchorage, AK 99501
(907) 272-1534

Special Needs Career and Vocational
Education
801 W.10th St.
Suite 200
Juneau, AK 99801
(907) 465-2970

Governor's Council on Disabilities and
Special Education
P.O. Box 240249
Anchorage, AK 99503
(907) 277-7325

AMERICAN SAMOA

Maternal & Child Health & Crippled
Children's Program
LBJ Tropical Medical Center
Division of Public Health
Pago Pago, American Samoa 96799
011 (684) 633-4606

Division of Special Education
State Department of Education
Pago Pago, American Samoa 96799
011 (684)-633-5237

ARIZONA

Division of Special Education
State Department of Education

1535 W. Jefferson
Phoenix, AZ 85007
(602) 542-1860

Children's Rehabilitative Services
Department of Health Services
1740 W. Adams
Phoenix, AZ 85007
(602) 542-1860

State Library for Blind and Physically
Handicapped
1030 No. 32nd St.
Phoenix, AZ 85008
(602) 255-5578
(800) 255-5578 (in Arizona)

Governor's Council on Developmental
Disabilities
1717 W. Jefferson
Phoenix, AZ 85007
(602) 542-4049

Raising Special Kids
(800) 237-3007
www.raisingspecialkids.org

ARKANSAS

Children's Medical Services
Department of Human Services
P.O. Box 1437, Slot #526
Little Rock, AR 72203
(501) 682-2277
(800) 482-5850 (in Arkansas)

Special Education
Department of Education
Arch Ford Education Bldg.
Room 105 C
Little Rock, AR 72201
(501) 682-4221

Governor's Developmental Disabilities
Planning Council
Freeway Medical Center
5800 W. 10th, Suite 805
Little Rock, AR 72204

Arkansas Disability Coalition
(800) 223-1330
www.adcpti.blueskywebsites.com/adcpti.
html

CALIFORNIA

Children's Medical Services Branch
714 P Street, Room #350
Sacramento, CA 95814
(916) 654-0499

Special Education Division
Department of Education
515 L Street, Suite 270
Sacramento, CA 95814
(916) 445-4568

California State Council on
Developmental Disabilities
2000 "O" St., Suite 100
Sacramento, CA 95814
(916) 322-8481

Exceptional Parents Unlimited
(559) 229-2000
www.exceptionalparents.org

Support for Families of Children with
Disabilities
(415) 282-7494
www.supportforfamilies.org

California Respite Association
(707) 644-4491
www.calrespite.org

COLORADO

Health Care Program for Children with
Special Needs
Colorado Department of Health
4300 Cherry Creek Drive South
Denver, CO 80222
(303) 692-2370

Special Education Services Unit
Colorado Department of Education
201 E. Colfax St.
Suite 300
Denver, CO 80203
(303) 866-6694

Developmental Disabilities Planning
Council
777 Grants St.
Suite 304
Denver, CO 80203
(303) 692-2370

Peak Parent Center, Inc.
(800) 284-0251
www.peakparent.org

CONNECTICUT

Children with Special Health Care Needs
Department of Health
999 Asylum Avenue
Hartford, CT 06106
(203) 566-3994

Connecticut Council on Developmental
Disabilities
90 Pitkin St. East
Hartford, CT 06106
(203) 725-3829

Early Childhood Unit
Department of Education
25 Industrial Park Rd.
Middletown, CT 06457
(203) 638-4204

Board of Education and Service for the
Blind
170 Ridge Road
Wethersfield, CT 06109
(203) 566-5800

Statewide Parent Advocacy Network, Inc.
(SPAN)
(800) 654-7726
www.spannj.org

Connecticut Lifespan Respite Coalition
(860) 513-0172
www.CTRESPITE.org

DELAWARE

Children with Special Health Needs
State Department of Public Health
P.O. Box 637
Dover, DE 19903
(302) 739-4735

Developmental Disabilities Planning
Council
Townsend Bldg.–Lower Level
P.O. Box 1401
Dover, DE 19903
(302) 739-3333

Delaware Lifespan Respite Care Network
(302) 831-4612
tbrooks@udel.edu

DISTRICT OF COLOMBIA

Health Services for Children with Special
Needs
State Department of Human Services
19th and Massachusetts Avenue S.E.
Washington, DC 20003
(202) 675-5214

Special Education Branch
District of Columbia Public Schools
Logan School
215 G St. N.E.
Washington D.C. 20002
(202) 724-4801

Developmental Disabilities Planning
Council
Department of Human Services
St. Elizabeth Campus
2700 Martin Luther King Ave. S.E.
Bldg. 801 East, Room 1301
Washington, DC 20032
(202) 232-2342

Advocates for Justice and Education
(888) 327-8060
www.AJE-DC.org

FLORIDA

Children's Medical Services Program
Department of Health and Rehabilitation
Services
1317 Winewood Boulevard
Building B, Room #128
Tallahassee, FL 32399
(904) 487-2690

Bureau of Education for Exceptional
Students
Department of Education
Florida Education Center
325 W. Gaines St. Suite 614
Tallahassee, FL 32399
(904) 487-2690

Developmental Service Program
Department of Health and Rehabilitation
1317 Winewood Blvd.
Bldg. B-Room 215
Tallahassee, FL 32399
(904) 488-4257

Developmental Disabilities Council
820 E. Park Ave.
Room I-100
Tallahassee, FL 32301
(904) 488-4180

Department of Education
Division of Blind Services
2540 Executive Center Circle West
203 Douglas Blvd.
Tallahassee, FL 32399
(904) 488-1330

Family Network on Disabilities of
Florida, Inc.
(800) 825-05736
www.fndfl.org

GEORGIA

Center for Exceptional Children
State Department of Education
1970 Twin Towers East
205 Butler St.
Atlanta, GA 30334
(404) 656-2425

The Governor's Council on
Developmental Disabilities
2 Peachtree St. N.W., Suite 3-210
Atlanta, GA 30303
(404) 657-2126

Children's Medical Services
Department of Human Resources
2600 Skyland Drive N.E.
Atlanta, GA 30319
(404) 679-2126

Emotional Disabilities
Child and Adolescent Mental Health
Division of Mental Health
Department of Human Resources
2 Peachtree St.-N.W. 3rd Floor West
Atlanta, GA 30303
(404) 657-2165

Parents Educating Parents and
Professionals for All Children
(800) 322-7065
www.peppinc.org

HAWAII

Special Needs Branch
State Department of Education
1430 Leahi Ave.
Honolulu, HI 96815
(808) 733-9055

Children with Special Needs
State of Hawaii Department of Health
741 Sunset Ave.
Honolulu, HI 96816
(808) 586-8100

State Planning Council of Developmental
Disabilities
Department of Health
919 Ela Moana Blvd., Room 113
Honolulu, HI 96814
(808) 586-8100

Child and Adolescent Mental Health
Division
Department of Health
3627 Kilauea Ave., Room 101
Honolulu, HI 96816
(800) 533-9684

Hawaii Parent Training and Information
Center
(808) 536-9684
www.ldahawaii.org/PTI.htm

IDAHO

Children's Special Health Program
Department of Health and Welfare
P.O. Box 83720, 4th Floor
Boise, ID 83720
(208) 334-5962

Bureau of Child Health
Department of Health and Welfare
P.O. Box 83720, 4th Floor
Boise, ID 83720
(208) 334-5967

State Department of Education
Special Education Section
P.O. Box 83720
Boise, ID 83720
(208) 334-3940

Idaho State Council on Developmental
Disabilities
280 No. 8th St., Suite 208
Boise, ID 83720
(208) 334-2179

Bureau of Community Mental Health
Division of Family and Community
Services
P.O. Box 83720
Boise, ID 83720
(208) 334-5512

Commission for the Blind and Visually
Impaired
341 W. Washington
Boise, ID 83720
(208) 334-3220

Idaho Parents Unlimited Inc.
(800) 242-4785
www.ipulidaho.org

ILLINOIS

Division of Specialized Care for Children
2815 W. Washington, Suite #300
Springfield, IL 62794
(217) 793-2350

Department of Specialized Education
Services
State Department of Education
100 No. 1st Street
Springfield, IL 62777
(217) 782-6601

Hearing and Visual Impairments
Philip Rock Center and School
818 Dupage Blvd.
Glen Ellyn, IL 60137
(708) 7090-2474

Family Matters Parent Training and
Information Center
(866) 436-7842
www.fmptic.org

Illinois Lifespan Respite Coalition
(312) 949-1808
www.Illinoislifespan.org/toolbox/respite/
respiteorgs.asp

INDIANA

Children's Special Health Care Services
Indiana State Department of Health
1330 W. Michigan
P.O. Box 1964
Indianapolis, IN 46206
(317) 383-6273

Division of Special Education
Department of Education
State House
Room 229
Indianapolis, IN 46204
(317) 232-0570

Developmental Disabilities
Developmental Disabilities Advisory
Council
Department of Mental Health
427 North Pennsylvania Street
Indianapolis, IN 46204
(317) 232-7885

INSOURCE
(800) 332-4433
www.insource.org

IOWA

Child Health Specialty Clinic
University of Iowa
247 Hospital School
Iowa City, IA 52242
(319) 356-1469

Visual Impairments
Department for the Blind
524 Fourth Street
Des Moines, IA 50333
(515) 281-7999

Developmental Disabilities
Hoover State Office Building–First Floor
Des Moines, IA 50319
(515) 281-7632

Hearing Impairments
Deaf Services Commission of Iowa
Department of Human Rights
Lucas State Office Bldg.
Des Moines, IA
(515) 281-3164

ASK Family Resource Center
(800) 450-8667
www.askresource.org

Iowa Respite and Crisis
(877) 255-3140
www.irccc.com

KANSAS

Services for Children with Special Health
Care Needs
State Department of Health and
Environment
900 S.W. Jackson, Room #1005-N
Topeka, KS 66612
(913) 296-1313

Developmental Disabilities
Kansas Planning Council for
Developmental Disabilities
Docking State Office Bldg.
915 Harrison, Room 141
Topeka, KS 66612
(913) 296-2608

Special Education Outcomes
Kansas State Board of Education
120 East Tenth Avenue
Topeka, KS 66612
(913) 296-7454

Families Together, Inc.
(888) 815-6364
www.familiestogetherinc.org

Kansas Lifespan Respite Coalition
(316) 687-5700
www.rockoinc.org

KENTUCKY

Commission for Children with Special
Health Care Needs
982 Eastern Parkway
Louisville, KY 40217
(502) 595-3264

Visual Impairments
Department for the Blind
Work Force Development Cabinet
427 Versailles Rd.
Frankfort, KY 40601
(502) 573-4754

Developmental Disabilities
Department of Mental Health
Cabinet for Human Resources
275 East Main Street
Frankfort, KY 40621
(502) 564-7842

Kentucky Special Parent Involvement
Network
(800) 525-7746
www.kyspin.com

LOUISIANA

Children's Special Health Services
Department of Health and Hospitals
Office of Public Health
P.O. Box 60630
Room #607
New Orleans, LA 70160
(504) 568-5055

Special Education Services
P.O. Box 4064
Baton Rouge, LA 70804
(504) 342-3631

Emotional Disturbance
Office of Mental Health
Department of Health and Human
Resources
4615 Government Street, Bldg B
Baton Rouge, LA 70806
(504) 925-1806

Project PROMPT
(800) 766-7736
www.projectprompt.com

MAINE

Bureau of Children with Special Needs
Department of Mental Health and Mental
Retardation
State House, Station #40
Augusta, ME 04333
(207) 287-4250

Developmental Disabilities
Maine Developmental Disabilities Council
The Nash Bldg., Station 139
Augusta, ME 04333
(207) 287-4213

Division of Special Education Services
State Department of Education
State House Station, No. 23
Augusta, ME 04333
(207) 287-5950
Maine Parent Federation
(800) 870-7746
www.mpf.org

State Point of Contact
UCP Respite Director
(207) 941-2955
www.ucpofmaine.org

MARYLAND

Children's Medical Services
Department of Mental Health
201 W. Preston Street, 4th Floor
Baltimore, MD 21201
(410) 225-5580

Division of Special Education
State Department of Education
200 W. Baltimore St.
Baltimore, MD 21201
(410) 767-0238

Developmental Disabilities Council
300 West Lexington Street–Box 10
Baltimore, MD 21201
(410) 333-8110

Parents Place of Maryland, Inc.
(800) 394-5694
www.ppmd.org

Maryland Respite Coalition, Inc.
(240) 453-9585
www.respitecoalition.org

MASSACHUSETTS

Division for Children with Special Health
Needs
Bureau of Family and Community Health
150 Tremont Street

Boston, MA 02111
(617) 727-3372

Emotional Disturbance
Department of Mental Health
25 Staniford Street
Boston, MA 02114
(617) 727-5608

Massachusetts Office on Disability
One Ashburton Place
Room 1303
Boston, MA 02108
(617) 727-7440

Federation for Children with Special
Needs
(800) 331-0688
www.fcsn.org

MICHIGAN

Children's Special Health Care Services
Department of Public Health
3423 N. Martin Luther King Boulevard
P.O. Box 30195
Lansing, MI 48909
(517) 335-8961

Developmental Disabilities
Developmental Disabilities Council
Departmental of Mental Health
Lewis Cass Bldg.
320 So. Walnut St.
Lansing, MI 48913
(517) 334-6123

Office of Special Education Services
Department of Education
P.O. Box 30008
Lansing, MI 48909
(517) 373-0923

CAUSE
(800) 221-9105
www.causeonline.org

MINNESOTA

Minnesota Children with Special Health
Needs
Division of Family Services
Department of Health

717 Delaware Street S.E.
P.O. Box 9441
Minneapolis, MN 55440
(612) 623-5150

Division of Developmental Disabilities
Department of Human Services
444 Lafayette Rd.
St. Paul, MN 55155
(612) 296-2160

Special Education Section
Minnesota Department of Education
Capital Square Bldg.
550 Cedar Street
St. Paul, MN 55101
(612) 296-6104

PACER Center, Inc.
(800) 537-2237
www.pacer.org

MISSISSIPPI

Children's Medical Program
P.O. Box 1700
Jackson, MS 39215
(601) 987-3965

Developmental Disabilities Council
239 No. Lamar St., Room 1101
Jackson, MS 39201
(601) 359-1288

Bureau of Special Services
Department of Education
P.O. Box 771
Jackson, MS 39205
(601) 359-3490

EMPOWER Community Resource Center
(800) 332-4852
http://msempower.org

MISSOURI

Bureau of Special Health Care Needs
Department of Health
P.O. Box 570
Jefferson City, MO 65102
(314) 751-6246

Visual Impairments
Rehabilitation Services for the Blind
Division of Family Services
619 E. Capitol Ave.
Jefferson City, MO 65101
(314) 751-4249

Developmental Disabilities
Department of Developmental Disabilities
P.O. Box 687
Jefferson City, MO 65102
(314) 751-3070

Missouri Parents Act (MPACT)
(800) 743-7634
www.ptimpact.com

MONTANA

Children with Special Health Needs
Bureau of Maternal and Child Health
1400 Broadway, Room #314
Helena, MT 59620
(406) 444-4740

Developmental Disabilities
Division of Social and Rehabilitative
Service
P.O. Box 4210
Helena, MT 59604
(406) 444-2995

Special Education Unit
Office of Public Instruction
State Capital
Helena, MT 59620
(406) 444-5661

Parents Let's Unite for Kids
(800) 222-7585
www.pluk.org

NEBRASKA

Medically Handicapped Children's
Program
Department of Social Services
301 Centennial Mall South
Lincoln, NE 68509
(402) 471-3121

Emotional Disturbance
State Mental Health Agency
Lincoln Regional Center
P.O. Box 94949
Lincoln, NE 68509
(402) 471-4444

Hotline for Disability Services/
Nebraska Child Find
Nebraska Department of Education
301 Centennial Mall South
Sixth Floor
Lincoln, NE 68509
(402) 471-3656

PTI Nebraska
(800) 284-8529
www.pti-nebraska.org

NEVADA
Children's Special Health Care Needs
Department of Human Resources
Kinkead Bldg.
505. E. King St.–Room 205
Carson City, NV 89710
(702) 687-4885

Developmental Disabilities
Developmental Disabilities Council
711 So. Stewart
Carson City, NV 89710
(702) 687-4452

Special Education Branch
Nevada Department of Education
400 West King Street
Capitol Complex
Carson City, NV 89710
(702) 687-3140

Nevada Parents Encouraging Parents
(800) 216-5188
www.nvpep.org

NEW HAMPSHIRE
Department of Special Medical Services
Office of Family and Community Health
Division of Public Health Services
6 Hazen Drive
Concord, NH 03301
(603) 271-4499
(800) 852-3345 (in New Hampshire)

Developmental Disabilities
New Hampshire Developmental
Disabilities Council
10 Ferry St.–Unit 315
Concord, NH 03301
(603) 271-3236

State Department of Education
101 Pleasant Street
Concord, NH 03301
(603) 271-3741

Parent Information Center
(800) 947-7005
www.parentinformationcenter.org

NEW JERSEY
Special Child Health Services
Department of Health, CN 634
Trenton, NJ 08625
(609) 292-5676

Department of Special Education
225 W. State St., CN 500
Trenton, NJ 08625
(609) 292-0147

Developmental Disabilities
Developmental Disabilities Council
32 West State Street CN 700
Trenton, NJ 08625
(609) 292-3745

Statewide Parent Advocacy Network, Inc.
(SPAN)
(800) 654-7726
www.spannj.org

NEW MEXICO
Children's Medical Services
State Department of Health
P.O. Box 968
Santa Fe, NM 87502
(595) 827-2574

Developmental Disabilities
Developmental Disabilities Division
State Department of Health
1190 St. Francis Drive
Santa Fe, NM 87502
(505) 827-2574

Emotional Disturbance
Division of Mental Health
1190 St. Francisco Drive
Santa Fe, NM 87502
(505) 827-2651

Parents Reaching Out
(800) 524-5176
www.parentsreachingout.org

NEW YORK

Physically Handicapped Children's
Services
Bureau of Child and Adolescent Health
Corning Tower Bldg.
Room 208
Empire State Plaza
Albany, NY 12237
(518) 474-2001

Emotional Disturbance
Office of Mental Health
44 Holland Ave.
Albany, NY 12229
(518) 474-4403

Office for Special Education Services
New York State Department of Education
One Commerce Plaza, Room 1624
Albany, NY 12234
(518) 474-5548

The Advocacy Center
(800) 650-4967
www.advocacycenter.com

Resources for Children with Special
Needs, Inc.
(212) 677-4650
www.resourcesnycdatabase.org

NORTH CAROLINA

Children's Special Health Services
Department of Environment, Health, and
Natural Resources
P.O. Box 27687
Raleigh, NC 27611
(919) 733-7437

Visual Impairments
Division of Services for the Blind
Department of Human Resources
309 Ashe Ave.
Raleigh, NC 27606
(919) 733-9822

Division of Exceptional Children
Department of Public Instruction
Education Building
301 North Wilmington
Raleigh, NC 27601
(919) 715-1563

Exceptional Children's Assistance Center,
Inc.
(800) 892-5028
www.ecac-parentcenter.org

NORTH DAKOTA

Children's Special Health Services
Department of Human Services
State Capitol
600 E. Boulevard Avenue
Bismarck, ND 58505
(701) 328-2436

Developmental Disabilities
Developmental Disabilities Division
Department of Human Services
State Capitol Bldg.
Bismarck, ND 58505
(701) 328-2768

Emotional Disturbance
Division of Mental Health
State Department of Human Services
600 East Blvd.
Bismarck, ND 58505
(701) 328-2766

OHIO

Bureau for Children with Medical
Handicaps
Division of Maternal and Child Health
P.O. Box 1603
Columbus, OH 43266
(614) 466-1700

Emotional Disturbance
Department of Mental Health
20. E. Broad St., 8th Floor
Columbus, OH 43266
(614) 466-2337

Developmental Disabilities
Office of Developmental Disabilities
Council
Department of Mental Health/
Developmental Disabilities
Eight East Long Street, Sixth Floor
Columbus, OH 43215
(614) 466-5205

State Point of Contact
(937) 298-8216
kinship@woh.rr.com

Ohio Coalition for the Education of
Children with Disabilities
(800) 373-2806
www.ocecd.org

OKLAHOMA

Special Health Care Needs Unit
Oklahoma Health Care Authority
Lincoln Plaza, Suite 124
4545 No. Lincoln Boulevard
Oklahoma City, OK 73105
(405) 530-3400

Special Education Services
State Department of Education
2500 No. Lincoln Blvd.
Oklahoma, OK 73105
(405) 521-3351

Developmental Disabilities
Developmental Disabilities Services
P.O. Box 25352, Room 510
Oklahoma City, OK 73125
(405) 521-3571

Oklahoma Respite Resource Network
(405) 522-0600
RoseAnn.Percival@okdhs.org

OREGON

Child Development and Rehabilitation
Center
P.O. Box 574
Portland, OR 97207
(503) 494-8095

Mental Health and Developmental
Disabilities Division
Department of Human Resources
2575 Bittern St. N.E.
Salem, OR 97310
(503) 378-2429

Emotional Disturbance
Mental Health Division
2575 Bittern Street. N.E.
Salem, OR 97310
(503) 378-2671

Oregon Lifespan Respite Program
(800) 442-5238
www.oregon.gov/DHS/spd/

Oregon Parent Training and Information
Center
(888) 505-2673
www.orpti.org/faqs.htm

PENNSYLVANIA

Division of Children's Special Health Care
Needs
Bureau of Maternal and Child
Preventative Health
State Department of Health
P.O. Box 90
Room #714
Harrisburg, PA 17108
(800) 852-4453

Bureau of Special Education
State Department of Education
333 Market St.
Harrisburg, PA 17126
(717) 783-6913

Developmental Disabilities
Developmental Disabilites Planning
Council
569 Forum Bldg.
Harrisburg, PA 17120
(717) 787-6057

Parent Education Network
(800) 522-5827
www.parentednet.org

Parent Respite Coalition
(412) 748-2863
maryjoa@thewatsoninstitute.org

PUERTO RICO

Crippled Children's Services
125 Diego Avenue
Puerto Nuevo, PR 00921
(809) 781-2728

Developmental Disabilities
Developmental Disabilities Council
P.O. Box 9543
San Juan, PR 00908
(809) 722-0590

RHODE ISLAND

Office of Special Needs
Department of Education
Roger Williams Bldg.
Room 209
22 Hayes Street
Providence, RI 02908
(401) 444-5685

Child Development Center
Rhode Island Hospital
593 Eddy Street
Providence, RI 02903
(401) 444-5685

Emotional Disturbance
Division of Children's Mental Health and
Education
Department of Children, Youth, and
Families
610 Mt. Pleasant Avenue
Providence, RI 02908
(401) 457-4514

State Parent Resource and Information
Center
(800) 464-3399
Schlesinger@ripin.org

SOUTH CAROLINA

Children's Rehabilitative Services
Division of Children's Health
Department of Health and Environment
Control
2600 Bull Street
Columbia, SC 29201
(803) 737-0465

Emotional Disturbance
Department of Mental Health
P.O. Box 485
Columbia, SC 29202
(803) 734-7766

Developmental Disabilities
Developmental Disabilities Council
1205 Pendleton Street, Room 372
Columbia, SC 29201
(803) 734-7766

Parent Training and Resource Center
(843) 266-1318
www.frcdsn.org

South Carolina Respite Coalition
(866) 345-6786
screspitecoalition@yahoo.com

SOUTH DAKOTA

Children's Special Health Services
Department of Health
445 E. Capital
Pierre, SD 57501
(605) 773-3737

Developmental Disabilities
Division of Developmental Disabilities
Department of Human Services
Hillsview Plaza
500 E. Capital
Pierre, SD 57501
(605) 773-3438

Office for Special Education
Department of Education and Cultural
Affairs
700 Governors Drive
Pierre, SD 57501
(605) 773-3678

South Dakota Parent Connection
(800) 640-4553
www.sdparent.org

TENNESSEE

Children's Special Services
Department of Health
Tennessee Tower, 11th Floor
312 Eighth Avenue North
Nashville, TN 37247
(615) 741-8530

Emotional Disturbance
Department of Mental Health
710 James Robertson Pkwy.
Nashville, TN 37243
(615) 532-6500

Developmental Disabilities
Developmental Disabilities Council
Gateway Plaza, Tenth Floor
710 James Robertson Pky.
Nashville, TN 37243
(615) 532-6615

Tennessee Respite Coalition
(888) 579-3754
www.tnrespite.org

Support and Training for Special Parents
(800) 280-7837
www.tnstep.org

TEXAS

Children's Health Division
Texas Department of Health
1100 W. 49th Street
Austin, TX 78756
(512) 458-7355

Texas Education Agency
Division of Special Education
1701 N. Congress Ave.
Austin, TX 78701
(512) 463-9362

Developmental Disabilities
Texas Planking Council for
Developmental Disabilities
4900 North Lamar
Austin, TX 78751
(512) 483-4080

Grassroots Consortium on Disabilities
Special Kids Inc.
(713) 734-5355
www.specialkidsinc.org

Partners Resource Network, Inc.
(800) 866-4726
www.partnerstx.org

UTAH

Children with Special Health Care Needs
Community and Family Health Services
Utah Department of Health
44 N. Medical Drive
Salt Lake City, UT 84114
(801) 584-8284

Special Education and Students at Risk
Utah State Office of Education
250 E.500 South
Salt Lake City, UT 84111
(801) 538-7702

Emotional Disturbance
Division of Mental Health
Department of Human Services
120 North 200 West, Fourth Floor
Salt Lake City, UT 84103
(801) 528-4270

Utah Parent Center
(801) 272-1051
www.utahparentcenter.org

VERMONT

Children with Special Health Care Needs
Department of Health
108 Cherry St.
Burlington, VT 05401
(802) 863-7338

Emotional Disturbance
Department of Mental Health
103 So. Main St.
Waterbury, VT 05671
(802) 241-2610

Visual Impairments
Division for the Blind and Visually
Impaired
Department of Aging
103 South Main Street

Waterbury, VT 05671
(802) 241-2210

Statewide Parent Advocacy Network, Inc.
(SPAN)
(800) 654-7726
www.spannj.org

Vermont Parent Information Center
(800) 639-7170
www.vtpic.com

(U.S.) VIRGIN ISLANDS

Services for Children with Special Health
Care Needs
Division of Maternal and Child Health
Department of Health
3200 Estate Richmond
Christiansted
St. Croix, VI 00820
(809) 773-1311

Division of Special Education
Department of Education
44-46 Kongens Gade
St. Thomas, VI 00802
(809) 774-4399

Developmental Disabilities
Division of Developmental Disabilites and
Rehabilitation Services
Department of Human Services
3011 Golden Rock
Christiansted
St. Croix, VI 00820
(809) 773-2323

VIRGINIA

Children's Specialty Services
Virginia Department of Health
1500 E. Main Street, Suite #135
Richmond, VA 23219
(804) 864-7708

State Mental Health Agency
Virginia Department of Mental Health
109 Governor Street
Richmond, VA 23214
(804) 786-5313

Visual Impairments
Virginia Department for the Visually
Handicapped
397 Azalea Ave.
Richmond, VA 23227
(804) 371-3140

WASHINGTON

Children with Special Health Care Needs
P.O. Box 47880
Olympia, WA 98504
(360) 753-0908

Special Education
Special Education Programs
Office of Public Instruction
P.O. Box 47200
Olympia, WA 98504
(360) 753-6733

Emotional Disturbance
Division of Mental Health
Department of Social and Health Services
P.O. Box 45320
Olympia, WA 98504
(360) 753-5414

Parent to Parent Power
(253) 531-2022
www.p2ppower.org

WEST VIRGINIA

Handicapped Children's Services
Office of Maternal and Child Health
Bureau of Public Health
1116 Quarrier Street
Charleston, WV 25301
(304) 558-3071

Special Education
Office of Special Education
Capitol Complex
Bldg. 6-Room B-304
Charleston, WV 25305
(304) 558-2696

Developmental Disabilities
Developmental Disabilities Planning
Council
110 Stockton Street
Charleston, WV 25312
(304) 558-0416

West Virginia Parent Training and
Information
(800) 281-1436
www.wvpti.org

WISCONSIN

Program for Children with Special Health
Care Needs
Department of Health and Social Services
1414 E. Washington Avenue, Room #167
Madison, WI 53703
(608) 266-7826

Developmental Disabilities
Council of Developmental Disabilities
P.O. Box 7851
Madison, WI 53707
(608) 266-7826

Division for Learning Support: Equity
and Advocacy
P.O. Box 7841
Madison, WI 53707
(608) 266-1649

Wisconsin Family Assistance Center for
Education, Training and Support
(877) 374-4655
www.wifacets.org

Respite Care Association of Wisconsin
(608) 222-2033
www.respitecarewi.org

WYOMING

Children's Health Services
Hathaway Office Bldg.
Room #462
Cheyenne, WY 82002
(307) 777-794

Developmental Disabilities
Governor's Planning Council on
Developmental Disabilities
Herschler Bldg.-Fourth Floor
122 W. 25th St.
Cheyenne, WY 82002
(307) 777-7230

Special Education Division
State Department of Education
Hathaway Office Bldg.
Cheyenne, WY 82002
(307) 777-7414

Parent Information Center
(800) 660-9742
www.wpic.org

U.S. Contacts for High-Risk Insurance

ALABAMA

Alabama Health Insurance Plan
(800) 513-1384 or (334) 353-8924

ALASKA

Alaska Comprehensive Health Insurance
Association
(800) 467-8724 or (907) 269-7900

ARKANSAS

Arkansas Comprehensive Health
Insurance Plan
(501) 278-2979

CALIFORNIA

California Managed Risk Medical
Insurance Program
(800) 289-6574 or (916) 324-4695

COLORADO

Colorado Uninsurable Health Insurance
Plan
(303) 863-1960

CONNECTICUT

Connecticut Health Insurance Association
(800) 842-0004

FLORIDA

(not open for new enrollees)
Florida Comprehensive Health Insurance
Plan
(850) 309-1200

IDAHO

Department of Insurance
(202) 334-4250

ILLINOIS

Illinois Comprehensive Health Insurance
Plan
(800) 367-6410 or (217) 782-6333

INDIANA

Indiana Comprehensive Health Insurance
Association
(800) 552-7921 or (317) 614-2000

IOWA

Iowa Comprehensive Health Association
(800) 877-5156

KANSAS

Kansas Uninsurable Health Insurance Plan
(800) 290-1366 or (316) 792-1779

KENTUCKY

Kentucky Access
(866) 405-6145

LOUISIANA

Louisiana Health Insurance Association
(800) 736-0947 or (504) 926-6245

MARYLAND

Maryland Health Insurance Plan
(866) 780-7105 or (410) 576-2055

MINNESOTA

Minnesota Comprehensive Health
Association
(952) 593-9609

MISSISSIPPI

Mississippi Comprehensive Health
Insurance Risk Pool
(601) 362-0799

MISSOURI

Missouri Health Insurance Pool
Northwest Missouri: (800) 645-8346
Remainder of state: (800) 843-6447

MONTANA

Montana Comprehensive Health
Insurance Association
(406) 444-8200

NEBRASKA

Nebraska Comprehensive Health
Association
(402) 343-3337

NEW HAMPSHIRE

New Hampshire Health Plan
(800) 578-3272

NEW MEXICO

New Mexico Comprehensive Health
Insurance Pool
(505) 271-4399

NORTH DAKOTA

Comprehensive Health Association of
North Dakota
(800) 737-0016 or (701) 282-1235

OKLAHOMA

Oklahoma Health Insurance High Risk
Pool
(800) 255-6065 or (913) 362-0040

OREGON

Oregon Medical Insurance Pool
(503) 373-1692

SOUTH CAROLINA

South Carolina Health Insurance Pool
(803) 788-0222

SOUTH DAKOTA

South Dakota Risk Pool
(800) 831-0785

TENNESSEE

TennCare Program
(615) 741-8642

TEXAS

Texas Health Insurance Risk Pool
(888) 398-3927 or (512) 441-7665

UTAH

Utah Comprehensive Health Insurance
Pool
(866) 880-8494 or (801) 333-5573

WASHINGTON

Washington State Health Insurance Pool
(800) 877-5187 or (360) 407-0380

WISCONSIN

Wisconsin Health Insurance Risk Sharing
Plan
(608) 264-7733

WYOMING

Wyoming Health Insurance Pool
(307) 634-1393

Toll-Free Numbers

Toll-Free Directory Assistance 1-800-555-1212
AIDS Hotline 1-800-232-4636
AMC Cancer Information Center 1-800-525-3777
American Council of the Blind 1-800-424-8666
American Kidney Fund 1-800-638-8299
American Speech-Language Association 1-800-638-8255
Better Hearing Institute 1-800-327-9355
Cancer Information Service 1-800-422-6237
Epilepsy Information Line 1-800-257-1227
International Hearing Society 1-800-521-5247
International Shriners Headquarters 1-800-237-5055
Shriners Hospitals–Canada 1-800-361-7256
Juvenile Diabetes Foundation 1-800-223-1138
Lung Line Information Service 1-800-222-5864
National Center for Stuttering 1-800-221-2483
National Cystic Fibrosis Foundation 1-800-344-4823
National Down Syndrome Congress 1-800-232-6372
National Down Syndrome Society 1-800-221-4602
National Easter Seal Society 1-800-221-6827
National Health Information Center 1-800-336-4797
National Center for Learning Disabilities 1-800-575-7373
National Technical Assistance Center 1-800-248-0822
Child Care Aware 1-800-424-2246
Childhelp USA 1-800-422-4435
Child Abuse Hotline 1-800-422-4453
National Child Care Association 1-800-543-7161
National Health Information 1-800-336-4797
National Immunization Information Hotline 1-800-232-2522
Loving Nannies 1-800-682-8154
National Mental Health Help Line 1-800-969-6642
U.S. Consumer Product Safety Commission 1-800-638-2772
Referral Service National Library Service for the Blind & Physically Handicapped
1-800-424-8567
National Rehabilitation Information Center 1-800-346-2743
National Spinal Cord Injury Hotline 1-800-526-3456
National SIDS Foundation 1-800-221-7437
Orton Dyslexia Society 1-800-222-3123
Prevent Blindness America 1-800-221-3004
RP Foundation Fighting Blindness 1-800-683-5555
Special Needs Network 1-800-471-0026

Spina Bifida Association for America 1-800-621-3141
Alzheimer's Association 1-800-272-3900
Arthritis Foundation 1-800-238-7800
Asthma Information 1-800-822-2762
Autism Society 1-800-328-8476
American Brain Tumor Association 1-800-886-2282
American Cancer Society Information 1-800-227-2345
AIDS Treatment Information Service 1-800-448-0440
Alcohol and Drug Helpline 1-800-821-4357
Food Allergy Network 1-800-929-4040
National Center for Alternative Medicine 1-888-644-6226
American Podiatric Association 1-800-366-8227
Trustline 1-800-822-8490

Questionnaire for Parents and Grandparents

FOR PARENTS

1. If your parents live close to you, what is the best way they can help with your child and any brothers or sisters?

2. What do you wish the grandparents would not do?

3. Do your parents accept all of your children equally or do they treat your special needs child differently?

4. If your parents live at a distance, what help would you like them to offer?

5. How did your parents react when they were first told of your child's special problem?

6. Please share any incidents or special accounts of how the grandparents have helped or not helped.

7. Please add anything else that would be helpful in a book for grandparents of special needs kids.

FOR GRANDPARENTS

1. What is the hardest thing about being the grandparent of a child with special needs?

2. Do you find it hard not to offer advice about how the parents care for your grandchild?

3. Do you spend one-to-one time with either the special needs child or any siblings?

4. If so do the kids open up and talk to you about their worries and concerns?

5. How do you handle your grief or worry about your grandchild?

6. Have you made any financial plans for your grandchild if you can afford to do so?

7. Are you comfortable talking with your friends about your grandchildren?

8. Where do you get the greatest support in your concern about your grandchild? Is it from friends, family, prayer, your church, synagogue, or mosque?

9. Do you have some special stories you would like to share with readers or suggestions about how to take care of themselves or their special needs grandchild?

Notes

1. Kübler-Ross, Elisabeth. (1997) *On Death and Dying.* New York, NY: Simon and Schuster
2. March of Dimes, 2007. www.marchofdimes.com
3. Martin, Patricia. (1975) "Marital Breakdown in Families with Patients with Spina Bifida Cystica." *Developmental Medicine and Child Neurology.* 17: 757-64.
4. Mann, Maureen, Tom Wharff, Mary Deaver. (1991) *Sexual Abuse of Handicapped Children.* Omaha, NE: National Research Hospital.
5. Conner, Bobbi. (2007) *Unplugged Play.* New York, NY: Workman Publishing.
6. Christie, Bryan. (2000) "Premature Babies have High Death and Disability Rate." British Medical Journal. 321: 467.
7. Lee, Sunmin (2003) "Grandmom's Little Health Hazard." *New York Times.* 11/ 4: D6.
8. Holbrook, M. Cay. (2006) *Children with Visual Impairments: A Parents' Guide.* Bethesda, MD: Woodbine House.
9. Legere, Henry. (2004) *Raising Healthy Eaters.* New York, NY: Perseus Book Group.
10. Tanguay, Pamela. (2001) *Nonverbal Learning Disabilities At Home.* Philadelphia, PA: Jessica Kingsley Publishers.
11. Conner, Bobbi. (1997) *The Parent's Journal Guide to Raising Great Kids.* New York, NY: Bantam Books.
12. Cole, Joanna and Stephanie Calmenson. (1991) *The Eentsy, Weentsy Spider: Fingerplays and Action Rhymes.* New York, NY: William Morrow.
13. Thomas, Pierre and Jack Date. (2006) *Students Dropping Out of High Schools Reaches Epidemic Rates.* Washington DC: U.S. Department of Education.
14. Carey, Benedict. (2008) "Calm Down or Else." *New York Times.* July 15, pg. D 1, D6.
15. Roberts, Timothy. (2008) *Tattoos and Body Piercing.* Elk Grove Village, IL: American Academy of Pediatrics.
16. Korpi, Mary. (2008) *Guiding Your Teenager with Special Needs through the Transition from School to Adult Life.* London and Philadelphia, PA: Jessica Kingsley Publishers.
17. Santora, Marc. (2008) "For the Disabled. Age 18 Brings Difficult Choices in Finding Health Care." *New York Times.* 5/14: C13.
18. Vignos, Paul, George Spencer and Kenneth Archibald. (1963) "Management of Progressive Muscular Dystrophy in Childhood." *Journal of the American Medical Association.* 184: 39-96.
19. Korn, Danna. (2001) *Kids with Celiac Disease.* Bethesda, MD: Woodbine House.
20. National Institute of Deafness (2007). www.nidcd.nih.gov
21. Wheeler, Maria. (2007) *Toilet Training for Individuals with Autism and Other Developmental Issues.* Arlington, TX: Future Horizons, Inc.
22. Korn, Danna. (2001) *Kids with Celiac Disease.* Bethesda, MD: Woodbine House.
23. Marshall, Catherine. (1991) *To Live Again.* New York, NY: Avon Books.

Index